MOON HANDBOOKS

ST. LOUIS

BROOKE S. FOSTER

D0951585

Contents

Maps

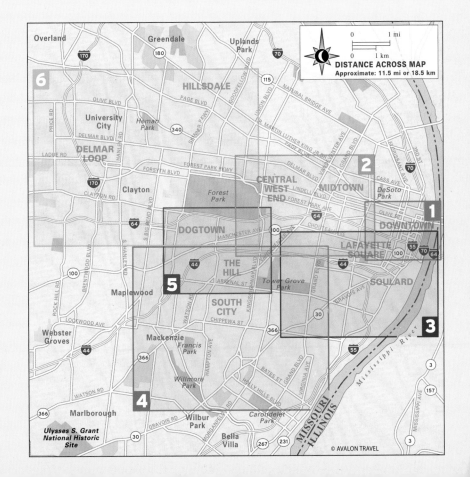

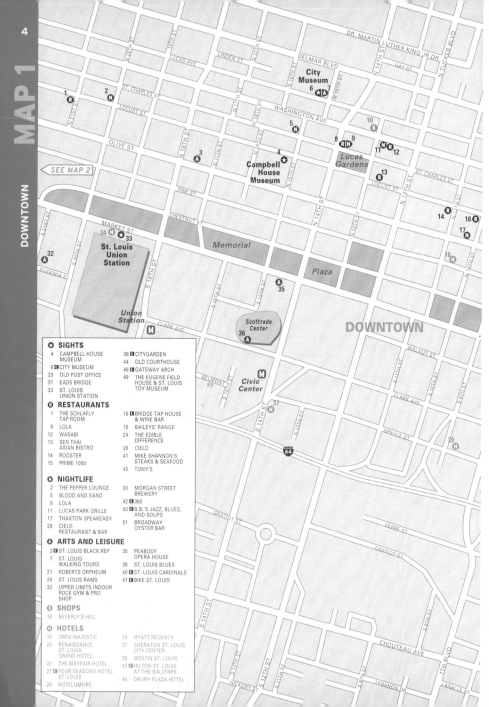

SEE MAP 2

DOWNTOWN

SIGHTS

4	CAMPBELL HOUSE MUSEUM	38	CITYGARDEN
6	CITY MUSEUM	44	OLD COURTHOUSE
23	OLD POST OFFICE	48	GATEWAY ARCH
31	EADS BRIDGE	49	THE EUGENE FIELD HOUSE & ST. LOUIS TOY MUSEUM
33	ST. LOUIS UNION STATION		

RESTAURANTS

1	THE SCHLAFLY TAP ROOM	16	BRIDGE TAP HOUSE & WINE BAR
8	LOLA	19	BAILEYS' RANGE
12	WASABI	24	THE EDIBLE DIFFERENCE
13	SEN THAI ASIAN BISTRO	26	CIELO
14	ROOSTER	41	MIKE SHANNON'S STEAKS & SEAFOOD
15	PRIME 1000	45	TONY'S

NIGHTLIFE

2	THE PEPPER LOUNGE	30	MORGAN STREET BREWERY
5	BLOOD AND SAND	42	360
9	LOLA	50	B.B.'S JAZZ, BLUES, AND SOUPS
11	LUCAS PARK GRILLE	51	BROADWAY OYSTER BAR
17	THAXTON SPEAKEASY		
28	CIELO RESTAURANT & BAR		

ARTS AND LEISURE

3	ST. LOUIS BLACK REP	35	PEABODY OPERA HOUSE
7	ST. LOUIS WALKING TOURS	36	ST. LOUIS BLUES
21	ROBERTS ORPHEUM	40	ST. LOUIS CARDINALS
25	ST. LOUIS RAMS	47	BIKE ST. LOUIS
32	UPPER LIMITS INDOOR ROCK GYM & PRO SHOP		

SHOPS

10	BEVERLY'S HILL

HOTELS

18	OMNI MAJESTIC	34	HYATT REGENCY
20	RENAISSANCE ST. LOUIS GRAND HOTEL	37	SHERATON ST. LOUIS CITY CENTER
22	THE MAYFAIR HOTEL	39	WESTIN ST. LOUIS
27	FOUR SEASONS HOTEL ST. LOUIS	43	HILTON ST. LOUIS AT THE BALLPARK
29	HOTELUMIÈRE	46	DRURY PLAZA HOTEL

COLE ST

CONVENTION PLAZA

Edward
Jones
Dome

25 A

CONVENTION PLAZA

CARR ST

26 27
R H

28 29
N H

DR. MARTIN LUTHER KING JR DR

MARTIN
LUTHER
KING
BRIDGE

LACLEDE'S LANDING

DELMAR BLVD

15
R

20
H

WASHINGTON AVE

M

Convention
Center

30
N

LUCAS AVE

21 A
22 H

Old Post
Office 23 A

19
R

OLIVE ST

LOCUST ST

31
R

Eads
Bridge

PINE ST

M

8th &
Pine

24
R

Arch-
Laclede's
Landing

M

WASHINGTON AVE

Citygarden
38

CHESTNUT ST

Kiener

Old
Courthouse
44

41 R
42 N H 43
45 R

MARKET ST
46 N

Plaza

47
A

Gateway
Arch
48

Jefferson
National
Expansion
Memorial

WALNUT ST

40 A

M Stadium

Busch
Stadium

CLARK AVE

70

SPRUCE ST

MISSOURI   ILLINOIS

Mississippi   River

The Eugene
Field House &
St. Louis
Toy Museum 49

64

50
N

51

POPLAR ST

POPLAR
STREET
BRIDGE

55 64 70

© AVALON TRAVEL

GRATIOT ST

CEDAR ST

GRATIOT ST

55

LOMBARD ST

SEE MAP 3

0   200 yds

0   200 m

DISTANCE ACROSS MAP
Approximate: 1.7 mi or 2.8 km

0   500 yds
0   500 m
DISTANCE ACROSS MAP
Approximate: 3.5 mi or 5.6 km

Pickett Playground

ENRIGHT AVE
DELMAR BLVD
WASHINGTON PL
WESTMINSTER PL
WATERMAN BLVD

DEBALIVIERE PLACE

SEE MAP 6

PORTLAND PL
WESTMORELAND PL

LINDELL BLVD

FOREST PARK PKWY

Forest Park

WASHINGTON BLVD
LENOX PL
PERSHING PL
MARYLAND AVE
MARYLAND AVE

DELMAR BLVD
WASHINGTON BLVD
WESTMINSTER PL
MCPHERSON AVE
OLIVE ST

D. BANKS AVE
W BELLE PL
ENRIGHT AVE

29
Cathedral Basilica of St. Louis

W PINE BLVD
LACLEDE AVE

CENTRAL WEST END

W PINE BLVD

Barnes-Jewish Hospital North
St. Louis Children's Hospital
Barnes-Jewish Hospital South

FOREST PARK AVE

28

JEFFERSON DR

FAULKNER DR

M
Central West End

MCKINLEY AVE
CLAYTON AVE
CLAYTON AVE

30

DUNCAN AVE

SARPY AVE

GRATIOT ST
PAPIN ST

66

CLAYTON AVE

I-64
OAKLAND AVE

BERTHOLD AVE
WISE AVE

KINGS OAK

WISE AVE

SEE MAP 5

FOREST PARK SOUTHEAST

GIBSON AVE
OAKLAND AVE
ARCO AVE
WICHITA AVE

MANCHESTER AVE

62   64
60

63 65
59 61
57 58

56
SWAN AVE
NORFOLK AVE
VISTA AVE

THE HILL

HUNT AVE

MACKLIND AVE
EAST RD

S KINGSHIGHWAY BLVD

S VANDEVENTER AVE

CENTRAL INDUSTRIAL AVE

BOTANICAL HEIGHTS

PARK AVE
FOLSOM AVE

MCREE AVE

NORTHRUP AVE
PATTISON AVE

I-44

SEE MAP 4

MCREE AVE
BLAINE AVE

© AVALON TRAVEL

○ SIGHTS

- 29 CATHEDRAL BASILICA OF ST. LOUIS
- 47 ERNEST TROVA AT SAINT LOUIS UNIVERSITY
- 54 SCOTT JOPLIN HOUSE STATE HISTORIC SITE

○ RESTAURANTS

- 1 DRESSEL'S PUBLIC HOUSE
- 3 LLYWELYN'S
- 17 COFFEE CARTEL
- 21 RASOI
- 24 BRASSERIE BY NICHE
- 25 TASTE
- 31 CAFÉ VENTANA
- 34 NADOZ
- 42 THE BEST STEAK HOUSE
- 45 VITO'S
- 52 PAPPY'S SMOKEHOUSE
- 53 HAMBURGER MARY'S BAR & GRILLE
- 57 SWEETIE PIE'S
- 60 EVEREST CAFÉ AND BAR

○ NIGHTLIFE

- 2 CLUB VIVA
- 7 CAFÉ EAU
- 10 MANDARIN LOUNGE
- 14 SUB ZERO VODKA BAR
- 16 BRENNAN'S WINE BAR AND CIGAR SHOP
- 22 34 CLUB
- 25 ROSIE'S PLACE
- 26 TASTE
- 30 THE SCOTTISH ARMS
- 44 JAZZ AT THE BISTRO
- 48 URBAN CHESTNUT BREWING COMPANY
- 49 PLUSH
- 50 CLUB DANTE
- 51 THE LOFT
- 55 THE FIREBIRD
- 58 ERNEY'S 32 DEGREES
- 59 SANCTUARIA
- 61 ATOMIC COWBOY
- 62 HANDLEBAR
- 63 JUST JOHN NIGHTCLUB
- 64 NOVAK'S BAR & GRILL
- 65 ATTITUDES NIGHTCLUB
- 66 JJ'S CLUBHOUSE & BAR

○ ARTS AND LEISURE

- 4 PHILIP SLEIN GALLERY
- 8 CHASE PARK PLAZA THEATER
- 28 STEINBERG SKATING RINK
- 32 MOOLAH THEATRE & LOUNGE
- 33 MUSEUM OF CONTEMPORARY RELIGIOUS ART
- 35 CONTEMPORARY ART MUSEUM ST. LOUIS
- 36 BRUNO DAVID GALLERY
- 37 PULITZER FOUNDATION FOR THE ARTS
- 38 SHELDON CONCERT HALL
- 39 SHELDON ART GALLERIES
- 40 POWELL SYMPHONY HALL
- 41 FOX THEATRE
- 43 HOTCITY THEATRE
- 46 THE MOTO MUSEUM
- 56 WHITE FLAG PROJECTS

○ SHOPS

- 5 CENTRO MODERN FURNISHINGS
- 6 LEFT BANK BOOKS
- 11 MORIS FASHIONS
- 12 WOLFGANG'S PET STOP
- 13 CASSIE'S
- 15 IVY HILL
- 18 Q BOUTIQUE
- 19 BIG SLEEP BOOKS
- 20 CENTRAL WEST END

○ HOTELS

- 9 THE CHASE PARK PLAZA
- 27 THE PARKWAY HOTEL
- 67 MARRIOTT RESIDENCE INN

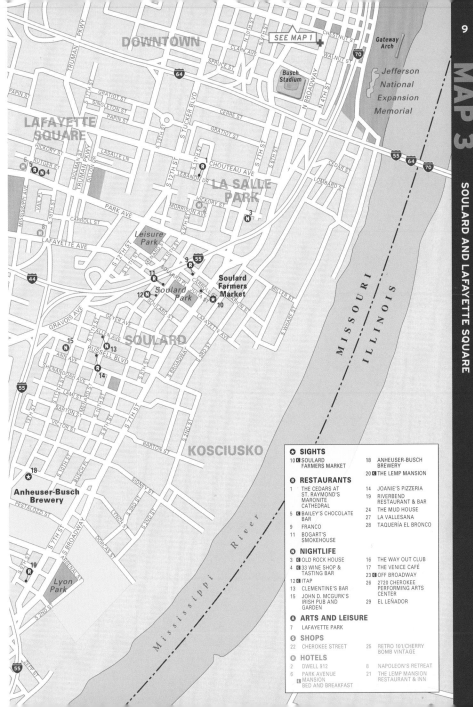

DOWNTOWN

SEE MAP 1

Gateway
Arch

Jefferson
National
Expansion
Memorial

Busch
Stadium

**LAFAYETTE
SQUARE**

**LA SALLE
PARK**

Leisure
Park

Soulard
Park

**Soulard
Farmers
Market**

MISSOURI

ILLINOIS

SOULARD

KOSCIUSKO

Mississippi River

**Anheuser-Busch
Brewery**

Lyon
Park

◎ SIGHTS
10 ⓒ SOULARD
FARMERS MARKET

18   ANHEUSER-BUSCH
BREWERY
20 ⓒ THE LEMP MANSION

ⓡ RESTAURANTS
1   THE CEDARS AT
ST. RAYMOND'S
MARONITE
CATHEDRAL
5 ⓒ BAILEY'S CHOCOLATE
BAR
9   FRANCO
11 ⓒ BOGART'S
SMOKEHOUSE

14   JOANIE'S PIZZERIA
19   RIVERBEND
RESTAURANT & BAR
24   THE MUD HOUSE
27   LA VALLESANA
28   TAQUERÍA EL BRONCO

ⓝ NIGHTLIFE
3 ⓒ OLD ROCK HOUSE
4 ⓒ 33 WINE SHOP &
TASTING BAR
12 ⓒ ITAP
13 ⓒ CLEMENTINE'S BAR
15   JOHN D. MCGURK'S
IRISH PUB AND
GARDEN

16   THE WAY OUT CLUB
17   THE VENICE CAFÉ
23 ⓒ OFF BROADWAY
26   2720 CHEROKEE
PERFORMING ARTS
CENTER
29   EL LEÑADOR

ⓐ ARTS AND LEISURE
7   LAFAYETTE PARK

ⓢ SHOPS
22   CHEROKEE STREET

25   RETRO 101/CHERRY
BOMB VINTAGE

ⓗ HOTELS
2   DWELL 912
6   PARK AVENUE
ⓒ MANSION
BED AND BREAKFAST

8   NAPOLEON'S RETREAT
21   THE LEMP MANSION
RESTAURANT & INN

SEE MAP 6

SEE MAP 5

GAYOLA PL
ZEPHYR PL
RANNELLS AVE
LOHMEYER AVE
LYNDOVER PL

BELLEVUE AVE

100

MCCAUSLAND AVE

44

HAMPTON AVE

COLUMBIA AVE

MANCHESTER AVE
SOUTHWEST AVE

CLIFTON
HEIGHTS

MCCUNE AVE
MAHMADUKE AVE

1
3
5
2
6
7
4

HAZEL AVE
MAPLE AVE
OAKLAND AVE
S BIG BEND BLVD

ODELL ST
HOFFMAN AVE

ARSENAL ST

Sublette
Park

MAPLEWOOD

FLORA AVE

CANTERBURY AVE

ELM AVE

SMILEY AVE
9   10

WATSON RD

SUNNEN DR

GREENWOOD BLVD

8

SCANLAN AVE

N
17

CAMBRIDGE AVE
OXFORD AVE

ELLENDALE AVE

BRADLEY AVE

11

TYLER AVE

HANCOCK AVE
12
13

ARTHUR AVE

HANCOCK AVE

Tiles
Park

MARQUETTE AVE
OLEATHA AVE

MARQUETTE AVE

HAMPTON AVE

PERNOD AVE
Lidenwood
Park

LINDENWOOD PL

LINDENWOOD

WATSON RD

PERNOD AVE
THOLOZAN AVE

MARDEL AVE
LINDENWOOD PL

366

14

JAMIESON AVE

LANSDOWNE AVE

CHIPPEWA ST

15
16

WINONA AVE
BANCROFT AVE

SUTHERLAND AVE
LANSDOWNE AVE

DEVONSHIRE AVE

51   N

NOTTINGHAM AVE

DEVONSHIRE AVE

MURDOCH AVE

NEOSHO ST
ITASKA ST

NEOSHO ST
ITASKA ST
DELOR ST

Francis
Park

52

WALSH ST

EICHELBERGER ST

EICHELBERGER ST

ROSA AVE

RIVER DES PERES

JAMIESON AVE

HAMPTON AVE

GOETHE AVE
MILENTZ AVE

ST. LOUIS
HILLS

RHODES AVE
53

HOLLY HILLS AVE

FINKMAN ST

KINGSHIGHWAY BLVD

LISETTE AVE

LOUGHBOROUGH AVE

GRESHAM AVE

PRINCETON
HEIGHTS

Willmore

DES PERES PKWY

Park

Saints Peter
and Paul
Cemetery

SIGHTS

23 MISSOURI BOTANICAL
GARDEN
24 THE "ANCIENT RUINS"
IN TOWER GROVE
PARK

29 COMPTON HILL
WATER TOWER
47 INTERNATIONAL
INSTITUTE OF
ST. LOUIS

RESTAURANTS

4 HOME WINE KITCHEN
5 ACERO
7 SCHLAFLY
BOTTLEWORKS
8 THE PICCADILLY AT
MANHATTAN
9 PIZZA-A-GO-GO
11 FARMHAUS
13 STELLINA PASTA CAFÉ
MOM'S DELI
19 COURTESY DINER
27 SWEETART

36 CITY DINER
37 MANGIA ITALIANO
39 KING & I
40 LEMONGRASS
41 BLACK THORN
PIZZA & PUB
42 PHO GRAND
46 MESKEREM ETHIOPIAN
RESTAURANT
49 GRBIC
53 ONESTO
PIZZA & TRATTORIA
58 IRON BARLEY

NIGHTLIFE

17 THE HIDEAWAY
PIANO BAR
18 SANDRINA'S
20 THE ROYALE
31 VAN GOGHZ MARTINI
BAR AND BISTRO
34 RILEY'S PUB
35 UPSTAIRS LOUNGE
38 MANGIA ITALIANO

43 ABSOLUTLI GOOSED
48 THE CIVIL LIFE
BREWING COMPANY
50 THE FAMOUS BAR
51 THE MACK
BAR AND GRILL
54 THE SILVER
BALLROOM
55 PEPPER'S GRILL & BAR
56 LEMMONS

ARTS AND LEISURE

1 SARATOGA LANES
2 FOCAL POINT
6 ART OUTSIDE
FESTIVAL

10 EPIPHANY LANES
25 FESTIVAL OF NATIONS
57 CARONDELET PARK

SHOPS

3 THE BOOK HOUSE
12 GROOMINGDALE'S
15 CATHOLIC SUPPLY
OF ST. LOUIS
16 T.F.A. THE FUTURE
ANTIQUES
21 LITTLE SHOP
AROUND THE CORNER

22 GRINGO JONES
IMPORTS
28 GROVE FURNISHINGS
32 BOTANICALS
DESIGN STUDIO
33 DUNAWAY BOOKS
44 GRAND SOUTH GRAND
45 CHEAPTRX
52 RECORD EXCHANGE

HOTELS

26 CASA MAGNOLIA BED
AND BREAKFAST

30 THE FLEUR-DE-LYS
MANSION

0   500 yds

0   500 m

DISTANCE ACROSS MAP
Approximate: 5.3 mi or 8.5 km

SEE MAP 2

THE HILL

Vigo
Park

SHAW AVE
DAGGET AVE
WILSON AVE

SHAW AVE

CASTLEMAN
AVE

SHAW BLVD
CASTLEMAN AVE
RUSSELL BLVD
FLORA PL
FLAD AVE
CLEVELAND AVE
SHENANDOAH AVE
BOTANICAL AVE

LAFAYETTE AVE
DE TONTY ST
44

Terry
Park

Compton
Hill Reservoir
Park

Compton Hill
Water Tower
29

RUSSELL BLVD
LONGFELLOW BLVD
HAWTHORNE BLVD

SHAW

30

BISCHOFF AVE

SOUTHWEST AVE

SHENANDOAH AVE

23

Missouri
Botanical
Garden

27

H

SHENANDOAH AVE

SOUTHWEST
GARDEN

MAGNOLIA AVE

26

31
N

REBER PL
ODELL ST

NORTHWEST DR

Tower Grove
Park

24 25

NORTHEAST DR

The "Ancient Ruins"
in Tower Grove Park

SIDNEY ST
MAGNOLIA AVE
HALLIDAY AVE

PESTALOZZI ST

18
N

KEMPER AVE

20

19
R

28

SOUTHWEST DR
ARSENAL ST
HARTFORD ST

SOUTHEAST DR
MAIN DR

34
N

TOWER GROVE
SOUTH

35

37 38
R N

HARTFORD ST

NORTHAMPTON

WYOMING ST
HUMPHREY ST

JUNIATA ST
CONNECTICUT ST

36

39 40
R

43

SEE MAP 3

McDonald
Park

MCDONALD AVE
PARKER AVE
FAIRVIEW AVE
POTOMAC ST
OLEATHA AVE
MIAMI ST

HUMPHREY ST

41 42
45

46
R

WYOMING ST

TYLER AVE
PARKER AVE
FAIRVIEW AVE
POTOMAC AVE
OLEATHA AVE
MIAMI ST

OLEATHA AVE
MIAMI ST
THOLOZAN AVE

FAIRVIEW AVE
POTOMAC ST
OLEATHA AVE
MIAMI ST

MCKEAN AVE

SOUTH
CITY

50
N

BECK AVE

366

THOLOZAN AVE

International
Institute of
St. Louis

Gravois
Park

47

CHIPPEWA ST

48
N

GRAVOIS AVE

PHILLIPS PL

OSCEOLA ST
BEETHOVEN AVE
TAFT AVE
ELLENWOOD AVE
NEOSHO ST
GANNETT ST

49
R

Amberg
Park

DUNNICA AVE
KEOKUK ST
ALBERTA ST

DUTCHTOWN
SOUTH

SOUTHAMPTON

54
N

DELOR ST
WILCOX AVE

EICHELBERGER ST

MORGANFORD RD

TAFT AVE
NEOSHO ST
ITASKA ST

BINGHAM AVE
MERAMEC ST

BEVO

Marquette
Park

MERAMEC ST

55

56
N

St. Matthew
Cemetery

CHRISTY BLVD

EICHELBERGER ST

BATES ST

WALSH ST

DELOR ST
WALSH ST

MT. PLEASANT ST
ITASKA ST

DELOR ST

55

WILMINGTON AVE
DOVER PL
LOUGHBOROUGH AVE

Carondelet
Park

57
A

CARONDELET

58
R

Mississippi
River

© AVALON TRAVEL

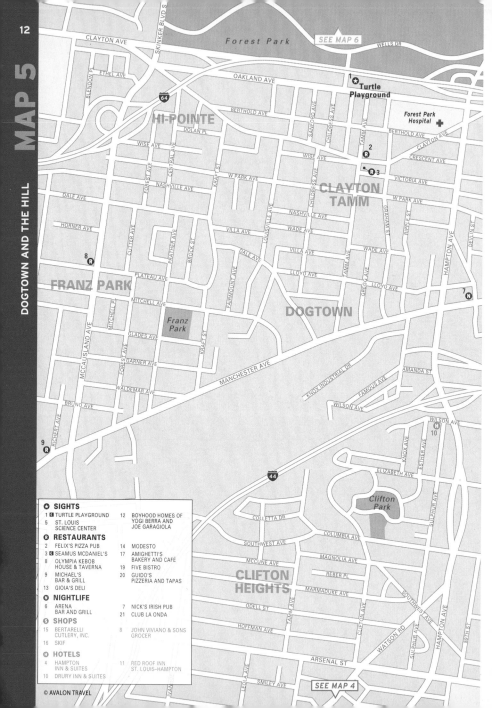

SIGHTS

| 1 | TURTLE PLAYGROUND | 12 | BOYHOOD HOMES OF YOGI BERRA AND JOE GARAGIOLA |
| 5 | ST. LOUIS SCIENCE CENTER | | |

RESTAURANTS

2	FELIX'S PIZZA PUB	14	MODESTO
3	SEAMUS MCDANIEL'S	17	AMIGHETTI'S BAKERY AND CAFÉ
8	OLYMPIA KEBOB HOUSE & TAVERNA	19	FIVE BISTRO
9	MICHAEL'S BAR & GRILL	20	GUIDO'S PIZZERIA AND TAPAS
13	GIOIA'S DELI		

NIGHTLIFE

| 6 | ARENA BAR AND GRILL | 7 | NICK'S IRISH PUB |
| | | 21 | CLUB LA ONDA |

SHOPS

| 15 | BERTARELLI CUTLERY, INC. | 8 | JOHN VIVIANO & SONS GROCER |
| 16 | SKIF | | |

HOTELS

| 4 | HAMPTON INN & SUITES | 11 | RED ROOF INN ST. LOUIS–HAMPTON |
| 10 | DRURY INN & SUITES | | |

SEE MAP 6

SEE MAP 2

CLAYTON AVE

CLAYTON AVE

64

Forest Park

GIBSON AVE

64

ARCO AVE

OAKVIEW PL

N 4

Forest Park
Community
College

OAKLAND AVE

OAKLAND AVE

St. Louis
Science Center ⊙ 5

WICHITA AVE

S TAYLOR AVE

SOUTH DR

MACKLIND AVE

EAST RD

BERTHOLD AVE

LAWN PL

HALF ST

WISE AVE

WISE AVE

WISE AVE

WISE AVE

CHELTENHAM

**KINGS
OAK**

N 6

W PARK ST

HUGHES PL

SWAN AVE

SEE MAP 2

PIERCE AVE

MANCHESTER AVE

SUBLETTE AVE

MACKLIND AVE

MCREE AVE

NORTHRUP AVE

S KINGSHIGHWAY BLVD

PATTISON AVE

21 N

44

44

H 11

Berra
Park

R 14

SHAW AVE

S 18

SHAW AVE

WILSON AVE

59TH ST

LILY AVE

R 13

15 S

R 20

DAGGETT AVE

S VANDEVENTER AVE

BISCHOFF AVE

WILSON AVE

THE HILL

S 16   19

R 17

MAURA AVE

ELIZABETH AVE

59TH ST

JANUARY AVE

DUGAN AVE

BISCHOFF AVE

EDWARDS ST

MARCONI AVE

HEREFORD ST

ELIZABETH AVE

SEE MAP 4

ALFRED AVE

Boyhood Homes of
Yogi Berra and
Joe Garagiola

BOTANICAL AVE

★ 12

BOTANICAL AVE

SHENANDOAH AVE

Missouri

COLUMBIA AVE

DALTON AVE

PEARL AVE

JANUARY AVE

SOUTHWEST AVE

TOWER GROVE PL

Botanical

HEGER CT

HEGER CT

Garden

COLUMBIA AVE

COLUMBIA AVE

REBER PL

MAGNOLIA AVE

BRANNON AVE

MAGNOLIA AVE

HEREFORD ST

MAGNOLIA AVE

Tower Grove Park

SUBLETTE AVE

REBER PL

REBER PL

REBER PL

*Sublette
Park*

SUBLETTE AVE

ODELL ST

**SOUTHWEST
GARDEN**

0   300 yds

0   300 m

DISTANCE ACROSS MAP
Approximate: 2.6 mi or 4.3 km

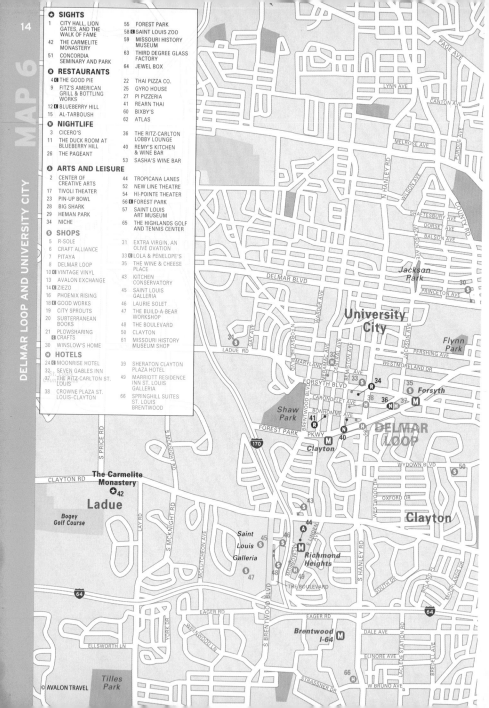

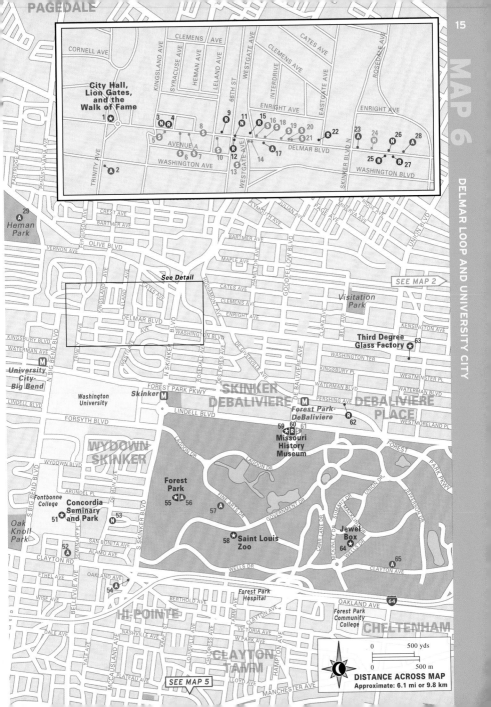

MAP 7

DISTANCE ACROSS MAP
Approximate: 15.5 mi or 25 km

0   1 mi

0   1 km

Normandie 1

Valhalla Cemetery

170

Butterfly House 2

Hanley Hills

OLIVE BLVD

University City

Haman Park

340

DELMAR BLVD

DELMAR LOOP

PRICE RD

HANLEY RD

LADUE RD

St. Louis Country Club

FORSYTH BLVD

Westwood Country Club

270 BALLAS

GEYER RD

67

Ladue

CLAYTON RD

170

Clayton

To 3 Faust Park

64 61

4

Log Cabin Golf Club

Galleria

CLAYTON RD

CLAYTON RD

Frontenac

5

WARSON RD

Tilles Park

LINDBERGH BLVD

BALLAS RD

6

BRENTWOOD BLVD

7

S. HANLEY RD

S. BIG BEND BLVD

100

To 8 American Kennel Club Museum of the Dog

61 67

Maplewood

9

100

10

MANCHESTER RD

ROCK HILL RD

KIRKHAM RD

270

Des Peres

DOUGHERTY FERRY RD

KIRKWOOD RD

WOODLAWN AVE

Glendale

Algonquin Golf Course

16,17

19,20

LOCKWOOD AVE

Magic House, Children's Museum 11

18

Old Webster Historic District

Webster Groves

21,22

Mackenzie

Kirkwood

12 13 14,15

ADAMS AVE

Westborough Country Club

44

366

Oakland

ELM AVE

CHIPPEWA ST

Resurrection Cemetery

366

BALLAS RD

St. Louis Community College

BIG BEND RD

Forever Oak Hill Cemetery

WATSON RD

Marlborough

To 23 Lone Elk Park and World Bird Sanctuary, 24 Shaw Nature Reserve, 25 Meramec State Park Cave Tour, and 26 Hidden Valley

S. LINDBERGH BLVD

WATSON RD

366

27

Emmenegger Nature Park

29 Laumeier Sculpture Park

Crestwood

Ulysses S. Grant National Historic Site

GRAVOIS RD

30

44

270

61 67

30

Sunset Burial Park

21

28

St. George

© AVALON TRAVEL

Greendale

St. Peters
Cemetery

Uplands
Park

Calvary
Cemetery

Bellefontaine
Cemetery

Hillsdale

Penrose
Park

O'Fallon
Park

Mississippi River

Natural Bridge Ave

Carter Ave

Fairgrounds
Park

Washington
University

DR. MARTIN LUTHER KING JR DR

Page Blvd

Delmar Blvd

CENTRAL
WEST
END

MIDTOWN

DeSoto
Park

Fontbonne
College

Forest
Park

Forest Park Ave

Saint Louis
University

Olive St

St. Louis

DOGTOWN

Manchester Ave

Chouteau Ave

DOWNTOWN

Jefferson
National
Expansion
Memorial

THE
HILL

LAFAYETTE
SQUARE

Park Ave

Lafayette
Park

Missouri
Botanical
Garden

Compton
Hill Park

Tower Grove
Park

Arsenal St

MISSOURI

SOULARD

SOUTH CITY

ILLINOIS

Francis
Park

Chippewa St

Willmore
Park

St.
Matthew
Cemetery

Saints Peter
and Paul
Cemetery

Carondelet
Park

Canokia

Wilbur
Park

Bella
Villa

North
Dupo

To Quail Creek
Golf Club

SIGHTS

2 BUTTERFLY HOUSE
11 THE MAGIC HOUSE,
   ST. LOUIS CHILDREN'S
   MUSEUM

18 OLD WEBSTER
   HISTORIC DISTRICT

NIGHTLIFE

12 KIRKWOOD ICE & FUEL

ARTS AND LEISURE

1 NORMANDIE
   GOLF CLUB
3 FAUST PARK
8 AMERICAN
   KENNEL CLUB
   MUSEUM OF THE DOG
13 STAGES ST. LOUIS
21 ST. LOUIS
   REPERTORY THEATER
22 OPERA THEATRE
   OF ST. LOUIS
23 LONE ELK PARK
   AND WORLD BIRD
   SANCTUARY
24 SHAW
   NATURE RESERVE

25 MERAMEC STATE
   PARK FISHER
   CAVE TOUR
26 HIDDEN VALLEY
27 POWDER VALLEY
   CONSERVATION
   NATURE CENTER
28 TAPAWINGO
   NATIONAL
   GOLF COURSE
29 LAUMEIER
   SCULPTURE PARK
30 QUAIL CREEK
   GOLF CLUB

SHOPS

4 MISTER GUY
   CLOTHIERS
5 PLAZA FRONTENAC
6 THE FACE & THE BODY
7 K. HALL DESIGNS
9 WEST COUNTY
   CENTER
10 KANGAROO KIDS

14 PAPERDOLLS
   BOUTIQUE
15 BLUSH BOUTIQUE
16 EUCLID RECORDS
17 YUCANDU
19 NATURALLY PURE
20 OLD WEBSTER

DISCOVER
St. Louis

St. Louis is a remarkable city, full of strange and beautiful secrets. The triumphs and follies of the past are visible everywhere in this red-brick town on the Mississippi River. This is where Lewis and Clark began their journey and Charles Lindbergh first took flight. In Forest Park—one of the largest urban green spaces in the nation—the pavilion from the 1904 World's Fair still stands. There's the soaring majesty of the Gateway Arch and the unearthly beauty of the Cathedral Basilica. On the city's south side sits the eerie home of the Lemp brewing family, who took their own lives after being pushed into insolvency by the Anheuser-Busch empire. The clubs and bars are filled with living blues legends—and with the memories of those who have come before.

Visitors will discover dozens of unique neighborhoods, from Grand South Grand, where you can find a halal meat market and a raucous Italian-restaurant-slash-rock-club within one block, to the Central West End, where bistros and boutiques occupy some of St. Louis's most architecturally stunning buildings, to Soulard, where you can stop in real-deal Irish pubs and dance-all-night clubs, all in shadow of the Anheuser-Busch brewery.

And because St. Louis is not widely heralded by glossy travel magazines and guidebooks, discovering the real St. Louis feels like your very own secret.

Planning Your Trip

Where to Go

Downtown

Visitors to downtown will find plenty to see and do—from the iconic Gateway Arch to shopping in one of the city's most cosmopolitan retail districts. After the bankers and lawyers head home at day's end, downtown's many restaurants and bars come alive. Whether you're looking for a sports bar packed with Cardinals fans or a chic martini lounge, you'll find it here.

Midtown and Central West End

Midtown is fast becoming the fine-arts hub of St. Louis, thanks largely to the reopening of the historic Fox Theatre and the development of Grand Center. In the Central West End, stately mansions nestle against modernist art galleries, which in turn neighbor high-end boutiques and rave-worthy restaurants.

Soulard and Lafayette Square

Soulard is home to pretty red-brick row-houses and friendly bars serving everything from draft beer to craft cocktails. In adjacent Lafayette Square, the Victorian-era mansions make this one of the most architecturally dazzling neighborhoods in the city. The many shops and restaurants hum with energy, and the bars and cafés that face historic Lafayette Park are particularly popular.

South City

The neighborhoods of South City are perhaps the most ethnically diverse in St. Louis. Within five city blocks of Grand South Grand, you can find three Vietnamese restaurants, a sushi restaurant, two Chinese restaurants, an Afghan restaurant, a Middle Eastern restaurant, and a halal meat market. At the Missouri Botanical Garden, visitors can

Dozens of small businesses have built lasting success in the once-residential Lafayette Square.

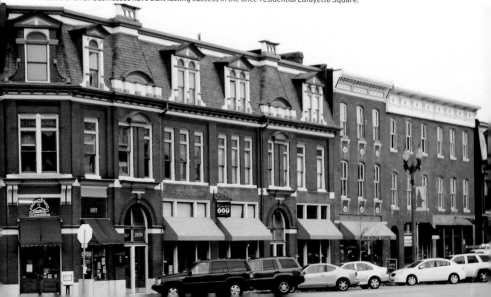

Yes, you can get *this close* to the gorgeous creatures at the Butterfly House, in Greater St. Louis.

explore the nation's oldest private botanical park and the first geodesic-dome greenhouse, the Climatron.

Dogtown and the Hill

The Hill is St. Louis's Italian neighborhood and a restaurant destination for visitors and native St. Louisans alike. On warm nights, it's not uncommon to see bocce tournaments unfolding on the neighborhood's lawns. Dogtown, to the north, is St. Louis's historically Irish neighborhood, and visitors won't be disappointed by the area's authentic Irish food and generous Guinness pours.

Delmar Loop and University City

The Delmar Loop spans both St. Louis and University City, and the area is constantly bustling with life. A visitor could spend an entire day in the Loop, shopping in boutiques and record stores, catching a movie at the art-house Tivoli Theater, attending a sold-out concert at The Pageant, and bowling till 3am at the Pin-Up Bowl.

Greater St. Louis

While some city-dwellers grumble about the homogenous nature of "the county," there are many suburbs with personalities all their own. There are stellar restaurants, hip boutiques, and great bars (including a craft brewery) in Ladue and Maplewood. Main Street in Webster Groves hearkens back to the turn of the 20th century. Best of all, most of these suburbs can be reached via the recently expanded MetroLink system, meaning that visitors can check out Greater St. Louis easily and affordably.

When to Go

As is true in many Midwestern cities, winter temperatures can dip into the single digits, while summer temperatures sometimes soar past 100 degrees. If extreme temperatures bother you, plan to visit St. Louis in April, May, September, or October. The city's vibe is downright joyous in the spring months, when people say goodbye to winter and make haste to St. Louis's many parks. In the fall, the tree-lined streets are awash in red and gold. If you don't mind some heat, pack plenty of shorts and sundresses and experience summer in St. Louis. The only time to avoid St. Louis is in the dead of winter: Freezing temperatures and icy roads can easily turn a fascinating city into a frustrating one.

The Two-Day Best of St. Louis

Day 1

► Start your first day in St. Louis off right—with a strong cup of coffee and delicious crêpe at Rooster.

► After your appetite has been sated (and your caffeine needs met), head due east on Locust Street. The Jefferson Expansion Memorial Park and world-famous Gateway Arch are just eight blocks away.

► After a tram ride to the Arch's observation deck, stop by the Old Courthouse for a mini-St. Louis history lesson, and then head southwest toward Busch Stadium to see the St. Louis Cardinals. Even if you don't have game tickets, it's worth walking around Busch's perimeter to get a sense of St. Louis sports history.

► The 8th Street MetroLink station is directly across the street from the stadium, and from there you can take the train to the Delmar Loop. Walk three blocks west of the Delmar Boulevard MetroLink stop, and you will find myriad shops and lunch options, including the landmark Blueberry Hill.

► Take the MetroLink to the DeBaliviere stop, then hop on the 90 or 3 bus into Forest Park. From the stop at the top of Art Hill, the Saint Louis Zoo is less than a five-minute walk away.

► By day's end, a cocktail will be in order, and there is no finer place (or view!) than Cielo in the Four Seasons hotel. Kick back at this elegant bar and watch the sun set over the Mississippi River.

► After whetting the appetite with a few

The Climatron houses tropical plants at the Missouri Botanical Garden.

The Old Courthouse played a key role in several major civil-rights cases.

small plates, head to Niche for dinner via car or the Four Seasons' limousine service. It's not every day that a *Food & Wine* Best New Chef and three-time James Beard Award finalist makes you dinner.

► Finish the evening at B.B.'s Jazz, Blues, and Soups for more drinks and some live music.

Day 2

► Start off your day with a delicious, leisurely breakfast at one of the delightful coffeehouses in the Central West End. The Central West End location of Pi Pizzeria offers delectable breakfast pizza (and some of the best coffee in town) 6am-11am every day. Coffee Cartel, a people-watching mainstay at the corner of Euclid and Maryland, whips up espresso drinks that will jump-start your morning. Then walk over to the Cathedral Basilica for a self-guided tour.

► From the cathedral, the Contemporary Art Museum St. Louis is only a short cab ride away; the fare clocks in at right around 5 bucks.

► After taking in the latest exhibition at the Contemporary, take another quick cab ride south to nearby Grand Boulevard. The Grand South Grand neighborhood, just past Tower Grove Park, offers some great shops and ethnic markets. Selecting a lunch spot can be challenging—given the overwhelming number of great spots—but you can't go wrong with the a steaming bowl of *pho* at LemonGrass or delicious homemade pasta at Mangia Italiano.

► Next, take a nice walk (or a quick ride on the 70 bus) to the Missouri Botanical Garden. After a stroll around the grounds, catch a cab or take the 8 bus to the intersection of Jefferson Avenue and Cherokee Street.

► A short jaunt down Cherokee puts you in the heart of the city's largest Latino neighborhood. Taquería El Bronco offers some great, fresh choices for an inexpensive dinner, and some good margaritas as well. Whether your preferred post-prandial activity is antiques shopping or club hopping, you'll find both options on Cherokee (most of the antiques stores stay open until 7pm). 2720 Cherokee Performing Arts Center, which serves as both a nightclub and a massive art space, is particularly fun.

Beer, Blues, and Barbecue

Anheuser-Busch beer wagon

BEER

No tour of this beer, blues, and barbecue town is complete without a visit to the **Anheuser-Busch Brewery.** But do be aware that A-B is no longer the beloved hometown employer. When the giant Belgian concern InBev took over in 2008, many St. Louisans lost jobs–and the entire city lost faith in this once-iconic company. Despite this, both beer fans and history aficionados will want to take a narrated tour of the King of Beer's erstwhile castle, and afterward, enjoy complimentary A-B products in the hospitality room.

To experience a true St. Louis brewing success story–one that's growing jobs rather than slashing them–head toward downtown to check out the popular local microbrewery **Schlafly Tap Room** at 21st and Locust. (You'll find a second Schlafly outpost, the **Schlafly Bottleworks,** in Maplewood. The Bottleworks serves up organic fare and hosts one of the area's most popular farmers markets through the spring and summer months.)

Sample a pint at **Urban Chestnut Brewing Company** near Midtown, and get a taste of another great St. Louis craft brewery–one that's symbolic of the craft-beer renaissance that's swept the city in the past few years. Other stellar local breweries include **The Civil Life Brewing Company** in South City

and **Morgan Street Brewery** on Laclede's Landing downtown. In Soulard, **iTap** wows even the choosiest beer connoisseur with its hundreds of bottles and drafts.

To keep up with what's hot on the St. Louis beer scene, check out the excellent **www.stlhops.com,** authored by hometown brew-scholar Mike Sweeney.

BLUES

Grab a table on the patio at the **Broadway Oyster Bar,** toss back a few chilled oyster shooters, and enjoy some great live blues. Live music plays pretty much every night at the Oyster Bar.

B.B.'s Jazz, Blues, and Soups is a legendary venue that serves up live tunes every night of the week alongside great Cajun classics like jambalaya and gumbo.

The **Old Rock House** is a fabulous refurbished saloon that serves up both blues *and* barbecue.

BARBECUE

When it comes to barbecue in St. Louis, the key word is pork. Lots and lots of pork. There are countless St. Louis restaurants that serve up their best pork steaks and country-style spare ribs every day. But to really satisfy your 'cue cravings, head to **Pappy's Smokehouse** in Midtown. This altar to smoked pig is the best barbecue restaurant in town.

Running a (very) close second is **Bogart's Smokehouse,** the wildly and deservedly popular Soulard barbecue shop opened by Pappy's own pitmaster, Skip Steele. Do not miss the house-made pastrami or the deviled-egg potato salad.

Want in on a barbecue secret (one so good we're almost reluctant to share it)? Some of the best ribs in town appear weekly at **The Piccadilly at Manhattan,** near the St. Louis-Maplewood border. Just how good are these ribs? Well, on nights when they're available, you're very likely to find Pappy's owner Mike Emerson enjoying a plateful and praising owner (and grill-master) Nick Collida.

SIGHTS

St. Louis is a city of iconic structures, from the soaring curve of the Gateway Arch to the shimmering dome of the Cathedral Basilica. A trip to St. Louis would not be complete without visiting such important sights—yet visitors also will not want to miss the smaller landmarks that make St. Louis the historical, beautiful, and downright quirky city that it is. Most of the region's architectural treasures are concentrated downtown, making it easy to walk from one stunning structure to the next. Every St. Louis neighborhood has its own special character, and this is reflected in the sights. Midtown is a thriving arts center, and sights include baroque theaters and Art Deco buildings. Life in the Delmar Loop and Central West End revolves around the 1,293-acre Forest Park, where many of the city's cultural institutions are located. The sights of Soulard reflect the city's strong French history, while South City boasts a proud amalgam of businesses and institutions built by immigrants from all points of the globe. Throughout the entire region, visitors will find gorgeous old churches, historically significant homes, and you-have-to-see-it-to-believe-it structures.

HIGHLIGHTS

LOOK FOR ℂ TO FIND RECOMMENDED SIGHTS.

ℂ **Best Civic Treasure:** Nothing brings the whole community together like the extraordinary **Citygarden,** which sprouts from the downtown concrete in a riot of color and form. This is the perfect destination for art lovers, kids, weary worker bees—everyone, really (page 27).

ℂ **Most Magical Museum:** There is no place in the world like **City Museum**—and that's not hyperbole. Spend an hour or a day in this artist-designed wonderland, and come away with experiences that include walking through an enchanted forest and clambering into a rooftop school bus that teeters over the city (page 28).

ℂ **Most Iconic Landmark:** At 630 feet, the **Gateway Arch** is the tallest national monument in the United States. Approximately one million visitors ride the tram to the top of the Arch each year (page 28).

ℂ **Best Escape to Europe:** The **Cathedral Basilica of St. Louis** rises like a gorgeous European landmark along historic Lindell Boulevard. Newer than most American cathedrals, yet imbued with the grandeur of centuries-old churches, the cathedral is well worth a tour for architecture and history buffs alike (page 32).

ℂ **Best Haunted Mansion: The Lemp Mansion** is beautiful and historic, to be sure—but it's also the home of dark local legends.

Take a tour of Lemp Mansion and you're certain to acquire new St. Louis knowledge (along with a few goose bumps) (page 33).

ℂ **Best St. Louis Microcosm:** Bustling with life all year round, the **Soulard Farmers Market** is more than just a one-stop shop for fresh produce. The market also hosts live entertainment, sells St. Louis delicacies (like Gus' Pretzels), and offers some of the best people-watching in the city (page 34).

ℂ **Best Place for Green Thumbs:** The 79-acre **Missouri Botanical Garden** features some of the best horticultural displays in the nation. Don't miss the Climatron, the first geodesic-dome greenhouse ever built (page 35).

ℂ **Best Roadside Attraction:** Sculpted by Bob Cassilly (the same genius behind the City Museum), the giant snapping turtles of **Turtle Playground** occupy a whimsical oasis off Highway 40. Visitors can stroll around these gigantic critters—and even climb on top of them (page 36).

ℂ **Best Free Attraction:** The City of St. Louis is wonderfully generous with its cultural institutions: The art museum, history museum, and many other attractions are free. But it's the world-renowned **Saint Louis Zoo** that has visitors and residents returning again and again to see the charismatic megafauna that call this place home (page 39).

Downtown   Map 1

CAMPBELL HOUSE MUSEUM
1508 Locust St., 314/421-0325,
www.campbellhousemuseum.org
HOURS: Wed.-Sat. 10am-4pm, Sun. noon-4pm
COST: $8 adult, free for children 12 and under

Thanks to a set of interior photographs from the early 20th century, the rooms in this historic downtown landmark were restored

precisely—right down to the placement of the original furnishings. This attention to detail is impressive, and the home is beautiful, yet visitors might also find their tour a bit disquieting. With just a glimpse out of the Campbell House's tall windows, one can see how much St. Louis has changed in the past two centuries.

Today, the meticulously restored Campbell

© GATEWAY ARCH EXPERIENCE

Citygarden

House seems out of place where it stands: a lovely anachronism. There is nothing else like it for blocks. Campbell House is all that remains of the once-prestigious Lucas Place, a neighborhood of row houses for which this avenue was the main drag. At the time of its development, the neighborhood's boundaries lay just outside the city's limits. The Campbell House is all that remains of this, St. Louis's first suburb.

◖ CITYGARDEN
8th St. between Market St. and Chestnut St., 314/241-3337, www.citygardenstl.org
HOURS: Daily sunrise-10pm
COST: Free

One of the city's greatest and newest civic treasures, Citygarden turns an often-trod two-square-block swath of downtown into an absolute wonderland. Plenty of the art world's biggest names—including Keith Haring and Mark di Suvero—have sculptures on display here, but it's Citygarden's ability to bring together an entire community that really makes it special. On any given day, you'll see jurors and judges taking their lunch break near the way-larger-than-life rabbit sculptures by Tom Claassen. You'll see little kids splashing gleefully in the fountains before taking a turn plunking out a tune on the giant piano. You'll see tourists, native St. Louisans, moms and dads, art aficionados, downtown worker bees—and the one unifying factor is the irrepressible smile on all of their faces, because Citygarden never fails to delight. Every piece of art here could be labeled "can't-miss"; particularly popular is Julian Opie's *Bruce and Sara Walking*, an LED panel that gives a whimsical send-up to everyday "Walk" signs. Igor Mitoraj's *Eros Bendato (Eros Bound)* makes an unforgettable addition to the intersection of 8th and Market Streets. The lush landscaping here is just as lovely as the human-made art. Like so many cultural gems in St. Louis, Citygarden does not charge an admission price—yet another destination that is truly meant for all to enjoy.

CITY MUSEUM

701 N. 15th St., 314/231-2489, www.citymuseum.org
HOURS: Mon.-Thurs. 9am-5pm, Fri.-Sat.
9am-midnight, Sun. 11am-5pm
COST: $12 general admission, $10 after 5pm on Fri.
and Sat., free for children 2 and under; $5 for The Roof;
additional $7.95 ($6 after 5pm on Fri. and Sat.) for
World Aquarium admission

There is no other museum on earth like this one. Here, visitors can wander through a 13,500-square-foot aquarium, climb through a 20-foot Slinky, explore an eight-story tunnel system made from conveyor belts, walk into the belly of a whale, and peek inside a school bus (which just happens to be teetering on the top of the building).

What is City Museum? It's what might result if a magic spell turned a Kilimanjaro-sized mountain of steel, stone, metal, plastic, and glass (salvaged from the relentless demolition of St. Louis buildings) into an enchanted playground. The imagination behind this 600,000-square-foot urban funhouse belonged to the late artist Bob Cassilly, lost far too young in a tragic accident in 2011. An urban revivalist in a city not known for its preservation, Cassilly dedicated his life to saving St. Louis's history from the wrecking ball. Cassilly's dream lives on as a team of 20 artisans piece together a never-ending puzzle, one abandoned city relic at a time.

EADS BRIDGE

Between Laclede's Landing and the Arch grounds (at the foot of Washington Ave.)
HOURS: Accessible 24 hours daily
COST: Free

Although not a frequent tourist destination, the Eads Bridge is both an impressive sight and a historically significant one. This 140-year-old dual-level, three-span steel-arch bridge, designed and built by Captain James Buchanan Eads, connects St. Louis to East St. Louis. It was the first large bridge to span the Mississippi River, and the first road-and-railway bridge. The Eads was built upon a caisson that descends more than 100 feet down into the bedrock below, and it represents a feat of engineering respected around the world.

The second level of Eads Bridge is open to foot traffic, but pedestrians share the 1,022-foot span with vehicles traveling at highway speeds. The view is spectacular, but those concerned with life and limb may find the walk anything but serene. The MetroLink (St. Louis's light-rail train), which travels smoothly along the deck below, offers a safer alternative.

THE EUGENE FIELD HOUSE & ST. LOUIS TOY MUSEUM

634 S. Broadway, 314/421-4689,
www.eugenefieldhouse.org
HOURS: Mar.-Dec. Wed.-Sat. 10am-4pm, Sun.
noon-4pm; tours in Jan. and Feb. by appointment only
COST: $5 adult, $1 child 4-11, free for children 3 and under

Roswell Martin Field occupies an important place in St. Louis—and U.S.—history. An attorney, Field defended the citizenship of Dred and Harriet Scott before the Supreme Court in the landmark Dred Scott case. His son, Eugene, was a writer best known for his children's poetry and humorous essays. Visitors can tour Eugene's boyhood home on Broadway, just outside the center of downtown. The home fell into disrepair during the Great Depression, but in 1936 children in the St. Louis Public Schools raised nearly $2,000 to restore the home to its former Victorian elegance. Admission includes a visit to an antique toy museum, and to this day, all St. Louis schoolchildren are admitted free of charge.

GATEWAY ARCH

St. Louis Riverfront, 877/982-1410,
www.gatewayarch.com
HOURS: Labor Day-Memorial Day daily 9am-6pm,
Memorial Day-Labor Day daily 8am-10pm
COST: Free entrance to the Arch; Journey to the Top
$10 adult, $7 with National Park Pass, $5 child 3-15

The Arch is to St. Louis what Lady Liberty is to New York: iconic. Reaching 630 feet at the apex, it is the tallest man-made monument in the United States. This stunning structure was designed by architect Eero Saarinen and structural engineer Hannskarl Bandel in 1947, although construction did not begin until 1963. By the time the Arch opened to the public in 1967, it was already writ large on the national

© GATEWAY ARCH EXPERIENCE

Gateway Arch

imagination. The Jefferson National Expansion Memorial, as the Arch and small national park on which it sits are officially called, symbolizes St. Louis's historic status as the "Gateway to the West," the jumping-off point for every Pacific-bound pioneer since Lewis and Clark.

Be sure to catch a screening of *Monument to the Dream,* a short documentary that chronicles the curve's construction, including how the left and right sides didn't exactly align at the top as work was nearly completed, forcing the St. Louis fire department to shrink the stainless steel plates a fraction of an inch by hosing them down with cold water. Finally, take a claustrophobic tram ride to the top (the elevator curves within the structure), feast your eyes on the fine view of the city, and think how much better the skyline would look with a giant, sleek, silver arch in the foreground.

OLD COURTHOUSE

11 N. 4th St., 314/655-1600, www.gatewayarch.com
HOURS: Daily 8am-4:30pm
COST: Free

The Old Courthouse plays an integral role in the history of American race relations. Unfortunately, that role wasn't always positive, as slaves were sold in estate sales on the courthouse steps. But then, the first trials of the Dred and Harriet Scott case—one of the main sparks that ignited the American Civil War—took place here.

Dred Scott, a slave who traveled with his owner to free territory, argued that he and his wife could no longer be enslaved after living in a free state. The Scotts even offered to purchase their freedom, but their master refused. In 1846, the Scotts filed suit at the Old Courthouse. The case was argued there the next year, and the Scotts lost on a technicality. After a second trial was granted and argued at the Courthouse in 1850, the Circuit Court of St. Louis County ruled in favor of the Scotts. In 1857, the United States Supreme Court ruled that Dred and Harriet Scott did not have citizenship or the right to be free. But while it seemed inevitable that this decision would expand slavery, it in fact caused abolitionists

RESURRECTING OLD NORTH

Few parts of St. Louis City have seen as much devastation as North St. Louis. Once a thriving industrial hub, North St. Louis lost much of its wealth—and much of its vitality—in the mid-20th century, as St. Louis suffered a breathtakingly sharp population decline. In the early 21st century, ruthless developers bought up huge swaths of land in North St. Louis, only to let the buildings rot with blight.

Fortunately, many St. Louisans are unwilling to sit by while a beautiful historic neighborhood falls victim to neglect and the wrecking ball. Civic leaders in this predominantly African American area are mobilizing residents to take back Old North, as the area just north of downtown is called, and bring it back to life. Quite a few visionary young city dwellers have joined the cause, leaving comfy middle-class neighborhoods to join the fight for Old North's survival. But make no mistake: The residents of Old North won't just stop at seeing their neighborhood survive; they're ready to see it flourish. Below are some can't-miss stops that provide a great introduction to Old North and its ongoing resurrection.

Crown Candy Kitchen: There's no better first stop in Old North St. Louis than Crown Candy Kitchen (1401 St. Louis Ave., 314/621-9650, http://crowncandykitchen.net, Mon.-Thurs. 10:30am-8pm, Fri.-Sat. 10:30am-9pm, Sun. 11am-5pm). Every day, this old-fashioned diner teems with life. Businesspeople, tourists, foodies, cops (and the occasional Food Network host) all crowd into this legendary space. Open since 1913, Crown Candy has remained a constant in Old North St. Louis's rise and fall and rise. Maybe that's because there's always a need for great comfort food at super-low prices. Try the excellent BLT, the egg salad sandwich, or the giant gourmet hot dog (when's the last time you had lunch for $4.49?). Crown Candy also boasts an amazing ice-cream-sundae menu, plus old-time favorites like malteds. Homemade candy is available by the pound. And when you eat at Crown Candy, you'll have a great view of Crown Square, the $32 million revitalization project that's bringing life back to this historic area.

Mullanphy Emigrant Home: After lunch at Crown Candy Kitchen, take a stroll or a quick drive up to the Mullanphy Emigrant Home (1609 14th St.). This building, once a triumph of late-19th-century masonry, is in dire need of saving. Owing to blight and natural disaster, Mullanphy has lost many of its extraordinary original details (including a round-topped cornice), but its beauty is still evident. Mullanphy Emigrant Home, as its name suggests, housed dozens of European immigrants in the waning days of the 19th century. In its 140-year-plus existence, it has also served as everything from a schoolhouse to a motorcycle repair shop. But although St. Louis's alt-weekly gave Mullanphy the dubious "Best Lost Cause" award in 2007, its hope for survival is far from dim. The Old North St. Louis Restoration Group, a hard-working neighborhood organization, has rebuilt parts of Mullanphy and plans to restore it to its former elegance.

New Roots Urban Farm: New Roots is a force for good in Old North St. Louis. While its ideals would no doubt be embraced by proponents of the Slow Food movement (and with all due respect to Slow Food), New Roots is not an organization devoted to making middle- and upper-class folks feel good about eating local. Rather, New Roots helps an impoverished area survive by sharing food—and food production methods—with its neighbors. New Roots describes its model as not just nonprofit but "antiprofit." Following the Catholic Worker Movement ethos, New Roots' goals are to nourish the community and to teach others how to nourish themselves. Throw in a healthy dose of environmentalism and pacifism, and you have a group that's doing some pretty revolutionary things in this Midwestern city. Stop by the farm (1830 Hogan St.) or see New Roots' wares at the North City Farmers' Market (right across from Crown Candy Kitchen, Sat. 10am-1pm).

© GATEWAY ARCH EXPERIENCE

Old Courthouse

to redouble their efforts to end slavery. Those fights were waged in newspapers, at town meetings, and ultimately on the battlefields of the Civil War.

The Old Courthouse is listed in the National Park Service's National Underground Railroad Network to Freedom, in recognition of the building's crucial place in abolitionist history. Many human- and civil-rights cases have been argued at the Old Courthouse; more than two decades after the Dred Scott decision, in the very same courtroom, Virginia Minor fought for women's voting rights. One of the building's courtrooms has been remodeled to reflect this monumental era, and the lobby features regularly revolving exhibits that trace the history of justice in St. Louis.

OLD POST OFFICE

815 Olive St., 314/436-0101, www.oldpostofficestl.com
HOURS: Mon.-Fri. 9am-5pm
COST: Free

Put the history of a once-thriving downtown into perspective by exploring one of the last remnants of its boom years. St. Louis's former Post Office and U.S. Customs House was dedicated in the optimistic years of the post-Civil War economy. Some urbanists say the demolition of the historic Century Building across the street irrevocably frayed the fabric of downtown St. Louis. Fortunately, the crown jewel of this historic square still survives. A massive renovation completed in 2006 preserved the Old Post Office's extravagant, Second Empire-style architecture and glass atrium for future generations of St. Louisans. This isn't a tourist attraction, per se, but visitors are welcome to explore the shared spaces of its first level. The Old Post Office is now home to the downtown branch of Webster University, offices of the Missouri Arts Council, a casual restaurant, and a branch of the St. Louis Public Library. Downtown St. Louis is currently making a thrilling comeback, and this gorgeous structure reminds natives and visitors alike of how vibrant the city can be.

ST. LOUIS UNION STATION

1820 Market St., 314/421-6655,
www.stlouisunionstation.com

HOURS: Mar.-Oct. Mon.-Sat. 10am-9pm, Sun.
10am-6pm, Nov.-Feb. Mon.-Sat. 10am-7:30pm, Sun.
11am-6pm (guided tours available by appointment only;
call in advance)

COST: Free

Union Station is the elegant transportation hub that began greeting visitors and returning residents in 1894. This national landmark now houses a luxury hotel and a less-than-stellar shopping mall, but it was once a full-scale train depot on the order of Chicago's Union Station.

At St. Louis's height, it was the largest, busiest railway station in the country, servicing 100,000 people a day. Despite its retrofitting, the station's elegant grand lobby remains intact. Its 65-foot barrel-vaulted ceiling, Romanesque archways, and stained-glass windows provide a beautiful glimpse of Union Station's true glory days. This iconic structure is best viewed from the exterior, unless you want to ask yourself this depressing question: Why in the world would anyone turn such an important building into a third-rate tourist trap of a mall? Visitors looking to complete their Hard Rock Café T-shirt collection will, unfortunately, find an outpost of the international chain here.

Midtown and Central West End   Map 2

CATHEDRAL BASILICA OF ST. LOUIS

4431 Lindell Blvd., 314/373-8200, www.cathedralstl.org

HOURS: Daily 7am-5pm (guided tours by appointment; call in advance to schedule)

COST: Free

As in many cities in Europe, the most impressive work of art in St. Louis isn't housed in the local museum but rather in the cathedral. As far as cathedrals go, this one is in its infancy—ground was broken in 1907, and construction was not completed until the late 1980s. Still, what the cathedral lacks in longevity, it makes up for in beauty. The 83,000-square-foot ceiling of the Cathedral Basilica, the emerald-domed jewel of the Central West End, is covered by a mosaic made of 41.5 million pieces of glass in more than 7,000 colors. The work took 20 different artists several decades to complete. The cathedral's beauty and magnitude rival the grandeur of cathedrals that are centuries older, and yet some of the intricate mosaic work reflects modern themes. Here and there, priestly vestments are replaced by suits and skinny ties. Look closely, and you'll even see a computer or two. Docent-led tours are offered a couple of times each week and are highly recommended. Pope John Paul II honored the cathedral as a basilica in 1997.

ERNEST TROVA AT SAINT LOUIS UNIVERSITY

221 N. Grand Blvd.

COST: Free

St. Louis's collection of public art is impressive. Among the artists responsible for these works-about-town was Ernest Trova, a renowned surrealist who was born in Missouri in 1927. A donation of 40 of his works led to the establishment of Laumeier Sculpture Park in Sunset Hills, and additional Trova sculptures can be found all over St. Louis. Enjoy works from Trova's *Profile Canto* series while taking a walking tour of the scenic Saint Louis University campus off Grand Boulevard in Midtown. Trova's dynamic works can also be seen in downtown Clayton; his *FM6 Walking Jackman*, at 98 N. Brentwood Boulevard, is particularly stunning. The artist made his home in St. Louis until his death in 2009.

SCOTT JOPLIN HOUSE STATE HISTORIC SITE

2658 Delmar Blvd., 314/340-5790,
www.mostateparks.com/scottjoplin.htm

HOURS: Feb. Tues.-Sat. 10am-4pm, Mar.-Oct.
Mon.-Sat. 10am-4pm; closed Nov.-Jan.

COST: $4 adult, $2.50 child 6-11, free for children 5 and under

Walk in the footsteps of the King of Ragtime by visiting his modest Delmar walk-up. A historical society has preserved the rooms where Joplin composed many of his most famous works, including the "Maple Leaf Rag." The musical history of St. Louis is rich, and Joplin's years here

(between 1900 and 1907) coincided with the birth of the city's burgeoning jazz culture. Joplin lived near the honky-tonk dives of Chestnut Valley and Gaslight Square—cultural hotbeds that would later foster the talents of Miles Davis, Josephine Baker, and Ike and Tina Turner.

Soulard and Lafayette Square   Map 3

ANHEUSER-BUSCH BREWERY
12th St. and Lynch St., 314/577-2626,
www.budweisertours.com
HOURS: Sept.-May Mon.-Sat. 10am-4pm, Sun. 11:30am-4pm; June-Aug. Mon.-Sat. 9am-5pm, Sun. 11:30am-5pm
COST: Free

St. Louis is a beer-making, beer-drinking, beer-loving town. Celebrate this heritage by touring the facilities of sudsy stalwart Anheuser-Busch (and be rewarded at the end of your tour with, you guessed it, a beer).

Before the invention of refrigeration, a vast network of natural caverns below St. Louis provided a consistent, cool temperature ideal for aging beer. By the mid-1800s, plenty of brewers wanted in on this sweet beer-cave deal, and St. Louis was home to nearly 50 breweries. But by 1950, thanks to factors like Prohibition, the Great Depression, and the wild success of the Anheuser-Busch family, only eight remained (including Griesedieck, Falstaff, and Lemp). Only A-B struck it rich and stood the test of time; it is now the largest brewer in the country and operates distributorships all over the world. (Please don't refer to it by the company's new name, Anheuser-Busch InBev, unless you want to get dirty looks from the locals; the company was sold to Belgian brewing giant InBev in 2008, and as a result many local jobs were lost.)

⬛ THE LEMP MANSION
3322 DeMenil Pl., 314/664-8024, 314/644-1814
for haunted history tour reservations,
www.lempmansion.com
HOURS: No regular hours; call ahead to schedule tour (reservations required)

COST: Free (haunted history tours are $20)

This 33-room mansion was once the estate of William Lemp, an industrious German immigrant who brought the hearty beer of his homeland to St. Louis in the 1840s. Lemp began producing lager, and he sold it in the grocery stores his family owned. The popularity of the lager soon outpaced the popularity of the stores, so Lemp left the grocery business and devoted his attention entirely to beer-making. He eventually became one of the city's wealthiest residents.

Today the Lemp family is a part of local legend—but that legend is a dark one. The Lemps were eccentric and suicide-prone, and the rumor is that not one descendant remains. The brewery closed a couple of years ago, after a very brief resurrection. The mysterious death of son Frederick was only the beginning of a tumultuous, fiercely secretive, 70-year family saga that included three suicides. Creep yourself out with a haunted tour led by medium Betsy Belanger. These tours are typically given on Monday night, but it's recommended that you call ahead. Tours are given more frequently in the weeks leading up to Halloween, when guests are given a half-hour lecture about the fascinating family, then led throughout the rooms. During the tour, Belanger points out family heirlooms, spends extra time in rooms where a death occurred, and tries to communicate with beyond-the-grave Lemps. Depending on your viewpoint, these tours are either totally scary or hilariously kitschy. But either way, they're quite interesting.

The historic home also serves as a restaurant and an inn.

◀ SOULARD FARMERS MARKET

730 Carroll St., 314/622-4180, www.soulardmarket.com
HOURS: Year-round Wed.-Thurs. 8am-5pm, Fri.
7am-5pm, Sat. 7am-5:30pm
COST: Free

Peruse the colorful offerings of local vendors and enjoy the spectacle that is Soulard Market, the oldest market west of the Mississippi River. A vital source of inexpensive foodstuffs, this historic market has survived through two centuries of relocations and transformations. It was even once a Civil War encampment for the Union Army.

The structure that the market now occupies was built in the 1930s and was restored only recently after a long period of decline. Stalls are open here Wednesday through Saturday, but the market sees most of its activity on Saturday. On this day only, every stall is open and stocked, and the thoroughfares are crowded with residents from all over the region. The Soulard Market offers something of a St. Louis microcosm, as people from all backgrounds gather to find good prices on fresh foods. The social aspect of a day at Soulard Market hearkens back to the ancient Greek ideal of an *agora*—a place where friendly conversation, political involvement, and cultural edification can coexist. To that end, Soulard Market allows everything from political canvassing (although it's rarely in-your-face) to strolling musicians. Soft pretzels, frozen custard, and cold beer are available for purchase, as are fresh flowers and numerous handicrafts.

South City   Map 4

THE "ANCIENT RUINS" IN TOWER GROVE PARK

Next to the Piper Palm House, on the upland north of Main Dr., 314/771-4424, www.towergrovepark.org
HOURS: Sunrise-sunset
COST: Free (docent-led group tour available for minimum donation of $40; call to schedule)

The broken stone columns along the north edge of Tower Grove Park's fountain pond are not the ancient ruins they appear to be. Rather, these faux-Greco curiosities were hand-selected by park benefactor Henry Shaw. They were plucked from the remains of the old Lindell Hotel, which burned to the ground shortly before Shaw deeded the land for Tower Grove Park to the city. Inspired by the spooky aesthetics of the fire-damaged blocks, Shaw had a pile of them transported to the park and arranged according to his design. The stone balustrade at the pond's southern shore was rescued from the U.S. Custom House and Post Office, which was demolished in 1939.

COMPTON HILL WATER TOWER

Grand Blvd. and Russell Blvd., in Reservoir Park, 314/552-9000, www.watertowerfoundation.org
HOURS: Occasional tours; call or visit the website for dates and times
COST: $5 adult, $3 child 6-12, free for children 5 and under

The observation deck of this 100-foot-tall retired French Romanesque water tower offers visitors a 360-degree view of the city and a glimpse into another era. The tower's staircase has 198 steps and seven landings. The water tower was built in 1898, when the population of St. Louis was just over half a million and quickly outgrowing its water-delivery system. It was renovated during the 1990s. The Compton Hill Water Tower is open for climbing just a few times per year, but visitors can stroll along the walks of the tower's beautifully landscaped 36-acre park, and around neighboring Stacy Park Reservoir, anytime.

INTERNATIONAL INSTITUTE OF ST. LOUIS

3654 S. Grand Blvd., 314/773-9090, www.iistl.org
HOURS: Tour available last Wed. of the month at 10am (reservations required)
COST: Donation requested

One of several international institutes in the

COURTESY OF MISSOURI BOTANICAL GARDEN

Missouri Botanical Garden

United States, this center for civic development serves St. Louis City's burgeoning international population by providing new Americans with English classes and other important transition services. Tours are available to interested parties, but the classrooms and offices of this South City sight are not so much a tourist destination as a place that enriches the very fabric of St. Louis.

The vibrant population of new Americans in this city is infusing some of its decaying neighborhoods with new life. If you're not in St. Louis on the last Wednesday of the month, consider visiting some of the city's immigrant-owned businesses. Browse in the Central American markets and Mexican *taquerías* along Cherokee Street. Stop in one of Grand Boulevard's many Vietnamese restaurants for a steaming bowl of *pho ga*. The International Institute is perhaps best experienced at the Festival of Nations, a weekend-long celebration of ethnic foods, art, and dancing held in Tower Grove Park every August.

MISSOURI BOTANICAL GARDEN

4344 Shaw Blvd., 314/577-9400, www.mobot.org

HOURS: Daily 9am-5pm, Memorial Day-Labor Day open Wed. until 9pm, grounds only Wed. and Sat. 7am-9am, closed Christmas Day; call for special holiday hours

COST: $8 adult, free for children 12 and under

Escape the din of the city for an afternoon and explore the setting of the nation's oldest private botanical park. Opened to the public in 1859 by botanist and civic leader Henry Shaw, the garden is internationally renowned for its botanical research and exploration. Tucked into the well-kept residential neighborhoods of South City, the garden's paved paths meander through 79 acres of some of the nation's greatest horticultural displays. Must-see attractions include the Climatron, the first geodesic-dome greenhouse ever constructed, and the sprawling traditional Japanese garden. Lesser-known but equally notable features include a six-million-specimen herbarium and an extensive historical library with volumes dating back to the garden's establishment.

Dogtown and the Hill   Map 5

BOYHOOD HOMES OF YOGI BERRA AND JOE GARAGIOLA
5400 block of Elizabeth Ave. on the Hill

St. Louis is a sports-loving town (to put it mildly), and so it's no great surprise that two of its most cherished heroes are baseball legends. Yogi Berra and Joe Garagiola were boyhood neighbors in the historically Italian, working-class Hill neighborhood, where one can imagine them playing baseball in the streets on 1940s summer afternoons. Berra and Garagiola lived across the street from one another on the 5400 block of Elizabeth Avenue (the late Jack Buck, a Hall of Fame baseball announcer and one of St. Louis's most beloved native sons, also lived on Elizabeth). Visitors can take a stroll through the baseball giants' old stomping grounds while also enjoying the array of Italian markets, delis, and restaurants for which the neighborhood is renowned.

ST. LOUIS SCIENCE CENTER
5050 Oakland Ave., 314/289-4400, www.slsc.org
HOURS: Mon.-Sat. 9:30am-5:30pm, Sun. 11am-5:30pm; planetarium shows hourly on the half hour
COST: Free general admission; parking $10; free parking for planetarium; admission fees vary for special exhibits

Although general admission to the St. Louis Science Center (SLSC) is free, an important distinction shared by many of the city's most popular attractions, no expense has been spared in its making. SLSC is one of the largest of its kind in the country, as well as one of the top five science centers in the nation. Two full stories, plus the neighboring James S. McDonnell Planetarium, boast hundreds of fun, interactive exhibits (many have admission charges) designed to teach visitors the basic principles of science. The state-of-the-art, four-story Omnimax theater (separate admission) screens everything from ocean documentaries to rock concerts.

◖ TURTLE PLAYGROUND
6401 Oakland Ave., south of Forest Park
HOURS: Daily dawn-10pm
COST: Free

The late Bob Cassilly was the powerful visionary behind the awe-inspiring City Museum. But before he dreamed up the great whale that greets visitors there, he was envisioning gigantic snapping turtles, red-eared sliders, and a snake crawling along Highway 40. Concrete sculptures of these Missouri wildlife natives now decorate a small park directly across from the zoo and Forest Park, and they are difficult to miss. Wondering if it's okay to climb atop the humongous turtles? Not to worry—locals do it all the time. They provide the perfect vantage point for watching the traffic go whizzing by on the freeway, which is actually much more relaxing than it sounds. Lie under the sun on the broad back of a Missouri snapping turtle for a few hours and the roar of the cars blurs into an unbroken wall of white noise, the perfect soundtrack for letting your mind drift while watching the clouds. In addition to the big turtles, there's a sandpit with sculptures of enormous turtle eggs in various stages of cracking open; the robust child (or daring adult) can perch atop these as well, and try to leap from egg to egg around the circumference of the pit. A nearby swing set offers more traditional recreation, but it's almost always empty (small wonder).

Delmar Loop and University City   Map 6

THE CARMELITE MONASTERY
9150 Clayton Rd., Ladue, 314/993-6899
HOURS: Always open
COST: Free

The spiritual focus of the Carmelites, a monastic order founded in the 12th century, is contemplative prayer. This Discalced Carmelite monastery, one of only 70 in the world, is intended for exactly that. The painstakingly maintained grounds offer visitors several settings for prayer and contemplation, including an inspiring chapel that is open to the public and holds a daily mass and benediction. No matter their beliefs, visitors are likely to find the quiet beauty of this place thoroughly moving.

CITY HALL, LION GATES, AND THE WALK OF FAME
6801 Delmar Blvd., University City, 314/862-6767,
www.ucitymo.org, www.stlouiswalkoffame.org
COST: Free

University City, one of St. Louis's oldest suburbs, is now widely considered one of its most liberal and diverse. Founded by publisher Edward Gardner Lewis in 1906, the city was a streetcar suburb in the late 19th and 20th centuries. The Beaux Arts architecture of the southern portion of the town, where the octagon-shaped City Hall and majestic Lion Gates stand, reflects this historic legacy and unique charm (and '80s-movie buffs might recognize the Lion Gates from *Back to the Future;* screenwriter Bob Gale is a U. City native). Just down the street from these signature sights, you'll find one of St. Louis's most popular entertainment districts—the Delmar Loop—and its eclectic assembly of shops, restaurants, and clubs.

The wide sidewalks of The Loop in University City are perfect for leisurely strolling and alfresco dining. And while the window-shopping is tempting, be sure to look down every once in a while and see St. Louis's very own walk of fame. The brass stars and bronze plaques embedded in the pavement (there are now more than 115) commemorate the lives and achievements of the city's most well-known residents. Honorees include Ulysses S. Grant, T. S. Eliot, Josephine Baker, Joseph Pulitzer, Charles A. Lindbergh, Betty Grable, and many others. The Walk of Fame began as the project of civic good-guy Joe Edwards, the Loop's foremost developer and tireless champion. Fans of 1970s crooner Michael McDonald will be pleased to see that he, too, has a star on the boulevard.

CONCORDIA SEMINARY AND PARK
801 Seminary Pl., Clayton, 314/505-7000, www.csl.edu
COST: Free

Located in the inner-ring suburb of Clayton, this meditative seminary campus is one of the largest in the country. The current Concordia campus was built in 1926, but the beautiful carved stonework of its main buildings and quadrangle has a mid-19th-century feel. Visitors will enjoy the pretty park that tumbles down the hill upon which the seminary is built. This lush park often bustles with life: It's a favorite study spot for Washington University students, a great place to take the dog for a run, and a destination for yoga and tai chi practitioners. Concordia is home to a 245,000-volume library and 49-bell carillon.

FOREST PARK
Between Skinker and Kingshighway,
www.forestparkforever.org
HOURS: Daily sunrise-sunset
COST: Free

Bordered by Kingshighway to the east and Skinker Boulevard on the west, this 1,293-acre urban oasis is larger than New York's Central Park. On a warm day, the park attracts visitors in the thousands. Its rolling grounds are home to the Saint Louis Art Museum, the Missouri History Museum, the Saint Louis Zoo, and multiple golf courses. The museums and zoo

TOP 10 PLACES TO TAKE THE KIDS

- **Best Place to Reenact a Scene from** *Big:* the giant piano at **Citygarden** (page 27).

- **Best Place to Climb Through a 20-Foot Slinky:** the enormous, whimsical **City Museum** (page 28).

- **Best Place to Cool Off During the Summer Heat:** the fountain near the children's garden at the **Missouri Botanical Garden** (page 35).

- **Best Place to See an Animatronic T-Rex:** the fun, interactive **St. Louis Science Center** (page 36).

- **Best Place for a Paddleboat Ride:** around the lagoon at **Forest Park** (pages 37 and 99).

- **Best Place to Lunch with Lions:** near the sea lions' pond at the **Saint Louis Zoo** (page 39).

- **Best Place to See Hundreds of Free-Flying Butterflies:** the **Butterfly House** at Faust Park (page 40).

- **Best Place to Solve a Math Problem on a Four-Foot Calculator: The Magic House, St. Louis Children's Museum** (page 40).

- **Best Place to Dream of Broadway:** at a show performed by the **Center of Creative Arts'** student acting company, where local kids hone big-time talent (page 87).

- **Best Place to Fill Up on Popcorn and Hot Dogs:** a **St. Louis Cardinals** game at Busch Stadium (page 104).

are free to visit. At the Boat House, guests can have a cocktail and a simple meal, then rent a paddleboat to tour the beautiful Grand Basin and canals. As part of a massive parkwide renovation project begun in the mid-'90s, this elegant water feature has been restored to its original state and recalls the glory days of the 1904 World's Fair.

If you need a break from sightseeing, head to **Art Hill** (just across the street from the Saint Louis Art Museum). On a warm afternoon, set up a picnic on this broad lawn and nap in the shadow of the monument to King Louis IX. Lazily contemplate the paddleboats in the Grand Basin below, and perhaps the golfers off to the north. Enjoy the breeze. Fall back asleep. (Freshly fallen snow in the winter makes this a popular sledding destination for locals, so you may want to restrict your sleepy Art Hill reveries to the summer months.)

JEWEL BOX

Wells Dr. and McKinley Dr. in Forest Park, 314/531-0080
HOURS: Mon.-Fri. 9am-4pm, Sat. 9am-11am, Sun. 9am-2pm

COST: $1; free Mon.-Tues. 9am-noon
The popularity of this Forest Park attraction has waned in the last 20 years, perhaps due to a renovation in which much of its display space and kitsch appeal were surrendered to the modern amenities of a full-scale event space. But the Jewel Box remains a compelling structure, and visitors to the park should not miss it. Resembling a Victorian terrarium, this elegant old world-style greenhouse was partly a WPA project. It was built in 1936, as the nation struggled through the first years of economic depression, and its beautiful, jewel-like floral displays beckon visitors through its doors year-round. It is a popular photo opportunity for local families—particularly during the holidays, when the house offers its traditional poinsettia display and a welcome reprieve from the dreary winter months.

MISSOURI HISTORY MUSEUM

Lindell Blvd. and DeBaliviere Ave. in Forest Park, 314/746-4599, www.mohistory.org
HOURS: Daily 10am-5pm, Tues. 10am-8pm
COST: Free; admission fees vary for special exhibits
This stately museum offers a rotating collection

SIGHTS

© 123RF.COM

Amur leopard resting in the shade at the Saint Louis Zoo

of themed exhibitions with a mainly regional focus. Well-attended events have included a Miles Davis retrospective and a 1904 World's Fair exhibit, and also a traveling exhibit from the National Baseball Hall of Fame. Museum officials seem to have a healthy appetite for audio tours, and several are usually available, but it's the wealth of supplemental events to the main exhibits that make the museum an everyday possibility. From presenting 15-minute plays about famous abolitionists to opening up the auditorium for a screening of home movies donated (temporarily) by area families to hosting the Urban Stories series, which pairs interesting guest speakers with unusual topics (how about Andre Royo of HBO's *The Wire* discussing "How Art Reflects Life" with his character Bubbles as the prism?), the Missouri History Museum makes a strong case for history being very much alive and very entertaining. While the special exhibits require a modest fee for entry, most if not all of the supporting programs are free; so once you've done the tour, you can stick around and make a full day

of it—and maybe catch a meal at the on-site café, Bixby's, which serves an excellent Sunday brunch.

◀ SAINT LOUIS ZOO

1 Government Dr. in Forest Park, 314/781-0900, www.stlzoo.org
HOURS: Early Sept.-late May daily 9am-5pm, late May-early Sept. Mon.-Thurs. 8am-5pm, Fri.-Sun. 8am-7pm, closed Christmas Day and New Year's Day
COST: Free

That's right, admission to the Saint Louis Zoo is free, by act of the Missouri state legislature. But don't let the budget-line admission fool you—this is a world-class zoo, with natural enclosures for the great apes (with heavy-duty glass instead of bars), a state-of-the-art Penguin & Puffin Coast where the only thing between you and the flightless waterfowl is a few inches of frosty air, and the River's Edge, a lengthy trail that shows you how the hippopotamuses live above and below the waterline. But the zoo doesn't just focus on the charismatic megafauna—the Monsanto Insectarium provides entry into the world of bugs and arachnids in horrifying, close-up detail (may not be suitable for the squeamish, but kids love it).

There's also a zoo within the zoo: The Children's Zoo requires an admission fee of $4 per person (free for children under 2), but it's free 8am-9am and worth being the first stop. Here's where the baby animals are tended to and kept on limited display, and educational programs on various small animals (such as birds and reptiles) are presented throughout the day. And no trip to the zoo is complete without taking a ride on the Zooline Railroad, a small-scale train that circles the entire park; tickets for this family favorite are $5 per person (free for children under 2), but hooting while going through the tunnels is free. Two well-stocked, sit-down cafés—the Lakeside Café and the Painted Giraffe—provide lunch options beyond burgers and fries.

THIRD DEGREE GLASS FACTORY

5200 Delmar Blvd., 314/367-4527, www.stlglass.com
HOURS: Mon.-Sat. 10am-5pm
COST: Free to visit; tours $12 (Mon.-Sat. 10am-4pm); classes and demonstrations available at varying rates

Third Degree Glass Factory is one of Delmar Boulevard's most interesting newcomers. The staff, volunteers, and team of instructors offer the city's only public-access glass-arts education center in a 12,000-square-foot space converted from a dilapidated 1930s service station. In this now-inviting space, visitors can take classes in the craft, watch demonstrations, rent studio space, and purchase the work of local glass artists. In addition to offering normal visiting hours, the organization holds well-attended art events like the Wall Ball throughout the year. If you're in St. Louis on the third Friday of the month, be sure to check out Third Degree's free open house (6pm-10pm).

Greater St. Louis   Map 7

BUTTERFLY HOUSE

Faust Park, 15193 Olive Blvd., Chesterfield,
636/530-0076, www.butterflyhouse.org
HOURS: daily 9am-5pm
COST: $6 adult, $5 senior, $4 child 3-12, free for children 2 and under

The Butterfly House is located on the elegant grounds of Faust Park in Chesterfield. A former home of Circus Flora, the grounds of this 8,000-square-foot garden feature a carousel, which only adds to the already whimsical nature of the place. Butterflies thrive in the glass house's humid environment; all told, the conservatory is home to 150 tropical plant species and more than a thousand tropical butterflies in free flight. Guests are free to walk among the fluttering creatures and can watch them emerge from their chrysalises in a fascinating "Miracle of Metamorphosis" display.

The Butterfly House was opened in 1998 to foster a better understanding of butterflies' life cycles and natural habitats. In addition to daily visiting hours, the facility offers educational

programs, special events, and lectures. Be sure to check the full-length mirrors upon leaving the conservatory, or you might accidentally take a monarch home in your hat.

THE MAGIC HOUSE, ST. LOUIS CHILDREN'S MUSEUM

516 S. Kirkwood Rd., 314/822-8900,
www.magichouse.org
HOURS: School year Tues.-Thurs. noon-5:30pm, Fri. noon-9pm, Sat. 9:30am-5:30pm, Sun. 11am-5:30pm; A Little Bit of Magic area opens from Tues.-Fri. at 10:30am, summer Mon., Tues., Wed., Thurs., and Sat. 9:30am-5:30pm, Fri. 9:30am-9pm, Sun. 11am-5:30pm
COST: $9.50 admission, free for children under 1

The Magic House gives kids (yes, of all ages) the chance to step into life-size science experiments. This huge Kirkwood house—more than double its original size thanks to a recent expansion—plays host to all manner of fun, educational activities. You can touch an electrically charged ball and make your hair stand on end, solve a math problem on a four-foot-tall

The Magic House, St. Louis Children's Museum

calculator, create your own TV newscast, and walk into a giant soap bubble. While it's true that the exhibits at the Magic House are designed to captivate the younger set, parents will appreciate the inventiveness of the exhibits. For a minimal admission, you and your happy brood can partake in more than 100 activities, and top off the experience by zinging down a three-story slide.

OLD WEBSTER HISTORIC DISTRICT

Roughly bounded by Allen Ave., Elm Ave., W. Lockwood Ave., and the Missouri Pacific Railroad tracks, www.historicwebster.org, www.webstergroves.org

The shady lanes and craftsman-built homes of this prized St. Louis suburb have a cinematic quality that has not gone unnoticed. For decades, filmmakers and journalists have looked to Webster Groves for images of the quintessential middle-American town. Beginning with the 1966 CBS documentary *16 in Webster Groves* and perhaps ending with photojournalist Laura Greenfield's portrayal in her best-selling book *Girl Culture,* Webster has always served as a microcosm of the Midwestern experience. Take it all in by joining the locals in a stroll down Lockwood Avenue. Enjoy this main drag's eclectic assortment of restaurants and shops, and then head south for a self-guided tour of the pristine residential neighborhoods. If the day is sunny and the air is warm, you may feel like the star of your very own Metro-Goldwyn-Mayer film.

RESTAURANTS

Over the past decade, St. Louis has shaken off its reputation as a culinarily timid town. For years, visitors associated St. Louis with good-but-unadventurous fare, including plates heaped with meat and potatoes and bowls of pasta sauced with sweet marinara. Fast forward to today, when fine-dining options can be found in practically every neighborhood and the city boasts James Beard nominees, *Bon Appétit* award winners, and two of *Food & Wine* magazine's "Best New Chefs" (that would be Niche's Gerard Craft in 2008, followed by Farmhaus's Kevin Willmann in 2011). Cozy bistros such as Brasserie by Niche and Franco serve food inspired by the French countryside, and hip spots like Five and Home Wine Kitchen try adventurous pairings that always seem to work out just right.

Of course, it's not always about haute cuisine and molecular gastronomy in this Midwestern city. True to its strong immigrant roots, the food scene in St. Louis is a delightful assemblage of Italian sandwich shops, Vietnamese noodle cafés, and Bosnian smokehouses. International options are particularly abundant in South City, where immigrant groups from Sarajevo to Addis Ababa have settled. St. Louis's Thai and Vietnamese restaurants are great bets for hungry vegetarians, as these spots turn out consistently delicious dishes loaded with tofu and fresh veggies.

There are plenty of gastronomic adventures to be had in the Gateway City. But make no mistake about it: St. Louisans also know their comfort food. After all, how better to withstand a harsh Missouri winter than with a

© SARA KETTERER

HIGHLIGHTS

LOOK FOR **(** TO FIND
RECOMMENDED RESTAURANTS.

(**Most Beautiful Restaurant: Bridge Tap House & Wine Bar** is one seriously gorgeous restaurant, with creative touches—glassware suspended from violin strings, chandeliers fashioned from antlers—that elicit as many "wows" as the amazing beer list (page 44).

(**Best Brewpub:** The world may know St. Louis as the hometown of Anheuser-Busch, but folks in the know favor **The Schlafly Tap Room.** Pair Schlafly's excellent microbrews with homemade soft pretzels, a bratwurst sandwich, or the best fish-and-chips in town. If you're visiting St. Louis during the winter, don't miss the Coffee Stout (page 47).

(**Best Barbecue:** In a town known as much for its barbecue as for its giant Arch, picking a favorite is tough. But when the (smoked-wood) chips are down, top honors go to **Pappy's Smokehouse.** Owner Mike Emerson serves up the finest 'cue in the city. The line often snakes through the restaurant and out the door, but the wait is worth it—and made totally tolerable by the abundant samples that travel through the queue, often handed out by Emerson himself (page 48).

(**Best Small Plates:** The term "small plates" is so common as to be almost meaningless, but **Taste** reclaims the phrase in a major way, thanks to its absolutely perfect culinary creations. The kitchen's playful take on street tacos will leave you smiling from ear to ear, as will the cocktails prepared by expert mixologist Ted Kilgore (page 49).

(**Best Soul Food:** A former backup singer for Ike Turner, Robbie Montgomery opened **Sweetie Pie's** in Forest Park Southeast in 2003. Offerings change daily and include pork steaks, okra, mac and cheese, and an oxtail stew that would give any high-end joint a run for its money (page 50).

(**Best Coffee Shop:** Tired of cookie-cutter coffee chains? Let **The Mud House** restore your faith in what a neighborhood coffee shop can truly be. Grab a seat, and spend the morning (or afternoon) sipping, snacking, and surfing at one of the hippest, friendliest places in town (page 51).

(**Best Place for a First Date:** With its sultry lighting, abundant red roses, and decadent desserts, **Baileys' Chocolate Bar** is the perfect first-date spot. Indulge in dark-chocolate martinis or nibble on a variety of truffles. Romance comes easy at this Lafayette Square gem (page 52).

(**Best Gourmet Experience:** Mention **Niche** (page 62) to any St. Louis foodie, and brace yourself for rapturous descriptions of what very well might be the best restaurant in town. Gerard Craft isn't afraid to make dishes like pork cheeks with bacon ice cream—and *Food & Wine* didn't hesitate to name him one of the Best New Chefs of 2008. In 2011, **Farmhaus** (page 56) head chef Kevin Willmann garnered that same auspicious *Food & Wine* award, thanks to his playful, divine takes on Gulf Coast cooking—including a prawn-and-escolar preparation that is the best seafood dish in town.

(**Best Pizza:** Fistfights have probably started over St. Louis pizza—that's how loyal St. Louisans are to their favorite pie. For perfectly crisp thin-crust pizza, try **Pizza-A-Go-Go** (page 58), a homey BYOB spot near the city's south side, or sample the authentic Neapolitan pizza at **The Good Pie** (page 63). If you crave a thicker crust, stop by the legendary **Black Thorn Pizza & Pub** (page 57).

(**Best Burgers:** Get your burger with a side of nostalgia at **Blueberry Hill** (page 61), where owner Joe Edwards's collection of Americana covers both levels of this Delmar Loop landmark. The burgers are perfectly seasoned (don't miss the onion rings). The burgers at super-friendly Irish pub **Seamus McDaniel's** (page 60) rival those at Blueberry Hill, and in the summer you can enjoy your meal on Seamus's huge patio.

heaping bowl of spaghetti or a blue-plate special? Visitors should not leave town without trying foods that are quintessentially St. Louis: We're talking toasted ravioli, thin-crust pizza topped with Provel cheese, barbecued pork steaks, and gooey butter cake.

PRICE KEY

$ Entrées less than $10

$$ Entrées $10-20

$$$ Entrées more than $20

Downtown   Map 1

AMERICAN
BAILEYS' RANGE $$
920 Olive St., 314/241-8121, www.baileysrange.com
HOURS: Mon.-Sat. 11am-1am, Sun. 11am-midnight
Baileys' Range is a burger wonderland for adults and kids alike. You can order a basic beef burger topped with your favorite cheese, vegetables, and condiments, or you can explore the menu of specialty burgers, like the swanky ABC (with apple, bacon, and Camembert cheese). Tired of plain old beef? Baileys' Range also has burgers made from bison, lamb, chicken, and black beans. (Whatever burger you choose, the fries are a must-have side.) Kids will love the shakes, which feature ice cream made in-house; adults will love such boozy shakes as the Sweet Sweet Bacon, made with bourbon, salted-caramel ice cream, and, yes, actual bacon.

◖ BRIDGE TAP HOUSE & WINE BAR $$
1004 Locust St., 314/241-8141, www.thebridgestl.com
HOURS: Mon.-Sat. 11am-1am, Sun. 11am-midnight
A great selection of wine and craft beer in one of St. Louis's most stunningly designed and decorated spaces: What more could you ask for in a hip downtown bar? Well, Bridge Tap House & Wine Bar also serves a fun menu of bar snacks (spiced popcorn and nuts) and plates of cheese and charcuterie that are a perfect match for your drink of choice. If you want a more substantial meal, Bridge can deliver that, too. There are sandwiches, salads, and a selection of small but tasty entrées like mac and

cheese with poblano peppers or coffee-braised beef with orzo.

THE EDIBLE DIFFERENCE $
615 Pine St., 314/588-8432,
http://edibledifferencestl.com
HOURS: Mon.-Fri. 7am-2pm
From early in the morning, the towering high-rises surrounding The Edible Difference teem with businesspeople. For these downtown worker bees, this café is the ideal breakfast and lunch spot. The casual, serve-yourself efficiency and great home-style breakfasts draw crowds that sometimes spill out onto the sidewalk. Menu offerings include everything from Create-a-Sandwich to a massive Cobb salad. Lunch specials change daily and are always inexpensive.

LOLA $
500 N. 14th St., 314/621-7277, www.welovelola.com
HOURS: Mon.-Thurs. 11am-midnight, Fri. 11am-2am, Sat. 9:30am-2am, Sun. 9:30am-midnight
You'll find Lola right around the corner from always-bustling Washington Avenue, but this restaurant and bar pulses with an energy that's uniquely its own. Here you can sip fancy cocktails and groove to local musicians and DJs until the wee hours of the morning—and then, after a brief snooze, you can return and enjoy chicken and waffles for brunch. Lola serves dinner, too, everything from savory crepes to steaks and seafood to a playful pairing of mac and cheese with a lobster tail corn dog.

EAT LIKE A LOCAL

Spend enough time in St. Louis–and by "enough time" we mean "really just a couple days"–and you will find certain foods listed on practically every restaurant's menu, from hot spots to corner dives. A few foods are so distinctively *St. Louis* that you'd be remiss not to try them at least once. Read the list, and understand why Tums were invented in St. Louis, too.

ST. LOUIS-STYLE PIZZA
Politics. Religion. Pizza. If you're looking for a good argument in St. Louis, bring up one of the aforementioned topics. St. Louisans take their pizza very, very seriously–even when outsiders consider it strange (or, even worse, mediocre). True St. Louis-style pizza starts with a cracker-thin crust topped with Provel cheese. It's the Provel that really incites debate. Delicious, melty pizza topping or inferior "cheese food"? Decide for yourself by visiting any outpost of the beloved local chain Imo's Pizza. Just don't out yourself as a tourist by asking for a "slice"– St. Louis-style pizza is served by the square.

TOASTED RAVIOLI
The origin story of the toasted ravioli varies from teller to teller. Some claim that toasted ravioli is the result of a happy accident, when a St. Louis chef mistakenly dropped stuffed pasta into the deep fryer. Others say that toasted ravioli got its (intentional) start at Oldani's restaurant on the Hill, now known as Mama's on the Hill. No matter where they came from, T-ravs (as the locals say) are a super-popular appetizer. You can order meat-filled or cheese-filled T-ravs (meat-filled are more traditional). The deep-fried delights have a structural integrity similar to that of a fried mozzarella stick, and are also served with marinara sauce.

PORK STEAKS
The pork steak is an absolute must-have at any St. Louis summertime barbecue–and plenty of local restaurants serve this popular cut, too. The pork steak comes from a pig's shoulder. While it isn't necessarily the best cut of meat, the pork steak is made fork-tender by simmering for hours in barbecue sauce.

ST. PAUL SANDWICH
Yes, it's a little strange that something called a "St. Paul sandwich" originated in St. Louis. And, in all honesty, the St. Paul sandwich itself is a little strange: Take an egg foo yong patty, apply a liberal amount of mayonnaise and a handful of dill pickles, and fold the whole shebang between two slices of Wonder bread. The St. Paul sandwich is getting harder and harder to find, but it can still be ordered at most chop suey places in the city.

GOOEY BUTTER CAKE
Don't call it a baked good–call it a baked *great*. So delicious that some sweet-toothed tourists have carried it back on the plane with them (or have it overnighted to their home), the gooey butter cake is a true St. Louis original. Recipes vary from bakeshop to bakeshop, but all start with a solid foundation of butter and yellow cake, topped with a cream-cheese mixture and sprinkled with confectioner's sugar. Saint Louis Bread Co., a café empire based here in town (it's called Panera elsewhere), serves gooey butter danishes. Park Avenue Coffee (1919 Park Ave.) offers gooey butter cake in 76 glorious flavors. There's even a shop on the south side devoted solely to the GBC (Gooey Louie, 6483 Chippewa St.).

THE CONCRETE
For more than 80 years, St. Louisans have flocked to Ted Drewes Frozen Custard shops. The legendary frozen custard, served out of two southside locations (one at 6726 Chippewa St., the other at 4224 S. Grand Blvd.), is unparalleled. The most popular Ted Drewes treat is The Concrete: thick custard blended with any number of ingredients and served in an iconic yellow cup. Before your server hands you The Concrete, she'll probably turn it upside down. Don't panic–that's just to prove that the custard's so thick that the spoon won't fall out. Try the Fox Treat, a Concrete with hot fudge, raspberries, and macadamia nuts.

MIKE SHANNON'S STEAKS & SEAFOOD ❸❸❸

620 Market St., 314/421-1540, www.shannonsteak.com
HOURS: Mon.-Fri. 11am-9pm, Sat.-Sun. 5pm-9pm; bar open daily until 10pm

Mike Shannon is one of St. Louis's best-loved native sons. A former Cardinals slugger, Shannon switched to the broadcast booth in the early 1970s and continues to call each game with his trademark giddy fervor ("A hit up the middle right now would be like a nice ham sandwich and a cold, frosty one!"). His downtown restaurant is half sports bar, half upscale steakhouse, and wholly filled with baseball-loving bonhomie. On game days, fans pack the bar to take in Cardinals action on the plasma TVs, and those who stick around past the bottom of the ninth are often treated to a visit by the man himself. Even people who care little about Redbird Nation will likely be impressed by the food. The dry-aged steaks are extraordinarily good, and side-item options include some of the best mashed potatoes you'll ever eat.

ASIAN

SEN THAI ASIAN BISTRO ❸

1221 Locust St., 314/436-3456, www.senthaibistro.com
HOURS: Mon.-Fri. 11am-2:30pm and 5pm-9:30pm, Sat.-Sun. 5pm-9:30pm

This section of downtown could use a quick-and-cheap noodle shop, but the more upscale Sen fills residents' curry cravings perfectly well. The menu can best be described as "Asian eclectic": a little Chinese, a little Vietnamese, a *lot* of Thai. While some local Asian restaurants dial down the spice for Midwestern palates, Sen creates dishes that are full of delicious, peppery heat. Try the *pad kapao* (spicy fried rice flecked with fresh basil and chiles), or tuck into the *bamee* barbecued pork. Just don't be too proud to ask for a glass of water.

WASABI ❸❸

1228 Washington Ave., 314/421-3500,
http://wasabisushibars.com
HOURS: Mon.-Thurs. 11am-2pm and 5pm-9pm, Fri. 11am-2pm and 5pm-10pm, Sat. 5pm-10pm, Sun. closed

Wasabi occupies an unassuming storefront on otherwise glitzy Washington Avenue. Visitors distracted by the strip's fashionable boutiques and trendy bars might walk right past the place, despite its red neon sign declaring the presence of "SUSHI." That, however, would be a mistake. The cavernous space behind Wasabi's door is far more impressive than its exterior, and the rolls and *nigiri* also draw raves.

BREAKFAST

ROOSTER ❸

1104 Locust St., 314/241-8818, www.roosterstl.com
HOURS: Mon.-Fri. 7am-3pm, Sat.-Sun. 8am-3pm

Rooster is one of the few breakfast options in downtown St. Louis, but it's worth seeking out on its own merits. Crepes are a house specialty, with both savory and sweet varieties available. Savory crepes range from simple combinations like brie-and-apple or cheddar-and-bacon to such fancier fare as basil-and-goat cheese. Sweet crepes include everything from an indulgent pairing of Nutella and strawberries to a simple and tasty lemon crepe with ricotta cheese. Sandwiches are available for lunch, and the brunch menu features excellent French toast and a classed-up version of that meat-tastic St. Louis staple, the slinger (a hamburger patty topped with sausage, two eggs, hash browns, chili, and cheese).

CONTEMPORARY AND NEW AMERICAN

CIELO ❸❸❸

999 N. 2nd St. (in the Four Seasons Hotel),
314/881-5800, www.fourseasons.com/stlouis
HOURS: Mon.-Fri. 6:30am-2:30pm and 6pm-10pm, Sat.-Sun. 7am-2:30pm and 6pm-10pm

Like the Four Seasons Hotel in which it's located, Cielo is elegant and expensive. But this is *not* your typical overpriced hotel food. Chef Fabrizio Schenardi turns out contemporary Italian fare that is both beautiful and delicious. Small plates shine brighter at Cielo than entrées (although if Schenardi's flawless ahi tuna on eggplant caponata is on offer, by all means order it), and the pastas are particularly good. Gnocchi and beer-braised short ribs are favorites. Cielo offers one of the best—if not *the* best—views in the entire city. Snag a table by the floor-to-ceiling windows, and you'll spend your meal gazing out at the hotel's rooftop infinity pool and, beyond that, the Arch.

PRIME 1000 ❸❸❸
1000 Washington Ave., 314/241-1000,
www.prime1000.com
HOURS: Mon.-Fri. 4pm-10:30pm, Sat. 5pm-11pm, Sun. closed

Are you in St. Louis—or Las Vegas? You might find yourself asking this question at this sleek downtown steakhouse. The steaks match the sizzle of the stylish decor, whether you splurge on prime, dry-aged rib-eye or choose (relatively) less expensive Black Angus or grass-fed cuts. Prime 1000 isn't simply a steakhouse, though. There are delicious pork, chicken, and seafood dishes, too. Even if you don't want a full meal, a glass of wine at the bar will give you a glimpse of some of the city's most beautiful people.

TONY'S ❸❸❸
410 Market St., 314/231-7007, www.tonysstlouis.com
HOURS: Tues.-Fri. 5:30pm-9:30pm, Sat. 5pm-10:30pm

Posh Tony's provides the ultimate old-school St. Louis experience from the front door to the final bill. Do you want to indulge your inner captain of industry with Osetra caviar and trophy California cabernet? Tony's is the place. Do you want to enjoy some of the city's best veal and lobster dishes? Tony's is the place. Do you want to enjoy the most pampering restaurant service of your life? Tony's is the place.

PUB FOOD
◖ THE SCHLAFLY TAP ROOM ❸❸
2100 Locust St., 314/241-2337, www.schlafly.com
HOURS: Mon.-Tues. 11am-10pm, Wed.-Thurs. 11am-midnight, Fri.-Sat. 11am-1am, Sun. noon-10pm

The home of one of St. Louis's first and finest craft breweries, the Schlafly Tap Room serves rustic American and British pub fare that complements the many different styles of beer created on premise: several different kinds of mussels; roast chicken; schnitzel; and the most excellent fish and chips in town. Service can be hit-or-miss, particularly during peak hours, but most servers are happy to recommend pairings when the menu does not. Housed in a beautiful historic building, the Tap Room is an ideal place for casual dining and leisurely drinking. But weekend diners, beware: Conversation becomes difficult when boisterous crowds fill the high-ceilinged dining room and adjacent bar.

Midtown and Central West End   Map 2

AMERICAN
THE BEST STEAK HOUSE ❸
516 N. Grand Blvd., 314/535-6033,
www.beststeakstl.com
HOURS: Mon.-Fri. 10am-9pm, Sat. 11am-9pm, Sun. 11am-8pm

Across the street from the historic Fox Theatre, The Best Steak House offers a great lunch at a great price, and is arguably one of the city's best-kept secrets. Visitors in the mood for simple, satisfying fare (think grilled beef, fried fish, Texas toast, and baked or French-fried potatoes) will not be disappointed. This cafeteria-style restaurant is nearly always crowded, and for good reason: The Best Steak House's crave-worthy, no-nonsense food is grilled right in front of diners, then handed over efficiently on red plastic trays.

HAMBURGER MARY'S BAR & GRILLE ❸
3037 Olive St., 314/533-6279,
www.hamburgermarys.com/stlouis
HOURS: Mon.-Tues. 11am-11pm, Wed.-Thurs. 11am-midnight, Fri.-Sat. 11am-1:30am, Sun. 10am-1:30am

Every day's a party at Hamburger Mary's, a gay-friendly burger joint in the city's up-and-coming Midtown Alley. The menu items—with sassy names like The Bird Cage of Paradise (a turkey club)—are a notch above your standard bar fare, but it's the excellent service and fun environment that make Hamburger Mary's worth a visit. Throughout the week, karaoke contests and drag shows keep things lively. Visit on a Tuesday evening to get two bucks off your Mary-tini.

BARBECUE
◖ PAPPY'S SMOKEHOUSE ◉
3106 Olive St., 314/535-4340,
www.pappyssmokehouse.com
HOURS: Mon.-Sat. 11am-8pm, Sun. 11am-4pm

When Pappy's Smokehouse opened its doors in early 2008, you could practically hear the chorus of hallelujahs (well, except from the pigs—they weren't too happy). This is the best barbecue restaurant in St. Louis. Mike Emerson, a barbecuing champ who got his start with local chain Super Smokers, serves meat so tender that knives are an afterthought. Ribs are absolutely perfect, whether you devour them dry or with one of Pappy's three sauces. Don't miss the sweet-potato fries; their salty-crunchy exterior gives way to a sweet-pillowy interior. This is also one of the few places where you can (and should) get Frito Pie: corn chips piled high with your choice of meat, onions, baked beans, and melted cheddar. Just be sure to call before you go—when the day's supply of barbecue runs out, Pappy's closes.

COFFEEHOUSES
CAFÉ VENTANA ◉
3919 W. Pine Blvd., 314/531-7500,
www.cafeventana.com
HOURS: Sun.-Wed. 6:30am-11pm, Thurs.-Sat. 6:30am-midnight

A favorite haunt of Saint Louis University students (it's within shouting distance of the campus), Café Ventana serves up stellar soups, sandwiches, and salads. Coffeehouse by day, totally chill hangout (complete with wine and beer specials) by night, this is a place where you can settle in for hours and not get the evil eye from employees. Gather with friends in the main building, relax on

the patio, or get some serious work done in one of the adjacent "think tanks" (private rooms with long tables, fireplaces, and audiovisual setup). Whatever you do, don't neglect to order a plate of beignets—some of the best this side of the Big Easy.

COFFEE CARTEL ◉
2 Maryland Plaza, 314/454-0000,
www.thecoffeecartel.com
HOURS: Daily 24 hours

Located at the busy corner of Euclid Avenue and Maryland Avenue, this popular neighborhood stop teems with life all hours of the day. Business is at its peak on sunny afternoons, when the café's enormous sidewalk patio welcomes a diverse crowd of coffeelovers. The Cartel also draws a large crowd most weekend evenings, when it plays host to the under-21, non-drinking set. During the week, local professionals stop in for caffeine fixes and deli sandwiches, and latenight hours make the Cartel a preferred haunt for college students. Visitors are advised to save room for dessert, as the café's most popular items include Edy's hard-serve ice cream and an alluring selection of cheesecakes and tortes.

NADOZ ◉◉
3701 Lindell Blvd., 314/446-6800, www.nadozcafe.com
HOURS: Mon.-Fri. 7:30am-4:30pm, Sat. 8am-4pm, Sun. closed

Located in the first floor of the renovated Coronado Building (a former hotel and current apartment complex), Nadoz is a slightly more upscale café with slightly more upscale prices to match. With a display case of chocolates and pastries that are as beautiful to look at as they are delicious to devour, Nadoz sets its sights a bit higher than your average corner bakery. Likewise, its sandwiches, panini, and crepes bring a European flair to the neighborhood, making it the ideal spot for a quick, light lunch. The grilled salmon BLT with pesto mayonnaise will haunt your dreams after one bite, and the café's salad creations take lettuce to delicious new heights.

CONTEMPORARY AND NEW AMERICAN
BRASSERIE BY NICHE $$$

4580 Laclede Ave., 314/454-0600,
www.brasseriebyniche.com

HOURS: Mon.-Thurs. 5pm-10pm, Fri. 5pm-11pm,
Sat. 10am-2pm and 5pm-11pm, Sun. 10am-2pm and
5pm-9pm

For a city founded by the French, St. Louis doesn't have very many French restaurants—but it doesn't need very many when it has Brasserie by Niche, part of renowned chef Gerard Craft's family of restaurants. Rekindle your love of Paris (even if watching *Ratatouille* is the closest you've ever come to visiting there), with stellar renditions of beef Bourguignon, steak frites, and trout with almonds. In pleasant weather, the restaurant's spacious patio is a great spot for a meal and people-watching.

◖ TASTE $$

4584 Laclede Ave., 314/361-1200, www.tastebarstl.com

HOURS: Mon.-Sat. 5pm-1am, Sun. 5pm-midnight

At Taste, the hip younger brother of Gerard Craft's acclaimed Niche, you can have a first-rate snack at the bar or share several small plates among friends. Whichever you choose, you'll have a smile on your face while you enjoy the melt-in-your-mouth ricotta gnocchi or the kitchen's spicy, playful take on Mexican street tacos. No visit to Taste is complete without sampling one of Ted Kilgore's cocktail creations. Tell him what you like to drink, and he'll make the best version of it you've ever sipped.

INDIAN AND NEPALESE
EVEREST CAFÉ AND BAR $$

4145 Manchester Ave., 314/531-4800,
www.everestcafeandbar.com

HOURS: Tues.-Thurs. 11:30am-2:30pm and 5pm-9pm,
Fri. 11:30am-2:30pm and 5pm-10pm, Sat. 11:30am-3pm
and 5pm-10pm, Sun. 11:30am-3pm and 5pm-9pm

It's not every day that you have the opportunity to eat Nepalese food, but after you taste the outstanding cuisine at Everest, chances are you'll want to eat Nepalese food...every day. Because of Nepal's geographic location, the nation's cuisine shares some traits with Chinese and Indian cooking. At Everest, the emphasis is on nutrition; all dishes are sourced from local ingredients and prepared without dairy products. The sizzling lamb *tarkari*, with its side of decadent (yet butter-free!) lentil soup, is particularly delicious.

RASOI $$

25 N. Euclid Ave., 314/361-6911, www.rasoi.com

HOURS: Mon.-Thurs. 11am-2:30pm and 5pm-10pm,
Fri.-Sat. 11am-2:30pm and 5pm-10:30pm, Sun.
11am-2:30pm and 5pm-9pm

Fans of Rasoi's affordable afternoon buffet might remember the restaurant's less auspicious beginnings in an unassuming storefront around the corner. This popular Indian restaurant has been in the Central West End for more than 10 years and opened the doors of its present location in late 2007. The bright, colorful, beautiful space is a more fitting showcase for the bright dishes served here, including lobster *dosa* (a rice crepe stuffed with lumps of tender sweet lobster meat, sweet potato, and South Indian spices) and classic *tikka masala*. The lunch buffet, which is still served daily, offers Rasoi's most popular dishes and comes highly recommended.

PIZZA
VITO'S $

3515 Lindell Blvd., 314/534-8486, www.vitosstl.com

HOURS: Mon.-Wed. 11am-10pm, Thurs. 11am-11pm, Fri.
11am-1am, Sat. 5pm-1am, Sun. 5pm-8pm

Vito's has flourished in the Midtown neighborhood by relying on the premise that people like really good pizza. It sounds simple, but in a town where cracker-thin pizza crust is a litmus test for St. Louis pride, Vito's stands by its Sicilian-style crust and above-average toppings (think pine nuts and portobello mushrooms). A long-time favorite of college kids and downtown businesspeople alike, the weekday lunch buffet (with all-you-can-eat pizza, salad, pasta, and soup) runs 11am-3pm. The dinner menu offers more Italian favorites, and both the comfy dining room and the airy patio make a great pre-show stop before going to the nearby

RESTAURANTS

Fox Theatre. Those looking for a late-night drink or snack will appreciate Vito's 1am closing time on Fridays and Saturdays—because, really, it's *always* time for pizza.

PUB FOOD

DRESSEL'S PUBLIC HOUSE ❺

419 N. Euclid Ave., 314/361-1060,
http://dresselspublichouse.com

HOURS: Mon.-Thurs. 11am-midnight, Fri.-Sat. 11am-1am, Sun. 10am-midnight; kitchen hours Mon.-Thurs. 11am-3:45pm and 5pm-10:30pm, Fri.-Sat. 11am-3:45pm and 5pm-midnight, Sun. 10am-3:45pm and 5pm-10:30pm

While Welsh food can be a tricky style to define, we know a thing or two about Welsh beers—clean, crisp, and with the perfect amount of bite. Luckily, Dressel's knows a few things about Welsh beers too, and the cozy bar and grill keeps more than a few on tap, along with more traditional Irish and English varieties of lager and stout. The menu takes several stratospheric steps above typical pub grub, thanks to the culinary genius of chef Michael Miller. Sure, you can find a burger here (and it happens to be one of the best in town). But keep reading through the bill of fare to find an extraordinary porchetta sandwich, ethereally flaky trout, and a juicy pan-roasted chicken breast. Preparations and ingredients change with the season, as Chef Miller takes his farm-to-table bona fides very seriously. Those looking for a place to enjoy a relaxing pint can retire to the Pub Above, where a fireplace, full bar, and pool table provide the ideal oasis away from the world outside.

LLYWELYN'S ❺

4747 McPherson Ave., 314/361-3003,
www.llywelynspub.com

HOURS: Bar hours Mon.-Sat. 11am-1:30am, Sun.

11am-midnight; late-night menu available Mon.-Sat. 10pm-midnight

There are four Llywelyn's outposts in St. Louis now, but the original location of this popular Welsh pub feels the coziest and most authentic. On nice days, patrons pack the patio and enjoy people-watching on the upscale, gallery-lined McPherson Avenue. (The beer garden out back is great, too.) Visitors can choose from an impressive selection of beers and brown spirits, as well as traditional Welsh and American pub dishes. The crisp fried pickle spears should not be missed—nor should Llywelyn's signature rarebit, which can be ordered with house-made chips or atop a grilled hamburger.

SOUL FOOD

🄲 SWEETIE PIE'S ❺

4270 Manchester Ave., 314/371-0304,
http://sweetiepieskitchen.com

HOURS: Tues.-Sun. 11:30am-8pm

Located in the historic Grove neighborhood, Sweetie Pie's may remind visitors of the soul-food cafeterias that are blissfully abundant in the South. This popular spot is owned by Robbie Montgomery, a former backup singer for Ike Turner whose musical talent is matched only by her culinary abilities. Every morning around 11, Montgomery's congenial staff places soul-food standards (okra, mac and cheese, oxtail stew) on the 14-foot line. (Thanks to Montgomery's star turn in *Welcome to Sweetie Pie's* on Oprah Winfrey's cable network, curious diners queue up around the block well before opening time.) Items are priced per piece, so just point to what you'd like and have it dished up by the heaping slotted spoonful. Crowd favorites include the bread pudding, fried chicken, and collard greens—but really, everything here is good. Just be sure that your schedule leaves time for an afternoon nap.

Soulard and Lafayette Square   Map 3

AMERICAN
FRANCO ❸❸❸
1535 S. 8th St., 314/436-2500, www.eatatfranco.com
HOURS: Mon.-Fri. 11am-2pm and 5pm-close, Sat. 5pm-close

The name refers to owner Tom Schmidt's nephew—look for the photograph of a toddler just inside the entrance—but Franco does in fact offer a contemporary American take on classic French bistro cuisine: escargot, house-made pâté, sweetbreads, and mussels. Don't miss the *pommes frites* (that's, uh, French for French fries), either on their own or with a juicy wood-grilled steak. Seafood dishes are also a good bet. With high ceilings, exposed brick, large windows, and a cool mural above the open kitchen, Franco is one of the most attractive dining spaces in town. The vibe suits both a romantic dinner for two and a night on the town with pals.

BARBECUE
BOGART'S SMOKEHOUSE ❸❸
1627 S. 9th St., 314/621-3107,
www.bogartssmokehouse.com
HOURS: Tues.-Thurs. 10:30am-4pm, Fri.-Sat. 10:30am-8pm

Skip Steele was already barbecue royalty in St. Louis after serving as pitmaster at Pappy's Smokehouse, but Bogart's Smokehouse has launched him into superstar status, thanks to incredible beef brisket, pulled pork, and ribs that he caramelizes at the last minute with a propane torch. Steele is also a mad genius. At Bogart's he offers incredible, unusual barbecue like prime rib and pastrami. Leave room for the sides, especially the beans cooked in brisket drippings and the deviled-egg potato salad.

CAJUN/CREOLE
RIVERBEND RESTAURANT & BAR ❸
701 Utah St., 314/664-8443, www.riverbendbar.com
HOURS: Mon. and Wed.-Thurs. 11am-3pm and 5pm-9pm, Fri.-Sat. 11am-3pm and 5pm-10pm

Craving a taste of that *other* historic Mississippi River town? Find a serious slice of NOLA—right in the shadow of the Anheuser-Busch Brewery—when you dine at Riverbend. This is the best Cajun food in town, served with a heaping side of Southern hospitality and Big Easy charm. During any given lunch or dinner, the owner (a New Orleans expat with one seriously amazing recipe collection) is likely to stop by your table, express sincere gratitude for your visit, and ask how everything was. The answer to that question: "Delicious." Big bowls of jambalaya and étouffée, po'boys piled high with deep-fried crawdads, and spicy soups will transport you right to the French Quarter. Don't miss Riverbend's oyster bread, and be sure to wash this addictive signature dish down with a cold Abita Turbodog.

COFFEEHOUSES
◖ THE MUD HOUSE ❸
2101 Cherokee St., 314/776-6599,
www.themudhousestl.com
HOURS: Mon.-Fri. 7am-5:30pm, Sat.-Sun. 8am-5:30pm

Does your Platonic ideal of the coffeehouse involve comfy seating, lightning-fast (and free!) WiFi, friendly service, delicious food, and—oh yes—high-octane coffee drinks that also happen to taste amazing? Well, then, welcome to paradise. Popular among stressed students and laid-back brunchers alike, The Mud House draws major crowds to its adorable Cherokee Street storefront. Place your order, and receive a hipster-vocab card to place on your table so that the baristas can find you (don't feel bad if you get "wack" or "played out"; you might get "dope" or "fresh" next time). The from-scratch food is always well worth the wait. Breakfast and lunch are both served any time, so don't be shy about ordering the Brioche French Toast at midday (or the out-of-this-world Crispy Confit Pork Shoulder before noon). Those who like their coffee on the decadent side will fall in

RESTAURANTS

love with the Iced Turtle latte, served up in a Mason jar.

DESSERT

ⓒ BAILEYS' CHOCOLATE BAR ⓢ

1915 Park Ave., 314/241-8100,
www.baileyschocolatebar.com

HOURS: Mon.-Sat. 4pm-1am, Sun. 4pm-midnight

Just *try* not to feel romantic at Baileys' Chocolate Bar. The restaurant's seductively dim lighting, flickering candle sconces, and surplus of red roses make it impossible not to feel a bit giddy. Dave Bailey (a young restaurant impresario who's also responsible for the fabulous downtown creperie Rooster) has crafted a menu of high-quality decadence. Sure, there are cheese plates and pizzettas, but locals flock here for the chocolate. Desserts include Fudgy Truffle Chocolate Cake, Chocolate Sundae Overdrive, and Chocolate Voodoo Bread Pudding. Want to have your chocolate and drink it too? Order from the extensive chocolate martini menu, which boasts varieties from Mint to White Chocolate Raspberry. Since its 2004 opening, Baileys' has been one of the most popular places in town—so be prepared to wait for a table on weekends.

MEXICAN

LA VALLESANA ⓢ

2801 Cherokee St., 314/776-4223

HOURS: Daily 10am-10pm

Beloved by neighborhood residents and out-of-town gourmands alike, the *taquería* La Vallesana is an absolute hive of activity during afternoon hours. In fact, La Vallesana has become so popular that a few years ago the owner tore down the original, brightly painted taco stand and built a larger building with a big patio. It's still one of the tastiest lunch bargains in the city. A generously stuffed burrito (with grilled chicken, steak, or shrimp) is only $7, and it comes with chips and a side of homemade guacamole. The ever-popular *torta* costs $7 or a taco can be had for a mere $1.99. La Vallesana is located in the Hispanic pocket of Benton Park, just a couple blocks west of

Cherokee Street's antiques row. Stop here after your antique-shopping adventure, and do stay for dessert. The handmade popsicles *(paletas)* are divine.

TAQUERÍA EL BRONCO ⓢ

2812 Cherokee St., 314/762-0691

HOURS: Mon.-Thurs. 9am-9:30pm, Fri.-Sun. 9am-10:30pm

This small, welcoming storefront *taquería* is just one of a handful like it in this predominantly Hispanic area, but it is among the very best. While many *taquerías* in the neighborhood only offer walk-up service, El Bronco features table service. This is the perfect place for a quick, inexpensive sit-down meal. From the treating-you-like-family service to the outstanding complimentary red and green salsas, El Bronco hits all the right notes. Menu standouts include *tacos al pastor* and chunky, impeccably fresh guacamole. This is also one of the few *taquerías* in town with a liquor license. Visitors can enjoy a great margarita or beer with their delicious from-scratch meal, making El Bronco a perfect first stop for a fun night on the town.

MIDDLE EASTERN

THE CEDARS AT ST. RAYMOND'S MARONITE CATHEDRAL ⓢ

939 Lebanon Dr., 314/241-8248, http://cedarsstl.net

HOURS: Wed. 11am-2pm

Every Wednesday, volunteers from St. Raymond's congregation gather to prepare a lunch of delicious Lebanese favorites. This midweek meal is a decades-old tradition—and a secret known only by locals, including high-ranking government officials from nearby City Hall. Traditional spinach and meat pies, *dolmas* (minced meat, rice, and parsley steamed in grape leaves), and *kibbeh* (fried mini-footballs of seasoned meats and bulgur) are served cafeteria-style beneath the mirror balls of The Cedars' banquet facility. Nothing costs more than $4, and visitors are likely to see some of the city's most influential residents casually chatting over their baklava.

simplicity and do-it-yourself ingenuity. And in a city peppered with plenty of fine delis, Mom's Deli stands tall in the St. Louis Hills neighborhood thanks to its old-school charm and, of course, the unbeatable sandwiches. The storefront shop houses fridges full of beer and soda and a fine selection of chips and snacks, but you're here for the meat counter. Sidle up and order any of the deli's signature sandwiches—Mom's Special is a best-seller, with a thick stack of turkey, ham, and roast beef brought to life by tangy 1,000 Island dressing. Better still is Ron's Special, a spicy mélange of salami, pepper jack cheese, and mustard. Be prepared to wait in line on the weekends, but once you have paid for your feast you can dine on one of the outdoor tables or picnic at one of the nearby neighborhood parks.

THE PICCADILLY AT MANHATTAN ❸

7201 Piccadilly Ave., 314/646-0016,
www.thepiccadilly.com
HOURS: Tues.-Sat. 11am-10pm
Many lifelong St. Louisans can't pinpoint the Ellendale neighborhood on a map of the city. Fans of the small but mighty Piccadilly at Manhattan wouldn't have it any other way. They know this family-owned tavern serves some of the area's tastiest bar food: fried chicken, burgers, pasta, and steak. True Piccadilly devotees won't be happy to have the menu's deepest secrets revealed: The patty melt and the baby-back ribs (an occasional special) are both extraordinary.

SCHLAFLY BOTTLEWORKS ❸❸

7260 Southwest Ave., Maplewood, 314/241-2337,
www.schlafly.com
HOURS: Mon.-Thurs. 11am-10pm, Fri.-Sat. 11am-11pm,
Sun. 11am-9pm
Visitors to the Schlafly Bottleworks in downtown Maplewood can tour the microbrewery's facilities, then enjoy the fruits of the brewers' labor in the clean, casual atmosphere of the adjacent restaurant. The Bottleworks offers a wide selection of locally sourced dishes, including an excellent free-range bison burger, and most items are listed with a recommended

beer pairing. Consider taking a refillable jug of freshly poured beer out with you when you leave—these half-gallon "growlers" make an excellent addition to the hotel mini-fridge.

ASIAN
KING & I ❸

3157 S. Grand Blvd., 314/771-1777, www.thaispicy.com
HOURS: Tues.-Thurs. 11am-2:30pm and 5pm-9:30pm,
Fri. 11am-2:30pm and 5pm-10pm, Sat. noon-3pm and
5pm-10pm, Sun. noon-3pm and 5pm-9:30pm
There is good Thai food all over the St. Louis region, but city dwellers have a special affection for King & I. This South Grand stalwart is one of the oldest—and best—Thai restaurants around. The menu sometimes veers into cutesy territory (Thai ravioli, Thai fajitas), but the perfectly prepared curries more than make up for the misguided attempts at Asian fusion. The green-curry dishes are particularly delicious; sweet coconut milk tempers the spicy, addictively good sauce. Soups, including shrimp *tom yum,* are also excellent. Service is brisk but friendly, and the prices are great. Plus, you can soothe your burning tongue with a traditional Thai iced coffee, the Thai beer Singha, or a "Siam Stinker"—that's rum, brandy, sloe gin, and fruit juice.

LEMONGRASS ❸

3161 S. Grand Blvd., 314/664-6702,
www.lemongrass-rest.com
HOURS: Sun.-Thurs. 11am-9:30pm, Fri.-Sat.
11am-10:30pm
Nestled in a sunny space on South Grand's ethnic-restaurant row, with kitschy-fabulous metal lobsters decorating the walls, LemonGrass offers some of the best Vietnamese cuisine in town. LemonGrass's menu seems as massive as a Pynchon novel, but don't worry: The servers are happy to recommend their favorites—and, besides, everything here is good. Traditional spring rolls are packed with smoky pork, cool shrimp, and fresh vegetables. Steaming bowls of *pho* (Vietnamese noodle soup) are the ultimate in comfort food. For a real treat, try *com thit nuong dac biet:* charbroiled pork, egg cake, and pork skin served over rice and topped with an over-easy egg.

PHO GRAND $

3195 S. Grand Blvd., 314/664-7435,
www.phogrand.com
HOURS: Sun.-Mon. and Wed.-Thurs. 11am-9:30pm,
Fri.-Sat. 11am-10:30pm

When it comes to good Vietnamese food, St. Louis is fortunate to have an embarrassment of riches. Pho Grand is perhaps the best-known Vietnamese restaurant in town, thanks to a decade-plus of serving authentic dishes to loyal crowds. The restaurant's popularity can lead to lengthy waits (particularly on Friday and Saturday nights), but your patience will be rewarded with great food and gracious service. Try the *banh xeo:* ethereally light rice-flour crepes, filled with pork, shrimp, and crunchy bean sprouts. Pho Grand is particularly accommodating of large crowds, which means the decibel level can get fairly high, but there are also plenty of nooks fit for quiet conversation.

BOSNIAN
GRBIC $$

4071 Keokuk St., 314/772-3100,
www.grbicrestaurant.com
HOURS: Tues.-Fri. 4am-10pm, Sat. noon-10pm, Sun. noon-8pm

You'll find Grbic in the predominantly Bosnian neighborhood south of Gravois Road, in a huge old building that was once a busy neighborhood dairy. The German masonry of this enormous space complements Grbic's Eastern European cuisine quite nicely. The menu features Hungarian goulash and German spaetzle, but branch out and try such Bosnian favorites as *cevapi* (spicy, finger-length beef sausages) and *palacinke* (dessert crepes filled with chocolate sauce, whipped cream, and walnuts). Members of St. Louis's Bosnian community frequently gather at Grbic to celebrate important occasions, and that warm, familial vibe is definitely extended to visitors.

COFFEEHOUSES
SWEETART $

2203 S. 39th St., 314/771-4278, www.sweetartstl.com
HOURS: Tues.-Fri. 9am-6pm, Sat. 9am-5pm
The "sweet" in the name of this cute neigh-

borhood café is Reine Bayoc, who presents a mouthwatering array of baked goods: cakes, cupcakes, cookies, and more. She also serves savory food, all of it vegetarian and/or vegan, including one of St. Louis's most beloved veggie burgers. (Don't worry, sweet-toothed vegans: Several of the baked goods are tailored to your diet!) The "art" is Reine's husband Cbabi, whose brilliantly colorful paintings adorn the walls.

CONTEMPORARY AND NEW AMERICAN
C FARMHAUS $$$

3257 Ivanhoe Ave., 314/647-3800,
www.farmhausrestaurant.com
HOURS: Mon.-Tues. 11am-2pm, Wed.-Fri. 11am-2pm and 5:30pm-10pm, Sat. 6pm-10pm

In 2011, *Food & Wine* magazine awarded Farmhaus owner and chef Kevin Willmann its coveted "Best New Chef" award. You'll be nodding your head in agreement after trying his flavorful and playful takes on Midwestern produce and Gulf Coast seafood, like the Breakfast (with pork belly, a poached egg, and corn blini) or the poached escolar with grilled prawns. Dishes are larger than appetizers but smaller than entrées: perfect for sharing. Reservations are strongly recommended, though you can land walk-in seats at the bar and the restaurant's Monday-Thursday Blue Plate lunch is first-come, first-served.

HOME WINE KITCHEN $$$

7322 Manchester Rd., Maplewood, 314/802-7676,
www.homewinekitchen.com
HOURS: Mon. 11am-10pm, Wed.-Sat. 11am-10pm, Sun. 10am-9pm

A visit to Home Wine Kitchen feels less like a restaurant than a fabulous dinner party. You won't know what you'll get till you walk in the front door of this cozy spot. Co-owner Cassandra Vires shakes up her menu of American bistro fare weekly, showcasing what's in season and what's caught her attention. On Mondays, she doesn't give you a menu at all. You'll eat what she wants you to eat, and you'll definitely like it.

ETHIOPIAN
MESKEREM ETHIOPIAN
RESTAURANT ❸

3210 S. Grand Blvd., 314/772-4442,
www.meskeremstl.com

HOURS: Mon.-Thurs. 11am-9:30pm, Fri.-Sat.
11am-10pm, Sun. 12:30am-9:30pm

Visitors seeking a unique dining experience have plenty of options on this ethnically diverse South City boulevard—but Meskerem surely offers one of the most distinctive. Locals love this Ethiopian restaurant's congenial staff, strong spiced tea, and authentic *wat* (savory stew). No utensils are on the tables here; just use your right hand and a piece of spongy *injera* bread to scoop up tender cubes of lamb, beef, and roasted bone-in chicken, as well as lentils and vegetables. A blend of traditional Ethiopian spices punctuates every plate, and the familiar staple ingredients make this unfamiliar cuisine thoroughly comforting, especially on a cold day. Vegetarians will adore the smoky, savory greens and refreshing *timatim* salad.

ITALIAN
ACERO ❸❸❸

7266 Manchester Rd., Maplewood, 314/644-1790,
www.fialafood.com/acero

HOURS: Mon.-Sat. 5pm-close

"Would you like the red sauce or the white?" is a question you'll hear at Italian restaurants all over St. Louis, but never at Acero. Here, restaurateur Jim Fiala and chef Adam Gnau serve the true, rustic cuisine of north Italy with an all-Italian wine list to match. Indulge in seductive fresh pasta dishes like a large raviolo encasing a farm-fresh egg yolk, or go whole hog for the *porchetta*, which is roasted for five hours. If you can't choose just one, Acero lets you build a four-course meal for $30.

MANGIA ITALIANO ❸❸

3145 S. Grand Blvd., 314/664-8585,
www.dineatmangia.com

HOURS: Sun.-Thurs. 3pm-10pm, Fri.-Sat.
3pm-10:30pm, brunch Sun. 11am-3pm

Mangia Italiano (just call it "Mangia" if you want to sound like a local) is a hip hangout that happens to serve absolutely delicious food. The pasta is the biggest draw—in fact, Mangia's handmade noodles are so popular that the restaurant packages them for sale at many local farmers markets and organic grocery stores. Perennial favorites include Vermicelli G.O.C. (garlic, olive oil, and cheese) and Porcini Tagliatelle in a sundried-tomato cream sauce. Nightly specials always make use of the freshest seasonal ingredients. If you don't want your pasta with a side of cigarette smoke and rock 'n' roll, be sure to arrive before 10pm—at that time, Mangia assumes its identity as one of the south side's most popular bars.

ONESTO PIZZA & TRATTORIA ❸❸

5401 Finkman St., 314/802-8883,
www.onestopizza.com

HOURS: Sun.-Thurs. 4pm-9pm, Fri.-Sat. 11am-10pm,
brunch Sun. 9am-2pm

Visitors to this casual bistro should seize the opportunity to try real fettuccine, served in the traditional style (topped with an egg yolk). Delicious brick-oven-baked pizzas include the Queen Margherita (fresh plum tomato sauce, mozzarella, and basil) and the Mad Cajun (shrimp, andouille sausage, fire-roasted peppers, and jalapeños).

STELLINA PASTA CAFÉ ❸

3342 Watson Rd., 314/256-1600,
www.stellinapasta.com

HOURS: Tues.-Thurs. 11am-9pm, Fri.-Sat. 11am-10pm

Ask a St. Louisan where to find the city's best sandwich, and you'll hear all sorts of different answers. Ignore them. The best sandwich in St. Louis is Stellina Pasta Café's South Side Smoke: pulled pork topped with caramelized onion and smoked gouda cheese on ciabatta bread seasoned with sea salt. Is it messy? Well, yes, but so is life. But if you must be fancy, co-owner and chef Jamey Tochtrop serves three pasta dishes each day, all of which feature fresh homemade pasta. A small gem worth seeking out.

PIZZA
🄲 BLACK THORN PIZZA & PUB ❸

3735 Wyoming St., 314/776-0534

RESTAURANTS

HOURS: Mon.-Sat. 5pm-11:45pm; bar open Mon.-Sat. until 1am, Sun. until midnight; Sun. kitchen open 5pm-9:45pm; Chicago-style pizza stops being served an hour before kitchen closes.

Black Thorn Pizza & Pub serves up a slice of southside life—in addition to Chicago-style pies so good that they justify the hour-plus wait. Order a pitcher of beer (Blackthorn keeps a nice rotation of microbrews and imports on tap), slide into a wooden booth, and see why St. Louisans have been coming here for more than 20 years. The laid-back neighborhood vibe and friendly competition (air hockey, anyone?) are appealing, to be sure. But it's the pizza—with its perfectly chewy crust, kicky tomato sauce, and bubbling mozzarella cheese—that makes this place legendary. If the super-dense Chicago-style pizza seems a bit daunting, go for an equally delicious thin-crust pie.

■ PIZZA-A-GO-GO ⑤
6703 Scanlan Ave., 314/781-1234, http://pizzaagogo.blogspot.com
HOURS: Sun.-Tues. and Thurs. 4pm-9pm, Fri.-Sat. 4pm-10pm

Pizza-a-Go-Go is a no-frills pizza joint. No checks. No credit cards. No beer—but you're welcome to bring your own. You order your pie at the window, then sit down in a vinyl chair to wait. So why make a special trip to Pizza-a-Go-Go? Because there is great happiness in simple pleasures, and this pizza is simply the best. Because this is a true St. Louis institution, open since 1964. Because Paul LaFata (son of Frank, the original owner) takes great pride in making from-scratch crust. The toppings run the gamut from Canadian bacon to anchovies, although you may want to do like the locals and order the Special: a classically delicious pie topped with sausage, pepperoni, mushroom, green pepper, and onion.

Dogtown and the Hill   Map 5

AMERICAN
FELIX'S PIZZA PUB ⑤
6335 Clayton Ave., 314/645-6565, www.felixspizzapub.com
HOURS: Mon.-Fri. 11am-1:30am, Sat. noon-1:30am, Sun. 11am-midnight

One of the best things about the Dogtown neighborhood is the gastronomic diversity found in such a small swatch of town. While you can find some of the town's best fried chicken and hamburgers in Dogtown, Felix's offers a slightly lighter menu and a more upscale (if still casual) vibe. The menu is heavy on appetizers, wraps, and single-serving pizzas, and the corner spot has become a haven for pork lovers thanks to its great barbecue ribs. But Felix's is as much a bar as it is a grill, as the locals who populate the barstools will tell you. There is a nice wine and martini list, and the dining room plays host to live local music a few nights a week.

CONTEMPORARY AND NEW AMERICAN
FIVE BISTRO ⑤⑤⑤
5100 Daggett Ave., 314/773-5553, www.fivebistro.com
HOURS: Tues.-Wed. 5pm-9pm, Thurs.-Sat. 5pm-midnight

Chef Anthony Devoti's acclaimed contemporary bistro is better than ever after relocating to a beautifully renovated building in the city's Hill neighborhood. The small menu features local producers, when possible, resulting in terrific beef and pork dishes and stunning vegetable preparations. A five-course tasting menu, with wine pairings, is a steal at $80. The restaurant frequently hosts special wine dinners and serves a special late-night menu (burgers, *pommes frites*) from 10pm to midnight Thursday, Friday, and Saturday.

GREEK
OLYMPIA KEBOB HOUSE & TAVERNA ⑤
1543 McCausland Ave., 314/781-1299

Delmar Loop and University City   Map 6

AMERICAN
BIXBY'S 🟡🟡
Missouri History Museum, 5700 Lindell Blvd.,
314/361-7313, www.bixbys-mohistory.com
HOURS: Mon.-Sat. 11am-2pm, Sun. 10am-2pm

No visit to the Missouri History Museum is complete without lunch or brunch at Bixby's, where the food on your plate is nearly as beautiful as the view of Forest Park from your seat. The lunch menu, served Monday through Saturday, includes a luscious cheeseburger on an English muffin and a trio of miniature crab cakes. Sunday brunch features all of your favorites, like omelets prepared to order and eggs Benedict. And be sure to try the incredible house-cured salmon.

🎵 BLUEBERRY HILL 🟡
6504 Delmar Blvd., University City, 314/727-4444,
www.blueberryhill.com

HOURS: Mon.-Sat. 11am-1:30am; Sun. 11am-midnight nighttime grill menu offered Mon.-Sat. 9pm-midnight, Sun. 9pm-11pm

Blueberry Hill is popular with hungry tourists looking to refuel after a day of shopping in the Loop. But this legendary Delmar Boulevard restaurant/bar/nightclub/museum of Americana is a favorite among locals, too. The menu features one of the best burgers in town, in addition to perfectly crisp onion rings, spicy "buffalo" fries, hearty daily soups, and much more. Blueberry Hill is owned by Joe Edwards, the beloved St. Louis visionary who is largely responsible for the Delmar Loop's success (and whose impressive collection of American kitsch is on full display throughout the venue). Service can be slow at times, but don't fret: Just drop a few more coins in the stellar jukebox or order another pint from Blueberry Hill's expansive beer list.

RESTAURANTS

© SARA KETTERER

Bixby's at the Missouri History Museum

© HOPE EDWARDS

Blueberry Hill

FITZ'S AMERICAN GRILL & BOTTLING WORKS $

6605 Delmar Blvd., University City, 314/726-9555, www.fitzsrootbeer.com

HOURS: Sun.-Thurs. 10:30am-9pm, Fri.-Sat. 10:30am-10pm

Located in the heart of the bustling Delmar Loop, Fitz's is brimming over with charm and nostalgia. As bottlers of fine, frothy root beer and orange pop (among other flavors), Fitz's hearkens back to the days of soda shops and dime stores, though its modern dining room is remarkably kitsch-free. The menu is fairly typical, offering a mishmash of American favorites and TGI Fridays-inspired concoctions, though its list of gourmet burgers is extensive. You would be remiss if you didn't try a frosty mug of the home-brewed root beer, and on certain days you can even see the bottling process take place in the restaurant's on-site bottling facility. Fitz's prides itself on being kid-friendly, so bring the youngsters.

◖ NICHE $$$

7734 Forsyth Blvd. in Clayton., 314/773-7755, www.nichestlouis.com

HOURS: Tues.-Thurs. 5pm-9pm, Fri.-Sat. 5pm-10pm

Niche owner and executive chef Gerard Craft is the brightest star of the current dining scene in St. Louis. In 2008, he was the first St. Louis chef to be named one of *Food & Wine* magazine's "Best New Chefs," and three times he has been a finalist for the James Beard Foundation's annual "Best Chef: Midwest" award. Despite all the acclaim, Craft's focus remains the food. With chef de cuisine Nate Hereford, he serves dishes that are beautiful, delicious and, with the addition of one unexpected ingredient (white chocolate with pork?), sublime.

ASIAN
REARN THAI $$

7910 Bonhomme Ave., Clayton, 314/725-8807

HOURS: Mon.-Thurs. 11am-8:30pm, Fri. 11am-9:30pm, Sat. noon-9:30pm, Sun. 5:30pm-8:30pm

Just a hop-skip-jump from central Clayton's downtown drag sits Rearn Thai, a paragon of

NIGHTLIFE

Don't let the hard-working Midwestern ethos fool you: St. Louis is *not* a city that turns in early. While it's tough to find a meal after midnight here, the drinking-and-dancing scene stays hot till at least 1:30am (and many places keep their doors open until 3am). The diversity of St. Louis's neighborhoods is reflected in the city's nightspots. In the trendy Washington Avenue district downtown, dressed-to-impress twentysomethings sample sushi and martinis, or order up premium bottle service at the many VIP booths. On the city's south side, a more relaxed vibe rules, although elegant wine bars are as common as smoky taverns. Bars near the major universities cater to the student demographic by offering cheap beer and well drinks, nightly food specials, and popular music.

Live music has always played a major role in St. Louis's cultural identity, from Miles Davis's early gigs to sold-out performances by hip-hop stars. St. Louis fosters a thriving jazz, blues, hip-hop, alt-country *and* indie-rock scene, so there are plenty of options on any given night. National touring bands also make it a point to stop here (although some bypass St. Louis in favor of the college towns of Columbia, Missouri, and Lawrence, Kansas), and with the exception of huge arena shows, ticket prices are very affordable. Local publications, such as *St. Louis Magazine* and *Riverfront Times,* do an excellent job of listing almost every upcoming show.

COURTESY OF URBAN CHESTNUT BREWING COMPANY

HIGHLIGHTS

LOOK FOR **(** TO FIND RECOMMENDED NIGHTLIFE.

(**Best Beer Selection:** Looking for a bar that serves more than just A-B products (and doesn't consider Sam Adams a "craft beer")? Cast your gaze no further than **iTap,** a Soulard hot spot with one heck of a great beer list. This is where St. Louis's true beer aficionados hang out, happily sharing their opinions on the best bottles and drafts (page 67).

(**Best View from a Bar:** Some bars have a view of a parking lot. Others, a streetscape. At the aptly named **360,** your view is the entire St. Louis skyline—and there's not a more breath-taking vantage point in town. Let the expertly mixed cocktails delight your taste buds, as the surrounding panorama provides a bird's-eye view of the Arch, the Cathedral, and all points in between (page 70).

(**Best Pub:** Spend an hour or two at **The Scottish Arms,** and you'll think you've been transported to Edinburgh. The Scotch selection is unparalleled, the kilt-wearing servers are friendly and knowledgeable, and there's always football—the real kind—on the television. Order haggis to complete the experience (page 72).

(**Best Late-Night Bar:** At some 3am bars, the late hours are the only selling point. Not so at **Atomic Cowboy,** where there are selling points by the score—including an expansive patio with an outdoor fireplace, stellar DJ nights, monthly burlesque shows, and perhaps the best margaritas in town (page 74).

(**Best New Old Bar:** The **Old Rock House** is a reincarnation of a legendary St. Louis saloon, and it's one of the most interesting places to open in the past few years. Enjoy live music on the main floor and the mezzanine, or head to the basement for scotch, cigars, and conversation. No matter where you are in the Old Rock House, you'll feel like part of St. Louis history (page 75).

(**Best Place for the Blues:** At **B.B.'s Jazz, Blues, and Soups,** passion for the blues is palpable. Late greats Johnnie Johnson and Bennie Smith had regular gigs here, and the place is always packed with casual fans, aficionados, and legends in the making (page 80).

(**Best Place to See Live Music: Off Broadway** is all about the music, and rare is the night when the place isn't packed. Off Broadway devotees truly support live shows, and the turnout is strong for local and national acts alike. Drinks are cheap, the sound is great, and the whole place is smoke-free (page 82).

(**Best Wine Bar:** Spending time at **33 Wine Shop & Tasting Bar** is a lot like hanging out in a really cool friend's amazing wine cellar. In this case, the friend is owner Jake Hafner, and his wine collection is both unparalleled and affordable. Enjoy your vino in the lovely smoke-free bar, or head outside to the lushly landscaped patio (page 84).

Bars

BREWPUBS
THE CIVIL LIFE BREWING COMPANY
3714 Holt Ave., no phone,
www.thecivillifebrewingcompany.com
HOURS: Tues.-Fri. 4pm-10pm, Sat. noon-10pm
COST: No cover
Map 4

The microbrew renaissance is a no-brainer for a town that's always been synonymous with Budweiser. Civil Life specializes in British, German, and American iterations of the hoppy stuff and offers perfect half-pints for a measly $2.50, so you can sample all the drafts without getting silly—remember, civility first. The warm wood tasting room is like a cozy log cabin tucked inside the brewery, and crowds often spill out onto the spacious patio.

ITAP

1711 S. 9th St., 314/621-4333,
www.internationaltaphouse.com
HOURS: Mon.-Thurs. 3pm-1am, Fri. 1pm-1am, Sat. 11am-1am, Sun. noon-midnight
COST: No cover
Map 3

Ordering wine at a place like iTap just isn't done. Sure, they serve it, but that doesn't make it okay. With 500 beers in house, more taps than you can shake a stick at, and bartenders who can introduce a new favorite brew even if you don't know a Zwickel from a porter, this Soulard saloon does one thing well and leaves the rest to the other guys. Feeling peckish after a few too many? Order a pizza from across the street, and no one will bat an eyelash when it's delivered to your barstool. The original iTap is still operating in a west-county strip mall, but this incarnation is better suited to the happy-hour crowd clad in business casual and to the party boys and girls who call Soulard home.

MORGAN STREET BREWERY

721 N. 2nd St., 314/231-9970,
www.morganstreetbrewery.com
HOURS: Mon. 4pm-midnight, Tues.-Sun. 11am-2:30am
COST: No cover
Map 1

Much of the once-thriving Laclede's Landing district has gone to seed in recent years. The district's anchor—the legendary rock club Mississippi Nights, which hosted everyone from Uncle Tupelo to Nirvana—was shuttered in 2007, and much of the Landing's "cool" factor seemed to go with it. Still, must-visit stalwarts remain, and one of those is Morgan Street Brewery. This spacious microbrewery blends in perfectly with the brick and cobblestone surrounding it, and the handcrafted beers are divine. Particularly good are the rich Doppelbock (available in winter) and the sweet-and-spicy Cobblestone Steam Lager (on tap year-round, thanks to its ability to pair well with absolutely everything). A nice menu, with dishes that are way beyond basic bar food, complements the beer selection.

URBAN CHESTNUT BREWING COMPANY

3229 Washington Ave., 314/222-0143,
www.urbanchestnut.com/home
HOURS: Mon. 11am-10pm, Tues.-Thurs. 11am-11pm, Fri.-Sat. 11am-1am, Sun. noon-10pm
COST: No cover
Map 2

It's not often a world-class brewmaster with a Munich pedigree finds a home in St. Louis, but Urban Chestnut's Florian Kuplent has spent two decades studying the art and brought his talents to roost in Midtown. The result is one of the most exciting developments in St. Louis brews since Schlafly. UCBC taps have found their way into most of the better restaurants and bars in the city, and fanatics flock to their lively tap room on Washington Avenue to answer the query "Revolution or Reverence?"—as in, do you want an experimental ale or a faithful take on a true-blue classic? Urban Chestnut's old-world-meets-new brewing philosophy sets it apart from the slew of lager lookalikes and pilsner pretenders. The unfiltered Zwickel and uber-hip STLIPA are obligatory, and the deposit required for their spiffy steins means you can steal your glass without the guilt.

COCKTAIL BARS
ABSOLUTLI GOOSED

3196 S. Grand Blvd., 314/771-9300,
www.absolutligoosed.com
HOURS: Mon.-Tues. 5pm-midnight, Wed.-Thurs. 4pm-midnight, Fri.-Sat. 4pm-1am
COST: No cover
Map 4

The classic martini had its resurgence quite a few years ago, along with zoot suits and swing music, but the modern drinker wants a little sweetness mixed in with the potent stuff. Drinkers know Absolutli Goosed as a haven of flavored cocktails: Many of the concoctions take inspiration from the candy aisle, while others offer updates on classic drinks like margaritas and cosmopolitans. The bar is successful

BAR-HOP LIKE A ST. LOUISAN

Sure, you can check out the bars that all the tourists know about—in fact, you *should*, because many of these nightspots are rich with St. Louis history. But if you really want to feel like a local, spend an evening visiting the city's more under-the-radar watering holes. Here, you're likely to meet interesting people and hear some great stories.

Start off at **The Royale** (3132 S. Kingshighway). Local impresario Steven Fitzpatrick Smith quickly turned this shotgun space into a favorite local hang, thanks to excellent DJ nights, way-above-average food, and tasty drinks. The libation menu itself is a crash-course in St. Louis neighborhoods and landmarks; try the River Des Peres, a martini turned deliciously dirty by kalamata olives.

If you can't find a seat at the super-popular Royale, check out the equally beloved but far less crowded **The Hideaway Piano Bar** (5900 Arsenal St.), a true dive bar (please, please, please do not order anything ending in -tini). The drinks are cheap, the folks are friendly, and you just might be invited to slow dance.

Soulard is the Holy Grail for many a bar-hopping St. Louisan. Cheap drinks and an impressive bars-to-block ratio make it easy and fun to check out plenty of spots. Don't-miss destinations include **iTap** (1711 S. 9th St.), with its jaw-droppingly extensive beer list; **Clementine's Bar** (2001 Menard St.), the city's oldest gay bar; and **Hammerstone's** (2028 S. 9th St., 314/773-5565, www.hammerstones.net), which frequently hosts great jazz and R&B acts.

Looking to catch a game? Blues, Cards, and Rams fans eschew the corporate-feeling sports bars and head instead to **Tom's Bar & Grill** (20 S. Euclid Ave., 314/367-4900, www.tomsbarandgrill.com). This Central West End institution has lots of screens, lots of beer, and lots of deep-fried bar fare. If you're feeling a bit fancier, head for **Maryland House** (4659 Maryland Ave.), a chic-but-cozy nightspot with a speakeasy vibe. Enter this bar through an unmarked door right next to Brennan's Bottle Shop & Bar, then ascend a narrow flight of stairs. Despite its being open for more than a decade, it seems many St. Louisans have yet to find out about Maryland House. Shh!

at attracting a mixed crowd from the diverse South Grand neighborhood, and it's a common sight to see gay, lesbian, and straight clientele rubbing elbows and tippling tall-stemmed drinks in the bar's tight quarters.

BLOOD AND SAND

1500 St. Charles St., 314/241-7263, www.bloodandsandstl.com
HOURS: Mon.-Sat. 5pm-close
COST: No cover
Map 1

A members-only restaurant is a tough sell in any metropolis, least of all in an unpretentious place like St. Louis, but Blood and Sand is raising the bar one truffled tater tot and eponymous cocktail at a time. Out-of-towners and first-timers can get in with a mere reservation, but everyone else has to fork over a fee to enjoy all the privileges—haute decor, excellent

deconstructionist cuisine, and really amazing cocktails. The service is exceptional if discursive, but there are a lot of things to explain here: the street that's really an alley, membership rules, and the fact that at this bar, only the bartender can give you permission to flirt with another patron. Each cocktail's ingredients barely fit in a Twitter missive, but after a few Silver and Sands (lemon ginger Scotch, Lillet Rouge, cherry liquor, egg white, grapefruit bitters) you might find that People are People (bourbon, grapefruit, cherry brandy, brown ale, bitters) and sometimes, Love Burns (aged rum, lemon, simple, Barolo Averna, grapefruit bitters, rose champagne).

CAFÉ EAU

212 N. Kingshighway Blvd., 314/633-3000, www.chaseparkplaza.com
HOURS: Mon.-Sat. 10:30am-1am, Sun.

10:30am-midnight
COST: No cover
Map 2

The Chase Park Plaza is legendary, and Café Eau is at its heart. Given the Chase's status as *the* hotel for visiting luminaries and well-heeled locals, the people-watching opportunities are ample. Café Eau has a decent wine list, but the expertly made cocktails are the real draw. It's hard not to feel elegant when sipping a martini in one of the city's most historic hotels. Patrons can also take their drinks to the poolside deck, where an outdoor fireplace keeps things toasty year-round.

LUCAS PARK GRILLE

1234 Washington Ave., 314/241-7770, www.lucasparkgrille.com
HOURS: Mon.-Wed. 11am-1:30am, Thurs.-Sat. 11am-3am, Sun. 10am-1:30am
COST: No cover
Map 1

Don't make the mistake of walking into Lucas Park after 10pm unless you're ready to become a human pinball—this popular nightclub on Washington Avenue is always full to bursting with a see-and-be-seen crowd—out-of-towners, county-commuters, college kids, and those young folks who seem to drink professionally all find themselves at home in this upscale space. By day Lucas Park operates as a trendy restaurant serving requisite fare like perfectly seared ahi tuna and crab cakes, but once the kitchen closes, swarms of over- and under-dressed young people descend and post up at the bar, so if you're lucky enough to belly up, order a double or two, because you may not make your way back.

THE RITZ-CARLTON LOBBY LOUNGE

100 Carondelet Plaza, 314/863-6300, www.ritzcarlton.com
HOURS: Sun.-Thurs. 11am-midnight, Fri.-Sat. 11am-1am, tea service Sat.-Sun. (call for reservations), sushi bar daily 5pm-9pm
COST: No cover
Map 6

Don't feel like shelling out big bucks for a night's rest at the Ritz-Carlton? You can still experience the hotel's legendary opulence and topnotch service by grabbing a drink in the Lobby Lounge. The room is absolutely beautiful, with dark woods and luxurious couches that practically demand intense, hours-long conversation. Drink specials change with the season, and by-the-glass wine selections are solid if not wildly interesting (the bottle list, on the other hand, is stellar). You'll pay a premium for drinking at the Ritz; glasses of wine are between $12 and $18, and cocktails are usually around $10. But the experience is worth it, and if you dress to impress, no one will know that you're just passing through for a drink.

SANCTUARIA

4198 Manchester Ave., 314/535-9700, www.sanctuariastl.com
HOURS: Tues.-Thurs. 5pm-1am, Fri.-Sat. 5pm-3am, Sun. 5pm-midnight
COST: No cover
Map 2

Handmade cocktails on draft? Yes, please! This tapas bar gets billed as "wild," and it's not hard to see why—the sumptuous decor is a little Day of the Dead, and the cocktail list is thick as a brick with more than 140 concoctions that will leave less intrepid imbibers scratching their heads and trying to remember what kind of base spirit they usually enjoy. Have no fear: The wonderful barkeeps and super-knowledgeable servers will assist in decision-making, and with a veritable warehouse of liquors, digestifs, bitters, and bottles at their disposal, there's no chance of getting out of here without a new favorite beverage and a new appreciation for this brand of exhaustive mixology. Join the cocktail club and work through that intimidating drink list, and the house will buy you a round for life.

SUB ZERO VODKA BAR

308 N. Euclid Ave., 314/367-1200, www.subzerovodkabar.com
HOURS: Mon.-Sat. 11am-1:30am, Sun. 11am-midnight
COST: No cover
Map 2

As one might expect, given the name, Sub

Zero offers an enormous selection of imported vodka and every mixer imaginable. But there's much more to the place than that, and a daytime visit is much different from a nighttime one. If you're interested in sipping a good martini in a lounge atmosphere, stop by during the late afternoon, when the place is almost sanctuary-like in its cool stillness. At night, Sub Zero caters primarily to the well-shod Baby Boomers who shuffle in from the city's suburban enclaves. Sushi and gourmet burgers are also available.

TASTE

4584 Laclede Ave., 314/361-1200, www.tastebarstl.com
HOURS: Mon.-Sat. 5pm-1am, Sun. 5pm-midnight
COST: No cover
Map 2

Let it be known: The craft cocktail movement in St. Louis started at Taste. Once named among the top 100 craft cocktail bars in the world, the original Taste on Sidney Street could only hold 18 people, but the cozy Central West End location is better equipped for a small crowd. Upscale booze hounds flock to Taste to sip incredible concoctions from beverage director and award-winning mixologist Ted Kilgore. Kilgore is a walking encyclopedia of spirits, and in his house, the drink is the thing. Hard-to-find bottlings, rare imports, and a sorcerer's lot of potions line the sleek wood bar, and every potation is guaranteed to please—or the knowledgeable barkeeps swiftly replace your cocktail for free. The small but mighty seasonal menu of small plates and snacks does credit to the Niche name, but the drinks, oh, the drinks are to die for.

◖ 360

1 S. Broadway, 314/241-8439, www.360-stl.com
HOURS: Mon.-Thurs. 4pm-1am, Fri.-Sat. 4pm-2am, Sun. 4pm-11pm
COST: No cover
Map 1

Boasting the best rooftop bar in River City, 360 on top of the Hilton St. Louis at the Ballpark is a swanky place to unwind after the game or as a last stop after a classy night on the town—just

ask Bono. He's been here. The inspired architecture gives you a bird's-eye view of downtown topography: the Arch, the Mississippi, Busch Stadium, and the Old Courthouse. On a clear night, you can see the inner-ring suburb of Clayton in the distance and even catch the seventh inning stretch without the price of admission. *Frites* with meyer lemon tarragon aioli, grass-fed local beef burgers, and infused cocktails are a vast improvement on concession-stand food and a warm brew anyhow.

VAN GOGHZ MARTINI BAR AND BISTRO

3200 Shenandoah Ave., 314/865-3345, www.vangoghz.com
HOURS: Tues.-Sat. 3pm-11pm, Sun. 9am-3pm
Map 4

Coffee shop by day and elegant cocktail lounge by night, Van Goghz shines in its two distinct roles. Free WiFi and a full-service brunch menu bolster this southside spot's daytime charms, while a seemingly endless list of wines, beers, and inventive martinis keeps the evening crowd coming back. This is a busy place, but the vibe is low-key, and there's never any pressure to vacate your seat. Quite the opposite; bartenders encourage leisurely conversation over drinks and small plates. The happy-hour specials (on both cocktails and food) make Van Goghz a popular stop with the after-work set. On nice nights, Van Goghz offers sidewalk seating.

TAVERNS AND SPORTS BARS
ARENA BAR AND GRILL

5760 W. Park St., 314/646-7171
HOURS: Mon.-Sat. 11am-1am, Sun. 11am-midnight
Map 5

The regulars at this quirky little Dogtown dive are fiercely loyal. Many have been coming here since the days of the old St. Louis Arena. That sports venue fell victim to controlled demolition in 1999, the Blues moved to Scottrade Center downtown, and this friendly bar is all that remains. If you're looking to drink on the cheap, the Arena is there for you. Drink specials often include $1 beer bottles and $2 shots. True Arena devotees head here for a two-martini lunch; the tiny corner kitchen serves up surprisingly great sandwiches and appetizers. You may not be a regular, but chances are you'll feel like one by the time last call rolls around.

THE FAMOUS BAR

5213 Chippewa St., 314/832-2211,
www.thefamousbar.com
HOURS: Mon.-Sat. 3pm-1:30am, Sun. 3pm-midnight; happy hour Mon.-Fri. 3pm-7pm
Map 4

Named in honor of the old Famous-Barr department store that used to anchor the nearby corner of Chippewa and Kingshighway, the Famous Bar has gained a bit of local fame in its own right for its speakeasy-esque atmosphere. It's hard to miss the throwback vibe upon entering the Famous Bar—the staff sport ties and blue jeans from behind the massive mirrored bar, and the cocktail and martini menu hearkens back to days of long-stemmed glasses and stiff libations. If you are a lighter drinker, don't fret: The bar has a nice selection of draft and bottled beers available, and the Bloody Mary menu is unrivaled (approach the Cajun Mary with caution—it kicks). The club books live blues, jazz, and rock on the weekends, and a cover charge applies on those nights.

THE HIDEAWAY PIANO BAR

5900 Arsenal St., 314/645-8822
HOURS: Daily noon-1:30am
Map 4

Beloved by local hipsters and septuagenarians alike, this dimly lit lounge offers a fun departure from the typical St. Louis bar scene. You won't find thumping bass or pink mixed drinks here. Instead, regulars order rail drinks or sip Budweiser from the bottle. Mark Dew, The Hideaway's blind pianist, takes requests from the crowd, and it's a rare night when *someone* doesn't get up to slow dance. Libations are cheap, the mood is relaxed, and the age range is fascinating—there aren't many other places that draw college kids *and* retirees.

JOHN D. MCGURK'S IRISH PUB AND GARDEN

1200 Russell Blvd., 314/776-8309, www.mcgurks.com

HOURS: Mon.-Sat. 11am-1:30am, Sun. 3pm-midnight
Map 3

St. Louisans love Irish pubs, and St. Louisans love patios. Enter John D. McGurk's: a classic Irish pub with one of the biggest, prettiest patios in town. The staff here is delightful, and the menu features well-prepared pub food with the occasional upscale twist. Those looking for a snuggly tête-à-tête will love McGurk's cozy hand-carved booths, which weave through the bar's three main rooms. If barroom conviviality is more your style, join in the raucous fun on the covered patio. The weekend crowd is young and collegiate—feel free to wear your university sweatshirt—and the party grows louder as the night goes on.

KIRKWOOD ICE & FUEL

215 N. Kirkwood Rd., 314/822-0494
HOURS: Mon.-Sat. 11am-1:30am, Sun. 5am-midnight
Map 7

A straightforward, just-good-folks bar in the heart of Kirkwood, Ice & Fuel pours some of the coldest drafts in the neighborhood. You shouldn't go out of your way to visit Ice and Fuel, but if you're already in the Kirkwood area, it's worth a stop. The bar keeps 15 beers on tap, and the kitchen turns out satisfying bar fare, including hot wings and sandwiches. The multiple TVs at this sports-themed bar make it a great place to catch a game. Just be sure that the words, "Go Cubs!" don't escape your lips.

THE MACK BAR AND GRILL

4615 Macklind Ave., 314/832-8199
HOURS: Daily 11am-1:30am
Map 4

Sometimes, upon stepping into a neighborhood bar, an out-of-town visitor feels ill at ease. That's never the case at The Mack (named after its location on Macklind Avenue), where the staff and the regulars are wonderfully welcoming. The vibe here reflects the hospitable, laid-back nature of the surrounding Southampton neighborhood—and the bartenders are happy to catch you up on all the local gossip. Buckets of beer are cheap, darts and air hockey are available in the back room, and if you're smart,

NIGHTLIFE

you'll come hungry. In-the-know locals swear by The Mack's food, which includes an awesome Mexican pizza and, on Sundays, stellar fried chicken. The hot wings are always a great accompaniment to the bar's $2 drafts.

PEPPER'S GRILL & BAR

5452 Gravois Ave., 314/352-9909,
http://peppersbarstl.com
HOURS: Mon.-Sat. 11am-1:30am, Sun. 11am-midnight
Map 4

Pepper's, a friendly pub in the Southampton neighborhood, boasts some great vintage details and fully stocked shelves. Something of a bartenders' bar, Pepper's attracts a crowd that's middle-aged and a little sedate, but the atmosphere provides a nice reprieve from the hubbub of the city's trendier nightspots. The quiet space, warm colors, and upholstered booths make this a great place to catch up with friends, and the food isn't bad either. Favorites include the outstanding house burger.

RILEY'S PUB

3458 Arsenal St., 314/664-7474
HOURS: Mon.-Fri. 4pm-1:30am, Sat. noon-1:30am
Map 4

Riley's Pub is only a couple of blocks east of South Grand Boulevard's bustling commercial strip, but this corner tavern still manages to feel like a neighborhood spot, a place where everyone might not know your name but sure are glad you came. Bottle and draft beer is reasonably priced, and in spite of the Budweiser memorabilia on the walls, a decent selection of brews is available. The kitchen turns out thin-crust pizzas to sate your munchies. The only potential drawback is the copious cigarette smoke.

ROSIE'S PLACE

4573 Laclede Ave., 314/361-6423
HOURS: Mon.-Sat. 11am-1:30am, Sun. noon-midnight
Map 2

Hidden among the expensive French restaurants and upscale nightclubs of the Central West End is Rosie's, a window into St. Louis's blue-collar, Budweiser-swilling soul. An eclectic mix of grizzled old barflies and slumming

Washington University grad students belly up to the bar of this tiny, narrow dive. It's cash-only and there's no beer on tap, just dirt-cheap bottles of Bud and some of the stiffest cocktails in town. The sole diversion is a jukebox heavy on Motown and Bon Jovi, which provides the soundtrack as the friendly bartenders, a muscle-bound ex-Mixed Martial Arts fighter and Rosie herself, do their best to keep the thirsty patrons from staggering home before last call.

THE ROYALE

3132 S. Kingshighway, 314/772-3600,
www.theroyale.com
HOURS: Mon.-Sat. 11:30am-1:30am, Sun. 11:30am-midnight
Map 4

This southside public house is an award-winning bar and restaurant that pairs local fare with outstanding sips and a slew of DJs spinning vinyl every night after 10pm. The cocktail menu features all the classics, like Corpse Revivers and Whiskey Daisies, as well as a bevy of beverages named after each ward in the city. Try a Baden Gimlet or a Holly Hills Daiquiri, and grab a seat on the patio whether it's May or December—the natural gas firepit is eco-friendly and keeps your drinkin' hand warm on even the most frigid evenings. Plus, the Royale has s'more kits at the ready for a bit of fun on those long winter nights.

◖ THE SCOTTISH ARMS

8 S. Sarah St., 314/535-0551,
www.thescottisharms.com
HOURS: Mon. 11am-2pm and 5pm-9pm, Tues.-Sat. 11am-2pm and 5pm-10pm, Sun. 10am-2pm and 5pm-9pm; bar open Tues.-Sat. until 1am, Sun.-Mon. until 11:30pm
Map 2

St. Louis has a glut of Irish bars, and even a few decent Welsh ones, but The Scottish Arms does more than its share to represent the British Isles. Owner Alistair Nesbit brings the spirit of his native Aberdeen, Scotland, to the heart of the Midwest. As befits a bar that hearkens back to the Highlands, the whiskey selection is among the best in town, and the beer list is heavy on

The Scottish Arms

dark, crisp U.K. brews. The dark wooden bar and low-glowing lights make for a suitably snug atmosphere, and the menu sails high above normal pub-grub fare. Delicacies like Scotch eggs (hard-boiled eggs cooked in sausage batter) and bangers-and-mash are must-haves, and the gastronomically adventurous will want to save room for haggis, the (in)famous Scottish dish of stuffed sheep's intestines.

34 CLUB
34 N. Euclid Ave., 314/367-6674
HOURS: Mon.-Sat. 3pm-1:30am
`Map 2`

Those who describe their favorite drinks with adjectives like "stiff" and "potent" will want to belly up to the 34 Club's bar. This shotgun space has little in common with high-rent neighbors like Sub Zero Vodka Bar and Brennan's Wine Bar, but it has a charm all its own. If your evening calls for something a little more down-and-dirty, make a beeline for the 34 Club. The clientele here is economically and culturally diverse, and while there are plenty of

regulars, they won't make out-of-towners feel out of place. Just look for the vintage neon window sign at the corner of Laclede and Euclid. That means you've arrived at the 34 Club, the neighborhood tavern that's been holding down this block for 60 years.

THE VENICE CAFÉ
1903 Pestalozzi St., 314/772-5994,
www.thevenicecafe.com
HOURS: Daily 4pm-1:30am
`Map 3`

The Venice Café might be a bit of a misnomer, as this popular joint doesn't serve food. Instead, people flock to Pestalozzi Street for the Venice's super-cool—and downright surreal—vibe. The patio could be described as "postmodern," or even "apocalyptic," with its combination of colorful mosaics, headless Barbie dolls, quirky fountains, and mannequin parts. The building's interior features more of the same, as well as a private second-floor bar that feels like the best treehouse ever. The Venice Café's wild whimsy attracts patrons of all ages. A small stage often hosts musicians and poets.

3AM BARS

C ATOMIC COWBOY

4140 Manchester Ave., 314/775-0775,
www.atomiccowboystl.com
HOURS: Mon.-Fri. 9am-3am, Sat.-Sun. 11am-3pm
COST: Occasional cover charge varies; call for more information
Map 2

Atomic Cowboy is a natural extension of owner Chip Schloss's magnetism and energy. Schloss is playing an instrumental role in the redevelopment of the entire Grove area, but Atomic Cowboy is at the epicenter of his efforts. The term "bar" does the venue an injustice, as it's also a lounge, dance club, art gallery, and late-night restaurant. On one side of the Cowboy, there are booths and high tables; on the other, there are living room-style arrangements of vintage Atomic Age furniture. The incredibly popular patio is shaded by a 1940s-style Quonset hut, and a roaring outdoor fireplace makes it possible to drink alfresco even on chilly nights. The crowd and the music are always eclectic, the Baja-Mexican food is tasty, and the atmosphere is 100 percent fun.

HANDLEBAR

4127 Manchester Ave., 314/652-2212,
www.handlebarstl.com
HOURS: Tues.-Sun. 11am-3am
COST: Occasional $5 cover on weekends after 10pm
Map 2

Nestled in the Manchester district known as The Grove, Handlebar is a bike-friendly watering hole smack in the middle of this covey of bars and nightclubs. Serving up local brews, sandwiches, and, oddly enough, borscht and pierogi (the adorable bike fanatic owner is Russian-born), this colorful 3am spot also houses bike art, murals by local artists, and a large patio for swilling Pabst alfresco. It's even got a tall bike sculpture out front for a ready-made photo-op.

LOLA

500 N. 14th St., 314/621-7277, www.welovelola.com
HOURS: Mon.-Thurs. 11am-midnight, Fri. 11am-2am,
Sat. 9:30am-2am, Sun. 9:30am-midnight
COST: Cover varies depending on entertainment
(rarely more than $10)
Map 1

Lola is a gin and jazz joint with an identity crisis, or perhaps just cultural attention deficit disorder. Entertainment on two stages ranges from hip-hop and soul to stand-up comedy and DJ sets on a rotating nightly basis, and after 10pm the place comes alive with a diverse crowd of revelers hell-bent on letting the good times roll. Incredible cocktails and inspired fare like Creole crepes or high-end chicken and waffles will sate your appetite for new American cuisine without the fussiness associated with the gustatory genre. The door charge is steep on the weekends, but if the music doesn't suit your mood, people-watching is all the entertainment you'll need.

MANGIA ITALIANO

3145 S. Grand Blvd., 314/664-8585,
www.dineatmangia.com
HOURS: Mon.-Sat. 3pm-3am, Sun. 11am-3am
COST: No cover
Map 4

Mangia Italiano may be beloved for its homemade pastas and cheap-and-tasty lunch buffet, but South Grand night owls know it as *the* place to be after midnight. Mangia is one of the very few 3am bars in the district, so it's not uncommon to see hordes of revelers heading here after the other bars call it an "early" night at 1:30am. The huge, inviting space features two bars, a subterranean space for special events, a small elevated stage, an expansive wall mural by legendary southside artist Wayne St. Wayne, and a charmingly mismatched assemblage of 1950s Formica tables and vinyl chairs. The seating is plentiful, making Mangia the perfect place for large groups who come here for the bar's weekly jazz gigs, rock shows, DJ sessions, and karaoke contests. Those sensitive to smoke should be aware that the bar gets a bit hazy as the night progresses.

Old Rock House

NICK'S IRISH PUB

6001 Manchester Ave., 314/781-7806,
www.nicksirishpub.com
HOURS: Mon.-Fri. 11am-3am, Sat.-Sun. 5pm-3am
COST: No cover
`Map 5`

Even if it is your first time coming through the doors, Nick's Pub will likely seem familiar: The green-and-white color scheme, the tall pints of beer, and the live folk music may make you think you've stumbled into an actual pub in Ireland. Every city needs a good Irish bar, and this is one of St. Louis's most comfortable. The menu offers good, greasy bar food, but the real draw is the pub's many facets: The beer garden is lovely in warm weather, and the upstairs area attracts all sorts of gamers. Dartboards, pool tables, and a slew of vintage arcade games await those with a competitive streak, and the shuffleboard table is perpetually packed. Nick's has a 3am license, making this a popular last stop for the under-30 crowd.

☾ OLD ROCK HOUSE

1200 S. 7th St., 314/588-0505,
www.oldrockhousestl.com
HOURS: Performance hours vary; see website
COST: No cover; ticket prices vary based on show
`Map 3`

The Old Rock House represents one of the more exciting developments near St. Louis's riverfront. Built as a reincarnation of the *original* Old Rock House—a rowdy riverside saloon rumored to draw everyone from shipping tycoons to Mark Twain himself—this new music venue is as gorgeous as it is ambitious. Thanks to an excellent renovation job, the Old Rock House seems like a historic landmark in the making. The original Old Rock House was demolished to make way for the Gateway Arch, but this new iteration takes the mantle quite effectively, with its intricate brickwork and gleaming wood floors. Within the venue's 6,000 square feet are three levels of seating; local and national bands rock out on the main floor and the mezzanine. The Old Rock House serves up great burgers and barbecue, and drink specials are abundant.

Those looking for quiet conversation can repair to the cigar-and-scotch lounge in the basement.

SANDRINA'S

5098 Arsenal St., 314/601-3456,
www.sandrinasstl.com
HOURS: Daily 4pm-3am
COST: No cover
`Map 4`

The old Sandrina's was a classic St. Louis Italian restaurant, serving the neighborhood with tasty if predictable red-sauce pasta and the like. The new Sandrina's features a revamped menu and a 3am liquor license. The food veers more towards bistro fare (pork chops, pizza, a few pasta dishes), but the nightlife provides a little snapshot of the surrounding Hill neighborhood. Once the area restaurants have shut down for the night, it seems that most of the waiters, bartenders, and kitchen staff make a beeline for Sandrina's to share war stories, a few laughs, and (of course) a couple more drinks. If the main floor gets too crowded, try the upstairs pool room, where an ancient 45-RPM jukebox spins out forgotten classics.

UPSTAIRS LOUNGE

3131 S. Grand Ave., www.upstairslounge.com
HOURS: Mon.-Sat. 6pm-1am, Sun. 6pm-midnight
COST: Cover varies depending on entertainment
`Map 4`

This pocket-sized bar is located directly above Mekong Restaurant, a Vietnamese restaurant at the corner of Grand Boulevard and Hartford Street. Mekong backs up to yet another smoky nightspot, the Jade Room, but the Upstairs Lounge is where the action is. The entrance is easy to miss—look for the lozenge-shaped Lounge sign above the door. A narrow set of stairs takes you past dingy, graffitied walls, but then the door opens on a scene of thumping music, friendly scenesters, and potent drinks. Do expect to pay a cover, and possibly a steep one. The Upstairs regularly hosts prominent out-of-town DJs, and you will be asked to pay a premium for them.

Dance Clubs

CLUB DANTE

3221 Olive St., 314/652-2369, www.clubdantes.com
HOURS: Call for hours
COST: $5 cover
`Map 2`

This spacious Midtown building has played host to a number of restaurants and clubs; as soon as one hot spot loses its luster, another moves in. Club Dante has been going strong for several years now—and shows no signs of slowing down. The place gets wall-to-wall packed on weekend nights. Dante is a European-style dance club with a large college-student following, and such top DJs as Tiesto, John Digweed, and Dave Aude spin here with surprising frequency. There are plenty of "theme" parties, too, so check the website to find a night devoted to your favorite kind of music (hip-hop, house, Latin, rock, and goth sets occur weekly). Despite its collegiate patrons and its proximity to Saint Louis University, Dante's isn't a place for cheap drinks. You won't find any dollar pitchers here; instead, the club stocks its back bar with premium liquors and offers a VIP bottle service. A lot of pretty people show up here, but Dante is no glorified meat market—this is a place where music lovers come to dance for hours on end.

CLUB LA ONDA

4920 Northrup Ave.
HOURS: Thurs.-Fri. 10pm-3am
COST: No cover
`Map 5`

La Onda just might be the most authentic Latino bar in the city, and it's certainly one of the most popular. Vast and warehouse-like, La Onda draws a mainly Hispanic crowd and features live bands throughout the week. The party vibe is strong, and the crowds are here to dance. Your high-school Spanish might draw good-natured jibes, but after a few rounds, you'll be able to take it all in stride. As is true in the best Mexican bars, tequila can be ordered by the shot or the bottle; the latter option is iced tableside. La Onda is in a transitioning neighborhood, and all revelers must pass through metal detectors. Once inside, though, the atmosphere is pure fun. On many weekend nights, real-deal Mexican-food vendors park their carts right outside the club—after a night of dancing and drinking, few things taste better than an authentic taco.

CLUB VIVA
408 N. Euclid Ave., 314/361-0322, www.clubvivastl.com
HOURS: Tues.-Sat. 8pm-1:30am
COST: $5 cover; Sat. $6; ladies free Thurs. until 10:30pm
Map 2

This hip Central West End nightspot is one of the few salsa clubs in town. Don't know how to salsa? Not to worry—just stop in a bit early, and take a free salsa class from 8pm-9pm Thursdays and Saturdays, before the dance floor heats up. The classes attract droves of people, all ready to let their hair down and learn one of the world's most sensual dances. The vibe at Viva is warm and welcoming, and despite being open since 1997, the club hasn't lost any of its panache. If you need a little liquid courage before you hit the dance floor, try the pisco sour.

THE LOFT
3112 Olive St., 314/225-2505
HOURS: Mon., Thurs.-Sat. 11am-2:30am, Tues.-Wed. 11am-9pm
COST: $10-30 cover
Map 2

There's no jazz at this so-called jazz loft, nor is there a loft, but there is a whole lotta hip-hop. Patrons look fresh off a video shoot nightly, and The Loft is an after-party requirement for any big-name rap artist who blows through the Fox Theatre or Scottrade Center. Local radio DJs do a live set from The Loft every Saturday, so book a booth ahead of time if bottle service is the end game. Weekend crowds can be huge,

but there's no better nightclub for Moscato and wings.

MANDARIN LOUNGE
44 Maryland Plaza, 314/367-4447, www.mandarinlounge.net
HOURS: Wed.-Thurs. 9pm-1:30am, Fri.-Sat. 8pm-1:30am
COST: $5 cover
Map 2

The Central West End's only rooftop club can, at first glance, seem like a secret club or a well-appointed tree house: Mandarin is accessible via a pedestrian walkway near the recently revamped Maryland Plaza Fountain. Soon after the doormen let you into the elevator, you'll enter the low-lit, red-walled lounge. The bar space is open and fluid, with a few snug booths available, but the real draw is the open-air rooftop bar, which offers a lovely view of the always-bustling West End nightlife. Like the bar's decor, the drink menu takes a few cues from the Far East, with cocktails like the Geisha Blossom (vodka, green tea, and peach nectar) and the Shanghai Cosmo (raspberry vodka, Cointreau, and white cranberry juice). You may not find yourself transported to an exotic locale in Asia when you party at Mandarin, but you will be able to dance and drink on one of the city's finest perches.

THE PEPPER LOUNGE
2005 Locust St., 314/241-2005, www.thepepperlounge.com
HOURS: Fri.-Sat. 9pm-3am, Sun. 10pm-3am
COST: $10-30 cover
Map 1

Although it's at a bit of a remove from Wash. Ave.—the city's main dancing-and-drinking drag—The Pepper Lounge is worth seeking out on it own merits. This club, built inside an old Eastman Kodak warehouse, is a favorite of many St. Louis trendsetters. Some clubs care more about raking in the cover charges than creating ambiance, but not The Pepper: It's as beautiful as it is popular. Some revelers may be bummed by the (tiny) size of the dance floor, but those looking to chill with friends will

NIGHTLIFE

Thaxton Speakeasy

be delighted by the expansive bar and ample, plush seating. (VIP booths are available for a steep premium.) The Pepper regularly hosts some of the best DJs in town, including a few who spin excellent old-school hip-hop.

THAXTON SPEAKEASY
1009 Olive St., 314/241-3279,
www.thaxtonspeakeasy.com
HOURS: Thurs.-Sat. 9pm-1:30am
COST: Call to inquire about cover
Map 1

Located in the historic Thaxton Building, the Thaxton Speakeasy is a sexy basement night-spot where the downtown crowd tipples and flirts the night away. Sidle up to the alley entrance, but be sure to check the website before-hand for the password for a couple bucks off the door charge. The beautiful antechamber on the main floor is definitely worth a long look, but head downstairs to dance the night away with an exclusive crowd of twenty- and thirtysomethings.

2720 CHEROKEE PERFORMING ARTS CENTER
2720 Cherokee St., 314/276-2700,
http://2720cherokee.com
HOURS: Call for hours
COST: $5-12 cover
Map 3

Whether it's an electronic DJ set, a low-key reggae night, or a gallery show with live art and body-paint clad models, it works in this three-story fun house, complete with hula hoop gangs and psychedelic objets d'art crammed in every available corner. (Think static-buzzing antique televisions, a busted spinet littered with tchotchkes, and a special shelf for *Star Wars* paraphernalia.) It takes all sorts to fill this 20,000-square-foot space, and the crowd is as unpredictable as the art for sale upstairs; it could be a hippie carnival, a black-clad hipster conference, or a subtle gathering of upwardly mobile artist-types, which is probably just another way of saying hipster. There's lots of space to boogie in this Cherokee Street mainstay, and an honest-to-goodness adherence to the old raver motto of peace, love, unity, and respect, because all are welcome, man.

Gay and Lesbian

ATTITUDES NIGHTCLUB
4100 Manchester Ave., 314/534-0044
HOURS: Call for hours
COST: No cover for 21+
`Map 2`
Today, the disco-style dance floor at this popular lesbian bar looks a little dated. Attitudes opened its doors more than 25 years ago, and it bears the hallmarks of LGBT clubs from the mid-1980s: nondescript building, tinted windows, tiny foyer. These secretive measures were put in place to protect patrons; while the Grove is now a flourishing gay-friendly neighborhood, that wasn't always the case. Still, even though Attitudes could use some sprucing up, it's a great place to drink and dance. And don't be scared off by the name—the attitudes on display here are friendly, outgoing, and laid-back.

CLEMENTINE'S BAR
2001 Menard St., 314/664-7869
HOURS: Mon.-Sat. 10am-1:30am, Sun. 11am-midnight
COST: No cover
`Map 3`
The city's oldest gay bar, Clementine's occupies a pretty brick building in the historic Soulard neighborhood. The bar primarily serves a leather crowd: Men come here to meet up, to hang out, and to have a bite at the adjoining Oh My Darlin' Café. Clementine's proximity to the annual Mardi Gras celebration makes it a particularly popular destination for the LGBT community each February.

ERNEY'S 32 DEGREES
4199 Manchester Ave., 314/652-7195
HOURS: Daily 6:30am-3pm
COST: No cover
`Map 2`
Sure, a gay bar with shirtless bartenders, a stripper pole, and urinals in every bathroom may seem a bit on the nose, but there's virtually no better place for a high-octane dance party than Erney's 32. Everything's just fabulous here,

from the shots available in the VodBox—32 degrees, don't ya know—to the pure white interior, made prismatic by the flatscreens sparkling throughout. Need some air? Right past the cage is a gorgeous, well-lit patio where someone will inevitably ask you for a cigarette. Saturday nights bring a kaleidoscopic view of St. Louis nightlife: industry folks winding down with some help from Jaeger, a gaggle of co-eds inexplicably dressed like they're in an exercise video from 1984, drag queens drawing approving looks from everyone. Just don't flirt with the bartenders; it's been done.

JJ'S CLUBHOUSE & BAR
3858 Market St., 314/535-4100, www.jjsclubhouse.com
HOURS: Daily 3pm-3am
COST: No cover
`Map 2`
This exclusively male gay bar on Market Street is the largest bear and leather scene in the city. Those looking for outgoing leather daddies will certainly find an active little enclave here, as well as pool tables (free Sundays and Mondays), dartboards, and a busy calendar of events. Every year, JJ's hosts the Mr. Midwest and Missouri Leather contests, the Mr. Heartland Bear contest, and a popular regional bear event called Hibearnation. This 3am spot welcomes people of other orientations, but female barhoppers should know that JJ's is not particularly touted for its friendliness to women.

JUST JOHN NIGHTCLUB
4112 Manchester Ave., 314/371-1333,
www.justjohnclub.com
HOURS: Mon.-Sat. 3pm-3am, Sun. noon-1:30am
COST: No cover
`Map 2`
One day the city of St. Louis may have to build a bridge from Novak's to Just John; though you could fly a paper airplane from door to door, these neighboring nightclubs are must-stops for dancing, divas, and drag. Just John is not what

COST: No cover; ticket prices vary based on show
Map 2

The Firebird is St. Louis's premier indie rock club, especially now that the tag "indie rock" is a fluid descriptor for all manner of nouveau-noisemaking. Rock, pop, electronic trickery, and even drone metal feel at home in this black-as-pitch space, located in an unassuming brick building on Olive Boulevard. The low-slung ceiling and snug black leather booths keep it cool, while the sounds pouring from the sub-woofers keep it hot no matter who's on stage. Bands that make their first-time St. Louis appearance at the Firebird often find themselves headlining The Pageant on their second visit, which is pudding-proof that the dudes running the place have a preternatural knack for trend-spotting.

LEMMONS

5800 Gravois Ave., 314/481-4812
HOURS: Daily 5:30pm-3am
COST: $5 cover
Map 4

Lemmons is an out-of-the-way club near South City's southern fringe, but fun-seekers have no trouble finding it. The venue's concert calendar reads like a who's-who in local music, but Lemmons is far more than just a rock club. The trivia nights (with accompanying hot-wing specials) are legendary. An all-you-can-eat pizza buffet and one-dollar drink specials are available during Lemmons's frequent movie nights. Worried that pizza at a rock club might be subpar? Don't fret. Lemmons serves the Black Thorn Pub's deservedly famous deep-dish pizza.

◖ OFF BROADWAY

3509 Lemp Ave., 314/773-3363,
www.offbroadwaystl.com
HOURS: Call for hours
COST: $5-10 cover
Map 3

Tucked away in the shadows of the long-dormant Lemp brewery (and not far from the Anheuser-Busch brewery and tour facility), Off Broadway is a little oasis of rock and folk music.

The tall ceiling and wood-paneled walls are reminiscent of an old-time saloon, and that vibe only intensifies when one of many local country-influenced bands performs in front of the stage's red velvet curtain. While Off Broadway is a favorite spot for local groups, many touring artists—including Andrew Bird, Jolie Holland, and the Hold Steady—have made the club their go-to spot when coming through town. The club is smoke-free (a welcome but rare thing in St. Louis), which reinforces Off Broadway's status as a listening room.

THE PAGEANT

6161 Delmar Blvd., 314/726-6161, www.thepageant.com
HOURS: Vary by show
COST: No cover; ticket prices vary based on show
Map 6

Built in 2000 on the eastern end of the Delmar Loop, The Pageant remains an anchor in this thriving cultural district. With a seating capacity of more than 2,000, The Pageant is *the* spot for mid- to upper-level touring bands. The balcony provides cushy seats and decent sight lines, although dedicated fans often prefer to nestle up to the stage on the ground floor. Bookings at The Pageant tend toward rock and pop, with the occasional hip-hop or hard-rock act thrown in. Most shows here are all-ages, though over-21 patrons can enjoy or a pre- or post-show drink at the attached Halo Bar, which serves until 3am.

PLUSH

3224 Locust St., 314/535-2686, www.plushstl.com
HOURS: Tues.-Thurs. 11am-9pm, Fri.-Sat. 11am-1am, Sun. 8am-1pm.
COST: Cover varies based on night and schedule (rarely more than $8)
Map 2

Every city has its next hip 'hood, and with the addition of Plush, Midtown Alley is definitely in the running. This four-story behemoth takes entertainment seriously, functioning as a concert hall, restaurant, espresso bar, game room, lounge, and private event space, with an art-forward attitude and plenty of room to grow. Whether you're looking to nosh after 9 or grabbing a hangover breakfast, Plush's scratch-made menu of diner-food-with-a-modern twist will keep you guessing (two words: meatloaf cupcakes), but it's the free local music nights that will keep you coming back.

THE SILVER BALLROOM
4701 Morgan Ford Rd., 314/832-9223,
www.thesilverballroom.com
HOURS: Mon.-Fri. 3pm-1:30am, Sat. noon-1:30am, Sun. noon-midnight
COST: No cover
Map 4

Buffeted by the booming Morgan Ford Strip to the north and the historic Bevo Mill neighborhood to the south, The Silver Ballroom is the perfect midpoint between old-school South City charm and new-city style. Aging rockers and rowdy young punks alike come for the three P's: Pabst, pinball, and punk rock. It's the only pretense about this place, and the combination is unbeatable. The legend above the bar reads "RETOX CENTER," so grab a highbrow—that's PBR and a shot of Jameson, for

the uninitiated—and you'll feel right at home in no time.

THE WAY OUT CLUB
2525 S. Jefferson Ave., 314/664-7638
HOURS: Wed.-Sat. 9pm-1:30am
COST: Cover varies based on night and schedule (rarely more than $10)
Map 3

Dropping by The Way Out Club is a simultaneous glance into the future and a step into the past: You can get a look at some of St. Louis's newest young bands while hanging out in a much hipper version of your grandparents' basement. The decor is a hodgepodge of beautiful trash—B-movie posters, old televisions, garage-sale junk, and vintage swag lamps mesh to create a one-of-a-kind atmosphere. Most bands that play the club veer towards loud, fast rock 'n' roll, and the slew of regulars will be happy to give you a thumbnail sketch of St. Louis's underground music history. While the musical performances can be hit or miss, The Way Out is worth stopping by, if only for a drink.

Wine Bars

BRENNAN'S WINE BAR AND CIGAR SHOP
4659 Maryland Ave., 314/361-9444,
http://cometobrennans.net
HOURS: Mon.-Sat. 3pm-1am, Sun. 3pm-midnight
COST: No cover
Map 2

Though located at a busy intersection frequented by people who want to see and be seen, Brennan's remains one of the best-kept secrets in St. Louis—many of the locals don't even know about this outstanding wine and cigar bar. Perhaps that's because this single address is home to four locales in one. You've got your main-floor wine and cigar storefront, which provides cash-and-carry wines by the bottle. During warm-weather evenings, the outdoor patio serves as an excellent post for people-watching, and on chilly winter nights,

the basement speakeasy Scotch bar provides a welcome coziness. Finally, the second-floor Maryland House is popular with both the primped and the laid-back, offering wines by the glass, cheese plates, and a casually cool vibe.

CIELO RESTAURANT & BAR
999 N. 2nd St., 314/881-2105, www.cielostlouis.com
HOURS: Sun.-Thurs. 11am-11pm, Fri.-Sat. 11am-1am
COST: No cover
Map 1

Anyone can mix a drink or pour a glass of wine, but very few get to do so with a million-dollar view at their back. Bypass the ostentatious Lumière Place casino and hotel, glide through the meditative lobby, and slide into a sumptuous seat at Cielo, the Four Seasons Hotel bar. Ah, sanctuary. This downtown destination plays host to footballers, St. Louis celebrities,

NIGHTLIFE

and visiting luminaries alike, and the rooftop lounge offers stellar sights, impeccable service, and five-star sips.

REMY'S KITCHEN & WINE BAR

222 S. Bemiston Ave., 314/726-5757, www.remyskitchen.net

HOURS: Mon.-Thurs. 11:30am-9:30pm, Fri. 11:30am-11:30pm, Sat. 5pm-11pm

COST: No cover

`Map 6`

A *Wine Spectator* Award of Excellence winner twelve times over, Remy's is a place that's serious about good wine. The good thing is, no one here takes *themselves* too seriously; the decor is at once classy and whimsical, the servers have great senses of humor, and the wine list is well-cultivated and creative. It's not uncommon to see a businessperson or professor tucked into a corner table, reading a book and working his or her way through a wine flight. The flights change monthly and offer sippers the opportunity to try some truly amazing vino. Summertime flights often include gorgeous Alsatian varietals, while winter flights showcase hearty Cab blends. The food at Remy's is hit-or-miss, but you can't go wrong with the cheese plate and the stuffed grapevine leaves.

SASHA'S WINE BAR

706 De Mun Ave., Clayton, 314/863-7274, www.sashaswinebar.com

HOURS: Mon.-Sat. 11am-1am, Sun. 10am-midnight

COST: No cover

`Map 6`

Sasha's Wine Bar & Market is exactly the kind of hidden-away, low-key spot people seek out to unwind over a glass of wine (or three). Situated in a quiet, residential neighborhood you'll wish you could call your own, Sasha's faces a tranquil park, making its outdoor seating a perfect refuge from the city's hustle-bustle. And when those patio tables are full, indoor patrons still can enjoy the benefit of a breezy summer night: The French doors are frequently flung wide, bringing the outdoors in. The lengthy wine list ensures there's something for every palate, and the crepes, pizzas, and other small plates guarantee you won't be drinking on an empty stomach.

◖ 33 WINE SHOP & TASTING BAR

1913 Park Ave., 314/231-9463, www.33wine.com

HOURS: Tues.-Sat. 3:30pm-1am

COST: No cover

`Map 3`

The 33 Wine Shop & Tasting Bar—33 to its regulars—is one of the city's hidden gems, a beautiful (and smoke-free) bar with a tremendous wine list, friendly and exceptionally knowledgeable staff, and one of the funniest menus that you'll ever read. The menu provides great choices at every price point, with only a modest markup if you enjoy a bottle (or two) at the bar. The beer selection is excellent, too. In nice weather, 33's backyard patio is a lovely place to while away an evening.

ARTS AND LEISURE

St. Louis boasts a thriving fine-arts scene, both in rarefied museum exhibits and in funky galleries. Entrepreneurial artists have turned much of the city's raw warehouse space into showrooms and studios for up-and-coming talent. St. Louis also reveals its wonderfully quirky side with museums that have nothing to do with portraits or Picassos—American Kennel Club Museum of the Dog, anyone?

Theater is also an important part of St. Louis's cultural identity, and the city hosts numerous theatrical companies. While the theater community sometimes argues over whether a midsize city can support so many different groups, most plays and musicals here are high-caliber. Particularly noteworthy is The Black Rep, one of the nation's largest African American theater companies.

Of course, entertainment in St. Louis isn't always about gallery openings and theatrical shows. This is a great city in which to let loose and have a great time; the sheer number of fairs and festivals practically mandates it. Visitors will find abundant options in any season, from the raucous Mardi Gras celebration (second only in size to New Orleans's annual party) in spring to the Festival of Nations in the summer to winter's Robert Burns Night.

Sports also are a key element of the city's cultural fabric. There are very few casual sports fans in St. Louis. Instead, there are sports lovers—and sports fanatics. The city is home to three major professional teams: the Cardinals (baseball), the Rams (football), and the Blues (ice hockey). Even when these teams are less than stellar (we're looking at you, 2008–2011

HIGHLIGHTS

LOOK FOR ◖ TO FIND RECOMMENDED ARTS AND ACTIVITIES.

◖ **Best Art Museum:** A work of art in itself, the **Contemporary Art Museum St. Louis** brings the world's most talented artists to the heart of St. Louis. But the museum also gives local talents plenty of credit—and it's that sense of community that makes the Contemporary so appealing, so respected, and so successful (page 87).

◖ **Best Acoustics:** Known as the "Carnegie Hall of St. Louis," the **Sheldon Concert Hall** does justice to many visiting luminaries with its near-perfect acoustics. The Sheldon also houses a small but beautiful art gallery (page 92).

◖ **Best Seat in the House:** With more than 4,000 seats, a gorgeous Baroque interior, and the renown of one of the largest Broadway houses in the nation, the **Fox Theatre** is the perfect place to see a musical, enjoy a concert—or just take a tour (page 92).

◖ **Best Theater Company: St. Louis Black Rep** is the largest African American theater company in the United States, and its shows are consistently stellar. Performances take place in the gorgeously renovated Grandel Theater in Grand Center (page 93).

◖ **Best Place for Movies and Martinis:** The **Moolah Theatre & Lounge,** a former Shriners Temple, boasts a full evening's entertainment under one roof. Grab a pre-show martini, watch a first-run movie (while sitting on a plush leather couch), and then repair to the basement for a few frames of bowling (page 94).

◖ **Best Summer Festivals:** The **Festival of Nations** (page 96) in Tower Grove Park is hosted by the International Institute and celebrates the food, dance, and art of St. Louis's many cultures. **PrideFest** (page 96) brings the city's LGBT community together for three days of parades, performances, and camaraderie.

◖ **Best Art Festival:** While some art fairs seem stuffy and staid, the **Art Outside Festival** brings a sense of pure fun (plus beer!) to the proceedings. Peruse awesome, affordable work by some of St. Louis's best artists; you're sure to find something you'll love (page 97).

◖ **Best Park for Joggers: Forest Park** is the perfect place for casual joggers and marathoners-in-training alike. The park's jogging path is 7.5 miles long and wraps around the circumference of St. Louis's urban oasis (page 99).

◖ **Best Urban Bike Route:** The **Bike St. Louis** route originally extended 20 miles from Forest Park Parkway to the Gateway Arch, and now it's been expanded by 50 miles. Along the way, colorful Bike St. Louis signposts direct cyclists to city neighborhoods, attractions, and other points of interest (page 101).

◖ **Best Way to Feel Like a True St. Louisan:** No matter how the team is doing—whether the season culminates in a World Series win or a pre-playoffs elimination—St. Louisans stay true to the **St. Louis Cardinals.** Take in a game at Busch Stadium, and be sure to wear red (page 104).

Rams), many St. Louisans stay loyal, and you'll find neighborhood sports bars packed on game nights.

While St. Louis isn't known for its die-hard citizen-athletes (no one will mistake St. Louis for, say, Denver or Austin in that regard), many St. Louisans lead very active lifestyles. The city's parks provide perfect terrain for joggers and runners. In recent years,

a dedicated group of cyclists has worked to make the city streets safer for those who commute on two wheels rather than four. Today, the bike trails and lanes are clearly marked, and the city's biking routes can provide visitors with a lovely tour de St. Louis. If you travel with your golf clubs, be sure to reserve a tee time at Forest Park; this beautiful course is open to the public.

The Arts

MUSEUMS

AMERICAN KENNEL CLUB MUSEUM OF THE DOG

1721 S. Mason Rd., 314/821-3647,
www.museumofthedog.org
HOURS: Tues.-Sat. 10am-4pm, Sun. 1pm-5pm
COST: $5 adult, $2.50 senior, $1 child
Map 7

If your idea of fine canine art involves dogs playing poker, you may want to expand your view at the American Kennel Club Museum of the Dog. This exhibition space, located in the gorgeous Queeny Park, is home to a vast collection of dog paintings. That may sound quirky, but the museum's aims are straightforward and sincere: They honor the elegance and faithfulness of the American dog. The paintings are touching homages to some of the world's most elegant breeds. Set aside an hour or two to see the 700 works on display here—and to admire the Jarville House, the lovely 18th-century home in which this collection is kept.

CENTER OF CREATIVE ARTS

524 Trinity Ave., University City, 314/725-6555,
www.cocastl.org
HOURS: Fall, winter, and spring hours: Mon.-Fri. 9am-9pm, Sat. 9am-6pm, Sun. 11am-6pm; Summer hours: Mon. and Wed. 7:30am-9pm, Tues. and Thurs.-Fri. 7:30am-6pm, Sat. 9am-5pm
COST: Varies based on exhibit or performance
Map 6

Located within shouting distance of the dynamic, artsy Delmar Loop, the Center of Creative Arts offers a vast variety of cultural experiences. COCA, as it's most commonly known, welcomes hundreds of visitors through its doors each year, for everything from fine-art exhibits to theatrical premieres to workshops on innovation in business. A favorite among St. Louis families, COCA offers dozens of classes for everyone from toddlers to seniors. Tourists are more than welcome here, too: Frequent gallery shows, wonderful kid-friendly entertainment, and a full schedule of art openings make COCA a can't-miss destination for anyone who wants to hear the artistic heartbeat of St. Louis.

CONTEMPORARY ART MUSEUM ST. LOUIS

3750 Washington Blvd., 314/535-4660,
www.contemporarystl.org
HOURS: Wed. 11am-6pm, Thurs.-Fri. 11am-9pm, Sat.-Sun. 10am-5pm
COST: $5 adult, $3 senior, free for students and children
Map 2

The Contemporary Art Museum St. Louis is the crown jewel of Grand Center, an area that is fast becoming the city's preeminent arts district. The Contemporary, St. Louis's premier institution for contemporary art and outreach, opened its doors in 2002 and hosts six to eight world-class exhibitions each year. The Contemporary's featured artists range from internationally acclaimed veterans to local rising stars. Past exhibitors include Yoshimoto Nara, Cindy Sherman, Jim Hodges, and Maya Lin. Don't miss the opportunity to peruse the Contemporary's Flat Files; you can open the files and peruse the works of artists of the Midwestern heartland. They are available to the public and provide a glimpse into the area's regional art communities. A free, docent-led stroller tour for families is offered the first Wednesday of every month at 9am, and a culinary and art tour is offered for $10 per person on the first Saturday of every month at noon.

LAUMEIER SCULPTURE PARK

12580 Rott Rd., Sunset Hills, 314/612-5278,
www.laumeier.com
HOURS: Daily 8am-30 minutes after sunset; gallery and museum shop open Tues.-Fri. 10am-5pm, Sat.-Sun. noon-5pm
COST: Free
Map 7

Laumeier Sculpture Park collects, commissions,

ARTS AND LEISURE

THE ART OF THE FAMILY VACATION

Families who visit St. Louis are in luck. Rather than being forced to seek out the local Chuck E. Cheese outpost, parents can introduce their kids to wonderful cultural activities. St. Louis's thriving art scene is kid-inclusive, thanks to places like the **Craft Alliance** (6640 Delmar Blvd.). Just down the street from the Craft Alliance, the **Center of Creative Arts** (524 Trinity Ave., University City) offers dance and theater workshops and a student acting company for the younger set. COCA's many performances are open to the public; affordable tickets make a COCA show the perfect choice for a family outing.

Kids who are fancifully inclined will love **Bob Kramer's Marionnettes** (4143 Laclede Ave., 314/531-3313, www.kramersmarionnettes.com). Kramer's beautiful marionettes—each of which takes nearly 1,500 labor hours to create—come to splendid life in offbeat shows like *The Magical Toyshop*.

If your kids aren't yet keen on "traditional" museums, take them to an out-of-the-ordinary place like **City Museum** (701 N. 15th St.) or the **American Kennel Club Museum of the Dog** (1721 S. Mason Rd.). Kids who grew up with Thomas the Train Engine will definitely want to check out **The St. Louis Museum of Transportation** (3015 Barrett Station Rd., Kirkwood, 314/965-6212, www.transportmuseumassociation.org), which is chock-full of model trains, automobiles, trolley cars, and full-size locomotives (there's even a mini-train on which kids can ride). At the **Saint Louis Artists' Guild** (2 Oak Knoll Park, Clayton, 314/727-6266, www.stlouisartistsguild.org), the Monsanto Children's Gallery always displays artwork by local students. Kids are sure to be inspired when they see their peers' work in such a beautiful setting.

and exhibits monumental contemporary sculptures. Laumeier's 100-plus acres of forest paths and broad lawns provide a backdrop for its internationally acclaimed permanent collection, as well as several touring exhibitions. Artists in the permanent collection include Donald Judd, Sol LeWitt, and Mark di Suvero. The park's small indoor museum displays additional works, including excellent photographs and drawings. Admission to both the sculpture park and the museum is free (except for special events). This is the perfect place for a picnic and afternoon stroll, and visitors should be sure to visit Laumeier's website for a calendar of fun outdoor events. During warm-weather months, the park plays host to live music, festivals, and outdoor movies.

THE MOTO MUSEUM

3441 Olive Blvd., 314/446-1805,
www.themotomuseum.com
HOURS: Mon.-Fri. 11am-4pm
COST: Free, $10 per adult for 30-45-minute tour
Map 2

Moto Museum founder Steve Smith maintains his rare and vintage motorcycles with the care and precision of a fine-art curator. The museum is, first and foremost, a workshop where Smith restores bikes that he has collected from all around the world. Moto also doubles as a super-cool event space.

MUSEUM OF CONTEMPORARY RELIGIOUS ART

3700 W. Pine Blvd., 314/977-7170, www.slu.edu/mocra
HOURS: Tues.-Sun. 11am-4pm
COST: suggested donation $5 adult, $1 student/child
Map 2

Saint Louis University is well-respected for its strong Jesuit mission, an approach that places scholarly pursuit far above dogma. The Museum of Contemporary Religious Art exemplifies this mission. The contemplative, sanctuary-like space is filled with pieces that have dialogue with, explore, and even critique matters of faith. The museum has an ecumenical approach, and the artwork here reflects themes of many world religions. Meditation and personal spirituality also inform MOCRA's

Contemporary Art Museum St. Louis

collection, and the museum hosted the largest-ever U.S. installation of Andy Warhol's *Silver Clouds.*

PULITZER FOUNDATION
FOR THE ARTS
3716 Washington Blvd., 314/754-1850,
www.pulitzerarts.org
HOURS: Wed. noon-5pm, Sat. 10am-5pm
COST: Free
Map 2

The Pulitzer Center's awe-inspiring galleries and elegant outdoor spaces sprang from the imagination of Pritzker Prize-winning architect Tadao Ando. The Pulitzer, a Modernist work of art in its own right, sits next to the equally stunning Contemporary Art Museum St. Louis (an impressive, much-beloved Richard Serra sculpture is on permanent display in the two museums' shared courtyard). The Pulitzer's artist roster changes somewhat frequently, and has in recent years included Dan Flavin, Hiroshi Sugimoto, Max Beckmann, and Cy Twombly. The Pulitzer also contributes to literary and

performing-arts programs. Visitors are advised to check out the museum's website in advance, as hours are limited.

SAINT LOUIS ART MUSEUM
1 Fine Arts Dr., 314/721-0072, www.slam.org
HOURS: Tues.-Sun. 10am-5pm, Fri. 10am-9pm
COST: Free (additional charge for select exhibitions)
Map 6

The Saint Louis Art Museum occupies a significant space in the St. Louis landscape, both figuratively and literally. The Beaux Arts-style building, designed in the late 19th century by famed architect Cass Gilbert, sits atop the aptly named Art Hill like a great white palace. Step inside, and you'll find an interior that's just as stunning—and a permanent collection that is both broad and well-culled. Of particular note is the modern-art wing upstairs, which includes one of the best German Expressionist collections in the nation. A large addition, simply called the East Building, opened in June 2013.

ARTS AND LEISURE

ART GALLERIES

BRUNO DAVID GALLERY

3721 Washington Blvd., 314/531-3030,
www.brunodavidgallery.com
HOURS: Wed. and Sat. 10am-5pm or by appointment
COST: Free
Map 2

The Bruno David Gallery is a great side stop for Pulitzer Center visitors attracted by its bright red door. This gallery aims to represent the bright young talents that museums like the Pulitzer and Contemporary typically miss, and those who follow their curiosity into the heart of this small space will appreciate the innovative and spirited work on display here. Bruno David exhibitions feature the creative projects of local and international talents side-by-side, and represent a variety of media, from sculpture and installation to video and illustration.

PHILIP SLEIN GALLERY

4735 McPherson Ave., 314/361-2617,
www.philipsleingallery.com
HOURS: Tues.-Sat. 10am-5pm or by appointment
COST: Free
Map 2

When St. Louis art collectors want the very best in cutting-edge art, they call up Philip Slein—or, better yet, they head to his new gallery in the Central West End. Thanks to his keen aesthetic sense and dynamic personality, Slein continually brings in artists who are at the top of their game. Frequent exhibitions make the work accessible to those who might not have deep enough pockets to make a purchase. Philip Slein helped bring renowned printmaker Tom Huck to national attention; today, Huck's gigantic and wonderfully grotesque works hang in some of the country's premier museums.

SHELDON ART GALLERIES

3648 Washington Blvd., 314/533-9900,
www.sheldonconcerthall.org
HOURS: Tues. noon-8pm, Wed.-Fri. noon-5pm, Sat. 10am-2pm
COST: Donation requested
Map 2

The Sheldon Art Galleries are on the basement level of the world-class Sheldon Concert Hall. Frequently missed by concert attendees (and even by astute gallery-goers), this collection represents one of the St. Louis art community's best-kept secrets. The Sheldon hosts a diverse array of artists and media; one exhibit featured photographs accompanied by carefully arranged found objects. The gallery also offers a full schedule of art talks, lunchtime lectures, and master-class workshops, in addition to a wonderful annual children's art show.

WHITE FLAG PROJECTS

4568 Manchester Ave., 314/531-3442,
www.whiteflagprojects.org
HOURS: Tues.-Sat. noon-5pm, or by appointment
COST: Free
Map 2

White Flag Projects offers art lovers an alternative to the often-stuffy exclusivity of the contemporary art world. The artists exhibited here run the gamut from progressive newcomers to internationally acclaimed veterans. The gallery's curators are not partial to any particular medium, but White Flag's focus is on fringe artists. Located in the burgeoning Grove neighborhood, this renovated industrial building provides the perfect backdrop for challenging art.

CONCERTS

FOCAL POINT

2720 Sutton Blvd., Maplewood, 314/560-2778,
www.thefocalpoint.org
Map 4

As the town of Maplewood continues to flourish with new restaurants and attractions, it's comforting to know that the area retains its small-town feel. Across the street from the one-of-a-kind bowlers' haven Saratoga Lanes stands the Focal Point, a listening room that plays host to all sorts of folk art from at home and abroad. Depending on the evening, you may come across a world-class Irish fiddler, a Cajun zydeco dancing exposition, or an expert banjo picker. The room is arranged with a small stage and a few rows of wooden seats, so every performance is intimate and memorable.

Most events take place on the weekend, and it's best to check the venue's website for upcoming events.

OPERA THEATRE OF ST. LOUIS

210 Hazel Ave., Webster Groves, 314/961-0644, www.opera-stl.org

Map 7

Opera Theatre of St. Louis's intimate home is located on the manicured grounds of Webster University. The company stages a nicely blended repertoire of classic and contemporary productions, from *Madame Butterfly* to *Una Cosa Rara*. The 2012 production of *Sweeney Todd* received universally rave reviews from critics and audiences alike. Opera Theatre of St. Louis also hosts an outdoor cocktail hour and picnic prior to several of its spring concerts—the perfect milieu for a date. Visitors are invited to bring their own wine and picnic food, and a local restaurant provides affordably priced boxed dinners for those who come without.

© ALISE O'BRIEN

Powell Symphony Hall

PEABODY OPERA HOUSE

1400 Market St., 314/499-7600, www.peabodyoperahouse.com

Map 1

The Peabody Opera House is, quite simply, one of the most gorgeous venues in the Midwest. Reopened in 2011 following a $78.7 million restoration, this cultural gem welcomes a wide variety of performers and performances. Performers from Norah Jones to Primus to the Rockettes have taken the stage at the newly renovated Peabody. Take a tour of the building and learn about its rich history. This opera house first opened to the public in 1934; over the decades, the best entertainers in the business (including Bob Dylan, Frank Sinatra, Ray Charles, and the Rolling Stones) have visited here and brought audiences to their feet. The architecture and stunning details are worthy of a standing ovation, too.

POWELL SYMPHONY HALL

718 N. Grand Blvd., 314/533-2500, www.stlsymphony.org

Map 2

This nearly 2,700-seat theater began its life as a vaudeville hall and movie palace. Today it is an acoustic marvel, thanks to a graceful mid-century renovation, and is home to the world-renowned Saint Louis Symphony Orchestra (SLSO). The Grammy-winning SLSO was founded in 1880 and took up residence at the Powell in 1966, thanks to a generous private donation. In addition to its beautiful Versailles-inspired decor, Powell Hall also boasts a permanent acoustic shell. There is simply not one bad seat in the house—the sound at the Powell carries perfectly.

ROBERTS ORPHEUM

416 N. 9th St., 314/588-0388, www.robertsorpheum.com

Map 1

This beautiful, Parisian-style venue began its life as the American Theater. The American was built in 1917 by Louis A. Cella, a self-made millionaire with a taste for vaudeville. When vaudeville acts waned in popularity, Warner

ARTS AND LEISURE

Brothers purchased the theater and converted it to a movie house. The American was reborn as a performance theater in the 1960s and has hosted hundreds of concerts, musicals, and other special events. Cary Grant, Mae West, Eartha Kitt, and Henry Fonda all performed here; contemporary acts such as Pearl Jam, Tori Amos, and the Red Hot Chili Peppers have also made appearances. The theater is now named for the Roberts brothers, the dynamic St. Louis duo who purchased it in 2003. Aided by their deep pockets and equally deep respect for local history, the brothers restored the theater to its original, dazzling elegance. Public events are rare these days at the Roberts Orpheum, which is mainly used as a rental space, but tours are available and well worth taking.

☾ SHELDON CONCERT HALL

3648 Washington Blvd., 314/533-9900, www.sheldonconcerthall.org
Map 2

The perfect acoustics of the intimate, early-20th-century Sheldon Concert Hall make it an ideal venue for the wide variety of engagements that take place within. Several chamber and solo concerts are scheduled at the Sheldon throughout the year, as are speaking engagements, jazz sessions, and blues concerts. Tickets are typically inexpensive (anywhere from $10 to $50) and can be purchased online at MetroTix.com. The Sheldon is located in St. Louis's Midtown arts district, behind the Fox Theatre, and enjoys the distinction of being one of the area's oldest concert halls.

THEATERS AND THEATER COMPANIES

☾ FOX THEATRE

527 N. Grand Blvd., 314/534-1678, www.fabulousfox.com
HOURS: Tues., Thurs., and Sat. 10:30am (tours)
COST: Tues. and Thurs. $5 per person; Sat. $10 adult, $8 senior, $5 child/student (organ presentation included on Saturdays)
Map 2

The Fox Theatre is one of the largest Broadway houses in the country. Considering its Baroque grandeur (and its 4,192 seats), it's hard to believe this ornate palace began its life as a movie theater—but indeed it did. Opened by cinema mogul William Fox in 1929, this theater was one of the first to show films with audio tracks. The Fox welcomed moviegoers until the 1970s, when the theater briefly served as a live-music venue. In the 1980s, a group of private investors purchased the Fox from the city of St. Louis and restored the theater to its original condition. Today the "Fabulous Fox" hosts touring Broadway shows and big-name performers. It is also the headquarters of Fox Theatricals, a Tony Award-winning Broadway production company.

HOTCITY THEATRE

501 N. Grand Blvd., 314/289-4063, www.hotcitytheatre.org
Map 2

In 2004, two of the city's most respected fringe theater companies, City Theatre and Hot House Theatre, combined forces to create HotCity. Today the company produces contemporary, issue-oriented theatrical works appreciated by both local and national audiences. HotCity's main-stage productions take place in Midtown's beautiful Kranzberg Arts Center, where the organization moved its offices in 2009. The company's annual GreenHouse New Plays Festival showcases theatrical debuts hand-selected by a jury. The festival has garnered international recognition and takes place during the months of June and July.

NEW LINE THEATRE

6501 Clayton Rd., Clayton, 314/773-6526, www.newlinetheatre.com
Map 6

New Line puts on some of the very best stage productions in the city. The company's challenging, buoyant productions have garnered praise from the nation's top theater critics, and the local following is strong. New Line's shows are first-rate—yet, refreshingly, tickets are never more than $20. The company often stages the U.S. premieres of shows by

© JOHN LAMB

HotCity Theatre

up-and-coming playwrights, and the directors and actors have a particular yen for wickedly entertaining musicals. Visit the company's website for show schedules.

STAGES ST. LOUIS

111 S. Geyer Rd., Kirkwood, 314/821-2407, www.stagesstlouis.org

COST: $55 preferred seat adult ($39 choice seat), $49 senior, $35 child for single tickets

Map 7

Stages St. Louis is one of the city's largest musical-theater production companies. Founders Jack Lane and Michael Hamilton established this professional, nonprofit company in 1987 after meeting on the New York theater scene. In addition to producing around five shows per year, Stages also teaches a host of popular theater workshops. The school, known as the Stages Performing Arts Academy, offers a year-round, comprehensive musical-theater curriculum in dance, voice, drama, and theory. The school moved in spring 2013 to the Kol Am building on Chesterfield Parkway East.

ST. LOUIS BLACK REP

1717 Olive St., 314/534-3807, www.theblackrep.org

Map 1

The St. Louis Black Rep is one of the nation's leading African American theater companies. Founded in 1976 by producing director Ron Himes (who is nothing less than a hero in local theater circles), the Black Rep stages plays that are at once challenging and entertaining. Himes has overseen the production of more than 100 shows at the company's home theater, the historic Grandel. The Black Rep is dedicated to the preservation and exultation of black culture through its plays and playwrights. The company produces plays and musicals, and favors inventive interpretations of modern classics by such scribes as August Wilson and Eubie Banks.

ST. LOUIS REPERTORY THEATER

130 Edgar Rd., Webster Groves, 314/968-4925, www.repstl.org

Map 7

The St. Louis Repertory Theater is a regional, professional playhouse at the top of its game. For more than 40 years, the Rep has staged high-caliber productions in the cushy Loretto-Hilton Center in Webster Groves. The main-stage selections can lean toward the predictable, but the theater's Off-Ramp Series more than makes up for that with its inclusion of excellent, daring selections like *The Lieutenant of Inishmore.* The season typically begins in early September, and the theater goes dark in mid-April. The excellent website includes a listing of all shows, along with online ticket-purchasing capabilities.

MOVIE HOUSES
CHASE PARK PLAZA THEATER

212 N. Kingshighway Blvd., 314/633-3000, www.stlouiscinemas.com/chase

COST: $9 adult, $7 student/senior, $6 child, $7 matinee

Map 2

Any time you see a movie at the Chase Park Plaza, it feels like an event. To reach the box office and theater, you must stroll through the

ARTS AND LEISURE

© ALISE O'BRIEN

Tivoli Theater

lobby of one of the ritziest hotels in St. Louis, passing limousines in the parking lot, tuxedos in the lobby, and an elegant bar where jazz drifts from the shiny baby grand. The theaters themselves are standard multiplex fare, with all the new releases and an occasional indie hit. But your departure from the theater is far classier than at other movie houses. As soon as the credits roll, ushers stand by the exit doors and offer mints and candy off a silver platter.

HI-POINTE THEATER
1005 McCausland Ave., 314/995-6273,
www.hi-pointetheatre.com
COST: $7 adult, $6 student/senior, $5 matinee
Map 6
This old-fashioned, single-screen cinema is named for its unique vantage point: The theater sits at the corner of Clayton Road and McCausland Avenue, the highest point in the city. The film du jour at the Hi-Pointe is almost always an acclaimed first-run indie flick. Some locals fear for the fate of their beloved little theater; the bar next door (also called the

Hi-Pointe) drew good crowds but was nevertheless shuttered in 2006. (Par, a ho-hum new bar with an unintentionally appropriate name, now fills that space.) Still, if you're in the mood for a good movie with a side of St. Louis-style nostalgia, you can't do much better than this.

◖ MOOLAH THEATRE & LOUNGE
3821 Lindell Blvd., 314/446-6868,
www.stlouiscinemas.com/moolah
COST: $9 adult, $7 student/senior, $6 child, $7 matinee
Map 2
If you set out to create the best movie theater ever, you would end up with the Moolah. For starters, there's a giant 45-foot screen and an ear-splitting sound system. There are plush leather couches, stadium seating with ample legroom, and a balcony that affords a bird's-eye view. Extras include a bar that serves theme drinks for each film (e.g., a Lord Voldemort Mojito for the *Harry Potter* franchise), a bowling alley in the basement, and a beautiful old building with a Masonic history. The Moolah

proves they don't build 'em like they used to—they build 'em better.

TIVOLI THEATER
6350 Delmar Blvd., 314/727-7271,
www.landmarktheatres
.com/market/St.Louis/TivoliTheatre.htm
COST: $9 adult, $7 student/senior, $7 matinee
Map 6

The Tivoli is one of the very few St. Louis theaters that screen foreign and independent films.

The theater has been open since 1924 and has the ambiance to accompany the history, including burgundy curtains in front of the screens, an orchestra pit in one auditorium, and a host of movie memorabilia that runs the gamut from a replica of the statue from *The Maltese Falcon* to a poster for hometown favorite *Meet Me in St. Louis*. Though the Tivoli was renovated in 1995, paring the original massive movie palace expanse into three smaller screening rooms, its iconic marquee remains.

Festivals and Events

WINTER
FIRST NIGHT
Grand Center, 314/289-8121, www.grandcenter.org/directory/festivals-events/first-night
HOURS: 6pm-midnight
COST: $10 adult, $5 child 6-12, free for children 5 and under
Map 2

This family-friendly New Year's Eve event takes place every year in the Midtown arts district. It was created in response to a public need for a fun, safe, and affordable event inclusive of families with children. Activities kick off at 6pm, with a quirky, spirited musical procession (often involving kazoos), and continue until midnight with a full schedule of unique music and comedy performances.

MARDI GRAS FESTIVAL
314/771-5110, www.mardigrasinc.com
COST: Free
This boisterous celebration is one of the city's most well-attended events—and it's also one of the largest Mardi Gras festivals in the entire nation. Usually celebrated in January or February, the eclectic schedule of events includes a pet parade, a Cajun cook-off, the Taste of Soulard restaurant showcase, and a Weiner Dog Derby. The architecture of Soulard, St. Louis's original French settlement, lends an air of authenticity to the proceedings. Attendees should strongly consider taking public transportation to the

event, as parking is quite limited. And while the parades are fine for small children, the street party is not.

SPRING
CINCO DE MAYO FESTIVAL
www.cincodemayostl.com
COST: Free
The Cinco de Mayo festivities in early May are the largest of St. Louis's annual Hispanic festivals and a testament to the city's booming Latino population. Things took off for the festival after planners partnered with the same folks who coordinate St. Louis's raucous Mardi Gras celebration. Three blocks' worth of Cherokee Street, the city's Hispanic hub, are blocked off to traffic. Vendors temporarily move their shops onto the street and peddle everything from tacos and empanadas to soccer jerseys and custom airbrushed Nikes. There are three stages for live music, with an array of acts from homegrown St. Louis rock to an 18-piece mariachi band. Drinko de Mayo, as the holiday that commemorates the Battle of Puebla is often called, is also the only time that sipping a *cerveza* is permitted on Cherokee, a part of town where liquor laws are unusually strict.

ST. PATRICK'S DAY PARADE
18th St. and Market St., 314/231-2598,
www.irishparade.org

ARTS AND LEISURE

COST: Free
Map 1

Every year, more than 250,000 St. Louisans celebrate their city's proud Irish heritage by attending a St. Patrick's Day Parade in mid-March. There are officially two, one downtown and the other in the formerly working-class, Irish neighborhood of Dogtown. The festival downtown has been taking place for more than three decades, and downtown is the "official" location of the event. City officials paint a path of green leprechaun footprints along Market Street each year in honor of the occasion, and a quirky afternoon festival features live Irish music and fare. Yet despite the popularity of this event, the Dogtown iteration is considered the more authentic of the two. Organized by members of the Ancient Order of Hibernians, the Dogtown party features far more local flair. The festival's eccentric little parade chugs down Tamm Avenue, and residents say—only half-jokingly—that the party starts at 6am.

SUMMER
ⒸFESTIVAL OF NATIONS
Tower Grove Park (Grand Blvd. and Arsenal St.), 314/773-9090, www.festivalofnationsstl.org
COST: Free
Map 4

Sponsored by the International Institute—itself a civic treasure—the Festival of Nations brings the world to Tower Grove Park each August. Given the sheer number of food stands, artisan booths, and cultural performances, visitors are wise to plan an entire afternoon around this festival. Entrance to the fest is free, as are primo lawn seats for the many stage shows, but food and drinks (and crafts, of course) cost extra. Adventurous gourmands will want to pass up the could-eat-it-anywhere booths selling fried rice and tacos, and head instead to the Bosnian, Peruvian, and Eritrean booths. The gorgeous artisanal items stretch for yards and include delicate silver jewelry, handmade instruments, and chic, vibrant dresses. Performances—many of them traditional dances, such as the Highland Fling—are not to be missed. This is the perfect place to introduce children to the big, big world around them—and to remind yourself that we truly are a nation of immigrants.

JAPANESE FESTIVAL
4344 Shaw Blvd., 314/577-5100, www.missouribotanicalgarden.org/things-to-do/events/signature-events/japanese-festival.aspx
HOURS: Sat. and Sun. 10am-8pm, Mon. 10am-5pm
COST: $15 adult, $5 child 3-12
Map 4

The Missouri Botanical Garden's annual Japanese festival is a Labor Day weekend tradition that draws visitors from all over the region. This is the garden's most popular yearly event, and pays tribute to the culture behind one of its finest features, the world-renowned Japanese Garden. Events during this jam-packed three-day weekend include sumo wrestling, *rakugo* Japanese comedy, and *taiko* drumming. Japanese food is also available for purchase. The nightly candlelight walks along the Japanese Garden's serene and meditative paths are worth the price of admission alone, but be sure not to miss the great bonsai exhibit in the main building.

ⒸPRIDEFEST
Kaufmann and Poekler Parks (Market Street and North Tucker Blvd.), 314/772-8888, www.pridestl.org
Map 4

St. Louis's annual PrideFest, like most other LGBT pride fests around the nation, takes place in late June to commemorate the 1969 Stonewall Riots in New York City. The concerts, barbecues, contests, dances, and parade at this three-day event attract 100,000 people each year. The majority of PrideFest activities take place in South City's beautiful Tower Grove Park. The dense residential area surrounding the park is known for its gay-friendliness and support of gay-rights issues. After sunset each day, the PrideFest fun continues in the Grand South Grand and Grove neighborhoods. Many bar owners block off streets and sidewalks to accommodate the enormous crowds. In 2013, St. Louis PrideFest celebrated its 34th year.

SHAKESPEARE FESTIVAL ST. LOUIS

Shakespeare Glen in Forest Park, 314/531-9800, www.sfstl.com

COST: Free; chair rental in front center available for $7 and $10

Map 2

Each year, the Shakespeare Festival St. Louis draws the city residents en masse to Forest Park. And with good reason: There are few better ways to spend a nice evening than with a picnic dinner and free theater. The festival sponsors a different Shakespearean work each season, and shows typically have a creative contemporary spin. Although the festival's mission is charitable in nature, this is professional theater. Productions employ nationally renowned directors, designers, and actors, and shows attract 50,000 people during their month-long run. Performances begin on Memorial Day weekend and run for four weeks; catch the pre-performance Green Show at 6:30pm and the mainstage show at 8pm every day but Tuesday.

ST. LOUIS PAGAN PICNIC

Tower Grove Park (Grand Blvd. and Arsenal St.), www.paganpicnic.org

COST: Free

Map 4

Regardless of one's spiritual inclinations, this yearly event in Tower Grove Park is a worthwhile experience. More a festival then a picnic, the Pagan Picnic is one-stop shopping for everything one needs to live the modern pagan lifestyle. Visitors will find a bevy of unique vendors, plus workshops on everything from building a coven and casting spells to tapping into the universal energy to gain spiritual enlightenment. Started in 1992, the popular two-day gathering takes place in June and is a labor of love for its supporters. The love is certainly evident in this all-are-welcome event.

TWANGFEST

www.twangfest.com

COST: $18 to $28

Every year in June, St. Louis's community radio station, KDHX (88.1 FM), hosts an eclectic music festival. Named for its down-home rock and country roots, Twangfest takes place over the course of a weekend and is one of the largest festivals of its kind in the nation. For three days and nights, local and national acts perform in venues all over the city, from the Duck Room in the Delmar Loop to the Schlafly Tap Room in Midtown. Past acts have included the Old 97's, Centro-matic, and the Waco Brothers. Proceeds from this perennially popular event support KDHX's excellent public programming.

FALL

◖ ART OUTSIDE FESTIVAL

7260 Southwest Ave., Maplewood, 314/241-2337, http://schlafly.com/events/annual-schlafly-festivals

COST: Free

Map 4

Taking place (not-so-coincidentally) the same weekend as the St. Louis Art Fair (usually the first Friday, Saturday, and Sunday in September), Art Outside offers an alternative to the traditional, pricey art sale. This yearly festival takes place in the enormous parking lot of the Schlafly Bottleworks and feels like a really great street party—that just so happens to feature really great art. Practically every medium is represented here, from photography to painting to sculpture to printmaking. One of the best things about Art Outside is that it makes art accessible; festival-goers can spend less than $50 and go home with an original work. Live music provides the soundtrack to your art perusal, and Schlafly keeps the suds flowing.

GROVE FEST

Manchester Ave. between Kingshighway Blvd. and Vendeventer Ave., www.thegrovestl.com/events/grove-fest

HOURS: Sat. 2pm-11pm

COST: Free

Map 2

This offbeat weekend festival, which usually takes place in September, celebrates the continued revitalization of the Forest Park Southeast neighborhood. A live-music stage hosts local bands, independent restaurants sell tantalizing food, street performers entertain the crowds, and visitors can browse a block's worth of arts-and-crafts booths. Throughout the festival, Grove residents work on a colorful new building mural, which is dedicated at the close of the festival. Thanks to this new tradition, there is plenty of public art to complement the Grove's rapidly gentrifying streetscape.

THE HISTORIC SHAW ART FAIR
314/615-3101, www.shawartfair.org
COST: $7, free for children 14 and under
This proud little weekend-long arts festival has been taking place in October for more than 20 years but has gained popularity and recognition in only the past few. Today it is one of the city's top art fairs, and it features the work of as many as 135 artists from around the country (including much of the city's nationally recognized local talent), in addition to a live music stage and food from area restaurants. One of the best things about Shaw Art Fair is its location: Stalls are set up along the elegant tree-lined boulevard of Flora Place, in South City's historic Shaw neighborhood. Southsiders love a good brunch, so consider attending the fair's opening-day breakfast feast. Partaking of this particularly well-attended neighborhood meal will net you free, early admission to the event.

ST. LOUIS ART FAIR
314/863-0278, www.culturalfestivals.com
HOURS: Fri. 5pm-10pm, Sat. 11am-10pm, Sun. 11am-5pm
COST: Free
The St. Louis Art Fair blossoms to life each year around the first weekend in September on the streets of downtown Clayton. While some art fairs are more kitsch than craftsmanship, the St. Louis Art Fair is the real deal. Price tags can be high, but the work is usually worth it. Spend a nice fall afternoon browsing original pieces by some of the nation's top artists, listening to live local music and enjoying food from more than 20 area restaurants. The artists and craftspeople featured here are hand-selected by a jury, and the St. Louis Art Fair deserves its great national reputation. Be prepared to walk quite a bit—this festival is attended by thousands of St. Louisans every year, so parking spots are at a premium.

ST. LOUIS HILLS ART IN THE PARK
Francis Park (bounded by Nottingham Ave., Tamm Ave., Eichelberger St., and Donovan Ave.), www.artintheparkstl.com
COST: Free
Map 4
The Southampton neighborhood's Art in the Park festival is a relative newcomer on what's quickly becoming the "St. Louis art fair circuit." The charm of this one-day fall gathering is its local focus. Much like Schlafly's annual Art Outside Festival, Art in the Park exhibits the crafts of local artists exclusively. Art in the Park also boasts a classic car show, along with a food court where local restaurant owners share *their* best work. Admission is free, and festivities take place in the neighborhood's beautiful Francis Park on the last Sunday in September.

Sports and Recreation

PARKS

CARONDELET PARK

S. Grand Blvd. and Loughborough Ave., 314/622-4800

HOURS: Daily 24 hours

Map 4

Many neighborhoods in south St. Louis are blessed with wonderful public parks. Carondelet, which is nestled in the charming Holly Hills area, is a reminder of the city park's historical role as the epicenter and main meeting place of a neighborhood. The park boasts a bevy of features in a relatively small space. A 1.5-mile walking/biking path surrounds a couple of baseball fields, tennis courts, a few playgrounds, and the best horseshoe pits around. The music stand hosts free concerts during the warm months, and a five-acre, fish-stocked lake attracts plenty of amateur anglers.

FAUST PARK

15185 Olive Blvd., Chesterfield, 314/615-8328, http://stlouisco.com/ParksandRecreation/ParkPages/Faust

HOURS: 7am-30 mins. after sunset

COST: Free

Map 7

Faust Park offers far more than the typical playground-and-picnic-shelter routine. In addition to miles of paved walking trails, super-clean picnic and restroom facilities, and a busy events calendar, several popular historic and tourist sites are here; admission costs are nominal. The Sophia M. Sachs Butterfly House is a can't-miss attraction here, as is the beautiful, fully restored 1920s carousel. A bit farther into the park, you'll find a restored 19th-century farm and historic village. This area is open for self-guided tours during the week and docent-led tours on weekends.

◖ FOREST PARK

Hwy. 40 between Skinker Blvd. and Kingshighway Blvd., www.forestparkforever.org

HOURS: Daily 24 hours

COST: Free

Map 6

Forest Park has captured St. Louis's civic imagination for well over 100 years. The huge, verdant park hosted the 1904 World's Fair, and native St. Louisans rightfully associate Forest Park with culture and history. But it's the perfect place for recreation, too. Biking enthusiasts will definitely want to take a bicycle tour, which covers 18 Forest Park attractions in 10 easy miles. Visitors up for an adventure should not miss the Segway tour; tours depart from the Saint Louis Science Center and (after a training session) send riders zinging through Forest Park. If a traditional jog is more your speed, take advantage of the wide, well-paved, seven-and-a-half-mile jogging trail. Paddleboats (which seat up to four adults) are available for rental at $15 per hour, and the views from Forest Park's Grand Basin are magnificent.

HEMAN PARK

7200 Olive Blvd., University City, 314/505-8617, www.ucitymo.org

HOURS: Daily dawn-dusk

COST: Free

Map 6

This wedge-shaped 85-acre park is a hive of activity during the warm-weather months. The Heman Park swimming pool is an important focal point for the community, as are the large playground and sports fields. Heman offers all of the amenities of a great city park—football and soccer fields, baseball diamonds, and lighted tennis courts can all be found here. Picnic areas are abundant, and restroom facilities are convenient (if not always spotless).

LAFAYETTE PARK

Park Ave. and Mississippi Ave., 314/622-4800

HOURS: Daily 24 hours

Map 3

This 29-acre, Victorian-era park was one of the first public parks to be established in St. Louis. It was dedicated in 1838 and is faced on all sides by some of the city's preeminent historic

ARTS AND LEISURE

Faust Park

COURTESY OF THE ST. LOUIS COUNTY PARKS DEPARTMENT

homes, including several meticulously restored Second Empire-style mansions. Behind the park's massive stone gates, visitors will find a one-acre lake, a playground, a park house, sports fields, and paved trails. Features include beautifully landscaped grounds, an 1870s police station and a pair of Revolutionary War-era cannons that once stood on the deck of a British war ship.

LONE ELK PARK AND WORLD BIRD SANCTUARY

1 Lone Elk Park Rd., Valley Park, 314/225-4390,
www.stlouisco.com/ParksandRecreation/ParkPages/
LoneElk, www.worldbirdsanctuary.org
HOURS: Daily 8am-5pm
COST: Free (donations encouraged)
Map 7

Many native St. Louisans have fond childhood memories of Lone Elk Park, of Sunday-afternoon drives along the road that snakes up and down its tumbling terrain. From the comfort of their vehicle, visitors can observe one of the nation's last remaining bison

herds, as well as the wild turkeys, waterfowl, elk, and deer that graze on the park's wild grasses. If you feel inspired to do some grazing of your own, pack a picnic and enjoy it in one of the park's several shelters. The World Bird Sanctuary at Lone Elk's entrance is open to visitors as well and keeps the same hours as the park.

POWDER VALLEY CONSERVATION NATURE CENTER

11715 Cragwold Rd., Kirkwood, 314/301-1500,
http://mdc.mo.gov
HOURS: Daily 8am-8pm; 8am-6pm (after Daylight Savings Time)
COST: Free
Map 7

Those seeking a quick and convenient break from the urban landscape will find it here, in a wild oasis set within the boundaries of the St. Louis suburb Kirkwood. Residents working in this area can enjoy its 112 acres of oak hickory forest and trails (some paved, some unpaved) during their lunch breaks. Travelers are urged to find respite as well. Just one word of warning: The cathedral lofts of Powder Valley's oaks frame views of the Highway 44/270 interchange, so one never quite escapes the sound of the highway here. But that matters little once you've seen the park's breathtaking vistas; from them, you just might acquire an appreciation for the convoluted beauty of nature interrupted by suburban sprawl.

SHAW NATURE RESERVE

Hwy. 100 and I-44, Gray Summit, 636/451-3512, www.missouribotanicalgarden.org/visit/family-of-attractions/shaw-nature-reserve.aspx
HOURS: Daily 8am-4:30pm
COST: $5 adult, $3 student/senior, free for children 11 and under
Map 7

The Ozark landscape of rural Missouri gives travelers a good idea of what this part of the country looked like to its earliest residents. This extension of the Missouri Botanical Garden, established in 1879, seeks to preserve a corner of this native environment for decades to come. Less than an hour's drive from the city, Shaw Nature Reserve's 2,500 acres boast a visitor center, a museum, and scenic hiking trails through marshlands, forests, glades, and prairies. The scientific data collected here in wildlife surveys is utilized by ecologists all over the world. The wildflower garden and views of the Meramec River are spectacular.

BICYCLING

BIG SHARK

6133 Delmar Blvd., 314/862-1188, www.bigshark.com
HOURS: Mon.-Fri. 10am-8pm, Sat. 10am-6pm, Sun. noon-5pm
Map 6

Avid cyclists and weekend cruisers alike will find the answer to all their bicycling needs at Big Shark, a friendly, one-stop retail and repair shop on the Loop. The staff at this stylish bike boutique is always courteous and knowledgeable. Whether in the market for a gear ratio built for speed and distance, a bicycle basket, or a powder-blue beach cruiser built for two, the

shopper will find answers here. Visit the shop's great website for special weekly discounts and the 411 on local cycling events.

BIKE ST. LOUIS

6174A Delmar Blvd., 314/436-7009, www.bikestlouis.org
Map 1

For too many years, St. Louis had a reputation of being inhospitable to cyclists. The Midwestern love affair with the automobile and the interstate system made it difficult for bikes to travel safely. Fortunately, Bike St. Louis is changing all of that. Congressman Russ Carnahan and Board of Aldermen president Lewis Reed spearheaded the project, which connects the city's parks to one another via bike-friendly commuter lanes. The original Bike St. Louis route was 20 miles, but a 2008 expansion added 57 more miles—and now cyclists can take the route as far as the River Des Peres Greenway in South St. Louis County and the Mississippi riverfront in North St. Louis. Colorful signs, designed by Kiku Obata & Company, guide riders as they take in St. Louis on two wheels.

GOLF

THE HIGHLANDS GOLF AND TENNIS CENTER

5163 Clayton Ave., 314/531-7773, www.highlandsgolfandtennis.com
HOURS: Daily 6am-8pm
COST: $23 weekdays, $24 weekends, $12 after 6pm
Map 6

The Bermuda-grass fairways and bent-grass greens of this historic nine-hole course are an urban oasis for St. Louisans. The tight fairways here are woven into the scenic landscape of beautiful Forest Park. The club's facilities include meticulously manicured grounds, an updated clubhouse, and a three-hole mini-course for pre-game practice. The course was established in 1897 to provide the public with low-cost athletic facilities, and it continues to fulfill this mission. A round here costs just $23 on weekdays. Cart rental is also available.

NORMANDIE GOLF CLUB
7605 Saint Charles Rock Rd., 314/862-4884,
www.normandiegolf.com
HOURS: Daily 6am-7pm
COST: Pricing varies and is updated on the website in real time
Map 7

Normandie Golf Club was established in 1901 and claims to be the oldest public 18-hole course west of the Mississippi. It's inarguably one of the longer courses in St. Louis and is prized by locals for its unique routing and tight fairways. Normandie was designed by a disciple of the Scottish legend Old Tom Morris and boasts gorgeous features reminiscent of that most famous Scottish course: St. Andrews. Normandie's management company, Walter Thomas, operates many of the area's best courses. Amenities here include a full-service pro shop.

QUAIL CREEK GOLF CLUB
6022 Wells Rd., 314/487-1988,
www.quailcreekgolfclub.com
HOURS: Daily 6am-8pm
COST: $18-59 (see website for details)
Map 7

The natural streams and narrow rolling fairways of this par-72 course have been the majestic backdrop of two USGA tournaments and a US Open qualifier. Quail Creek is one of the area's most challenging public courses from its back tees and boasts a slope rating of 141, though it does a great job of hosting all play levels. The atmosphere here is casual, and the front tees are playable by all. Quail Creek is only a 25-minute drive southwest of downtown. Its amenities include a full-service pro shop and casual restaurant.

TAPAWINGO NATIONAL GOLF COURSE
13001 Gary Player Dr., Sunset Hills, 636/349-3100,
www.tapawingogolf.com
HOURS: Daily 7am-6pm
COST: $25-70 (see website for details)
Map 7

Tapawingo is a Native American word for "place of joy," a fitting summary of the hardwood forests, rolling prairies, and 27 championship holes at this lovely course. Tapawingo is a 20-minute drive from downtown and offers play for golfers of all levels. An undulating front nine and links-style back nine bookend a total of three 18-hole combinations. This par-36 course was designed by golf legend Gary Player, and rates are reasonable considering the amenities, which include majestic 3,520-yard fairways and practice greens regularly visited by wild turkeys, geese, and deer.

BOWLING
EPIPHANY LANES
3164 Ivanhoe Ave., 314/781-8684
HOURS: Call for hours
Map 4

Epiphany Lanes has all the ambiance of a church basement, but really, that's part of its charm. That, and the rock-bottom prices, which will leave you wondering if it's 1972 again. At only $3 per game ($2 before 6pm), bowling at Epiphany is one of the cheapest dates in town. This church-owned eight-lane bowling alley is near the corner of Jamieson and Arsenal, adjacent to its sister parish, and is one of the last of its kind in the country. Though amenities here are basic, visitors will find everything they need, from shoe rental ($1.50) to a well-stocked bar and basic grill.

PIN-UP BOWL
6191 Delmar Blvd., 314/727-5555, www.pinupbowl.com
HOURS: Mon.-Thurs. 3pm-3am, Fri.-Sun. noon-3am
Map 6

Bowling alley and restaurant by day, see-and-be-seen hot spot by night, this nightclub hybrid is *the* place to go after a concert at The Pageant or dinner on the Loop. Pin-Up Bowl's location is great. It's in one of the city's prime nightlife districts, and just a couple doors down from one of the city's most popular concert venues. The fun here revolves around classic cocktails, late-night snacks, and midnight bowling. Under the watchful gaze of a museum's worth of Vargas prints, Pin-Up's humming bar serves cocktails until 3am. The kitchen is open nearly as late as the bar (and turns out fun,

Pin-Up Bowl

nostalgic items like grilled-cheese sandwiches and Campbell's tomato soup), and bowling on the 12 full-length lanes is available all night for just $3.50-5 a game.

SARATOGA LANES

2725 Sutton Blvd. #A, Maplewood, 314/645-5308, www.saratogalanes.com
HOURS: Mon.-Fri. noon-1am, Sat.-Sun. 2pm-1am
Map 4

Saratoga Lanes in Maplewood is one of the last second-floor bowling alleys in the country, and despite the humble appearance of its modest brick facade, it is the pulse of quite a scene. This is a favorite haunt of more than a few St. Louis country-rock legends (and plenty of aspiring ones). There are only eight lanes at Saratoga, and scoring is figured the old-fashioned way. Checkerboard floors and a wall of rec-center lockers make for a retro, kitschy utopia, or at least a worthy tribute to your Uncle Buck's basement bar. No less fabulous for it, the ambiance evolving here seems to be purely accidental.

TROPICANA LANES

7960 Clayton Rd., Richmond Heights, 314/781-0282, www.tropicanalanes.com
HOURS: Mon. 3pm-11pm, Tues.-Thurs. 10am-midnight, Fri.-Sat. 10am-1:30am, Sun. 10am-11pm
Map 6

This way-popular bowling behemoth is within throwing distance of downtown Clayton and is certainly deserving of its "bowling center" appellation. A good deal broader than any other local alley, Tropicana boasts an impressive 52 lanes, a banquet facility, a lounge, a game room—you name it—and is roughly the size of two *Air Force One* airplane hangars. This is the perfect place to join a league, host a child's birthday party, or get in a couple of last-minute sets. The sheer size of this place means that there's almost always an open lane waiting, and electronic scoring makes single play a breeze.

SPECTATOR SPORTS
ST. LOUIS BLUES

Scottrade Center at 1401 Clark Ave., 314/421-4400, http://blues.nhl.com

ARTS AND LEISURE

COST: $18-235
Map 1

Located right off I-64 near Union Station and City Hall, Scottrade Center plays host to rock concerts and the occasional basketball tournament, but the tall glass structure is best known as the home of the St. Louis Blues. The hockey squad remains the only St. Louis sports franchise that lacks a championship, but even without Lord Stanley's Cup, the Blues have turned out consistent teams in the past few seasons and made it admirably far in the playoffs. The oval seating plan makes for ideal viewing from nearly any angle in the arena, and the cushy blue-and-purple seats make for the most comfortable viewing short of your at-home easy chair. Tickets are fairly easy to come by and can often be purchased on the cheap.

ST. LOUIS CARDINALS
Busch Stadium at 700 Clark Ave., 314/345-9000, http://stlouis.cardinals.mlb.com
COST: $16-185
Map 1

Fans of the St. Louis Cardinals fancy themselves the best fans in baseball, and their loyalty was rewarded in 2006 with a brand-new stadium. The grand structure stands adjacent to the site of the old Busch Stadium. During their first year in their new digs, the Cards won the World Series (then they did it again in 2011), so you would be forgiven for thinking there's a little bit of magic in these red bricks. The sight lines are better at the new Busch (check out the center-field view of the Old Courthouse), and the kid-friendly concessions and accoutrements—including an on-site Build-A-Bear Workshop—make a Cards game an ideal family outing. Single tickets can be purchased in advance or at the box office on the day of the game.

ST. LOUIS RAMS
Edward Jones Dome at 901 N. Broadway, 314/342-5201, www.stlouisrams.com
COST: $40-125
Map 1

The Rams came to St. Louis from Los Angeles in 1995, and the Edward Jones Dome has

been the football team's home turf since then. Attached to the America's Center convention complex, the dome can hold almost 67,000 football fans, and all those seats were filled during the Rams' 2000 run to the Super Bowl. As is the case with many indoor stadiums, the experience of watching a Rams game can be a little like watching a TV show taping—the bright lights and white roof give the impression of a soundstage, although the action on the gridiron is (ideally) much more engrossing.

GUIDED AND WALKING TOURS
MERAMEC STATE PARK
FISHER CAVE TOUR
115 Meramec Park Dr., 573/468-6072, www.mostateparks.com/meramec.htm
HOURS: Call for tour hours
COST: $8 adult, $7 teen, $6 child, free for children 5 and under
Map 7

This 6,896-acre park offers year-round camping, picnicking, and hiking. Great amenities include inexpensive rental cabins, raft and canoe rentals, and a visitors center, but a trip here isn't complete without a tour of Fisher Cave. Lantern-lit paths lead visitors along an underground stream, past caverns horned with thousands of calcite columns (some of them more than 30 feet tall). This is just one of the park's 40-plus caverns, and it offers some of the most beautiful cave scenes in the country. Naturalist-led tours are available seasonally, between April and October, and travelers should check out the visitors center's cool aquarium display afterward.

ST. LOUIS WALKING TOURS
701 N. 15th St., Suite 502E, 314/368-8818, http://stlouiswalkingtours.com
HOURS: Scheduled public walking tours available Apr.-Oct.; check website for specific dates and tour times
COST: $10-35 for scheduled public walking tours or $60 up to 4 adults in a private tour
Map 1

The narrated art and architecture tours of downtown St. Louis introduce travelers to the city's rich and dramatic history through its most important landmarks. Stops include the Wainwright Building (the oldest steel skyscraper on earth) and the world-famous Gateway Arch, the tallest manmade monument in the United States. The history covered here begins with the territory's early days as the burial grounds of the country's largest tribal culture and then covers the first years as a cultured French Creole village. Bring a pair of comfortable shoes. Tours are 2.5-5 hours long.

OTHER RECREATION

HIDDEN VALLEY

17409 Hidden Valley Dr., 636/938-5373, www.hiddenvalleyski.com

HOURS: Mon.-Thurs. 1pm-9:30pm, Fri. 1pm-10pm, Sat. 9am-10pm, Sun. 9am-8pm

COST: $33-77 (price includes ski rental)

Map 7

The Midwest is hardly known for its alpine wonders, but those who hit Missouri with a strange desire to ski *do* have a few options. One of these is Hidden Valley, a pocket-sized ski spot

with one lift and 12 runs of varying difficulty. Slopes open in mid-December and close in early March, weather depending, and snow here is predominantly artificial. A popular feature at Hidden Valley is its "Moonlight Marathons." Beginning on December 23, on Fridays and Saturdays, skiers can hit the slopes until 3am.

STEINBERG SKATING RINK

400 Jefferson Dr. (in Forest Park), 314/361-0613, www.steinbergskatingrink.com

HOURS: Sun.-Thurs. 10am-9pm, Fri.-Sat. 10am-midnight

COST: $6; skate rental $4

Map 2

Anyone seeking a wintertime idyll should make skating at Steinberg a priority. For more than 50 years, St. Louis families have flocked to this outdoor rink, which is nestled into Forest Park and provides a picture-perfect winter tableau. On Friday and Saturday nights, the rink stays open till midnight, making it a favorite date destination. The nearby Snowflake Café offers sandwiches and pizzas, plus beer and wine.

© CHRIS LEE

Upper Limits Indoor Rock Gym & Pro Shop

During the warmer months (March 1 through mid-November), Steinberg hosts sand-volley-ball leagues—but it's the ice-skating that brings people back again and again.

UPPER LIMITS INDOOR
ROCK GYM & PRO SHOP

326 S. 21st St., 314/241-7625, www.upperlimits.com

HOURS: Mon.-Fri. 11am-10pm, Sat. 10am-8pm, Sun. 10am-6pm

COST: $12 adult day pass, $10 child day pass, $45 family day pass (harness included), $60 family day pass (includes harnesses, shoes, 2 belay devices and 2 chalk bags)

Map 1

Urbanites interested in honing their mountain-climbing skills—and novices looking for a way to try out the thrilling experience—don't have to travel far. Upper Limits' indoor climbing facilities offer artificial rock faces, equipment, and advice for climbers of all experience levels. The training gym boasts 10,000 square feet of climbing area, experienced instructors, and plenty of classes. Upper Limits is also a great resource for meeting other climbers and planning that next big out-of-state excursion. The gym is only five minutes from downtown, behind Union Station. Yearly memberships are available for repeat visitors.

SHOPS

No one is going to mistake the shopping promenades of St. Louis for those of New York or Los Angeles. That's perfectly fine, because what St. Louis lacks in breadth, it makes up for in quality, ingenuity, and affordability. The relatively low cost of living here makes nearly all price points lower, from the tab at the bar to the receipt from the mall. And the affordable rents allow young entrepreneurs to make a go of it, which is why you'll find many chic stores in up-and-coming districts (such as Maplewood and The Grove). Many St. Louisans are devoted to patronizing independent businesses, and this devotion has kept money in the local economy and brought new life to many sleepy neighborhoods. The consortium Build St. Louis (www. buildstlouis.org) provides support for local merchants and posts great information about St. Louis businesses on its frequently updated website.

No matter what you're looking for, you're likely to find it in St. Louis. If it's boutique shopping you seek, head downtown to Washington Avenue for high-end pieces by still-under-the-radar designers (labels like Prada and Michael Kors can be found in the shops of Ladue and Clayton). Each neighborhood offers its own unique shopping opportunity. Browse for vintage clothing, rare recordings, and striking home accents in the Delmar Loop. Find antique radios, Chippendale desks, and 1920s jewelry on Cherokee Street. Discover shelves of used books and fabulous 1950s toasters on Grand South Grand. Wherever your St. Louis travels take you, fun shopping is bound to be right in the neighborhood.

© PETER WILSON

HIGHLIGHTS

LOOK FOR ◖ TO FIND
RECOMMENDED SHOPS.

◖ **Best Gift Store:** There are dozens of wonderful gift shops in St. Louis, with items ranging from the elegant to the quirky. But it's **Plowsharing Crafts'** mission that makes it doubly wonderful; the money spent here goes directly back to artisans in developing nations (page 109).

◖ **Best Independent Bookstore: Left Bank Books** is a St. Louis landmark, and with good reason. Not only does this lovely shop carry the best in literary fiction and creative nonfiction, it also has an excellent used-book selection, hard-to-find periodicals, and a schedule of author readings that rivals those in far bigger cities (page 110).

◖ **Best Music Store: Vintage Vinyl** is staffed by music lovers; these guys and gals know music up and down, and they can make some great recommendations. Be diligent when searching the CD racks, as local music journalists and DJs frequently offload parts of their collections here (page 111).

◖ **Best Women's Boutique: Ziezo** is paradise for the woman with great fashion sense and a little cash to burn. This Loop boutique keeps pace with the latest fashions without ever drifting into trendy impracticality (page 113).

◖ **Best Furniture and Home Decor: Good Works** is in the Delmar Loop, on the very same street where Charles Eames has a star on the St. Louis Walk of Fame. That's some nice synergy, as Good Works sells modern, often minimalist furniture undoubtedly inspired by Eames (but at a fraction of the price) (page 114).

◖ **Best Shop for the Home Chef: Kitchen Conservatory** provides everything a great home chef could ever desire, from All-Clad pots to Emile Henry ceramic Dutch ovens (page 118).

◖ **Best Kids' Store:** If you're tired of Dora, Elmo, and all of their sing-songy comrades, head to **City Sprouts.** This adorable Loop shop sells beautiful wooden toys, classic illustrated books, and too-cute-for-words baby duds (page 119).

◖ **Best Place to Pamper Your Pet:** Want a tiny plush Porsche for your kitten to nap in? Need a wee Cardinals jersey for your bichon frise? Head to **Lola & Penelope's.** If your pet is traveling with you, make sure to treat her to a pawdicure (page 120).

◖ **Best Aromatherapy:** Cassie Buell's Central West End shop, the eponymous **Cassie's,** is an olfactory treat. Customize your own perfume or body wash with the dozens of scents available at Cassie's, or treat yourself to an Earthly Body's Suntouched soy candle—it burns down into warm massage oil (page 123).

Arts and Crafts

CRAFT ALLIANCE
6640 Delmar Blvd., University City, 314/725-1177, www.craftalliance.org. Second location: 501 N. Grand Blvd., 314/534-7528.
HOURS: Tues.-Thurs. 10am-5pm, Fri.-Sat. 10am-6pm, Sun. 11am-5pm
Map 6

Visit Craft Alliance one day, and you'll see a beautiful display of handmade clothing. Stop in the next day, and one-of-a-kind home accessories will sparkle in the window. The inventory may change regularly, but one thing is certain: Craft Alliance is no mere gift shop. It is also a thriving community art center where people of all ages learn glass-blowing, ceramics, textile-making, and more. On the second floor of this well-established Loop space, working artists bustle about in their studios. Craft Alliance now operates a huge second store in Grand Center, Midtown's rapidly emerging arts district. No matter which location you choose, your purchase will benefit Craft Alliance's superlative outreach programs.

PLOWSHARING CRAFTS

6271 Delmar Blvd., University City, 314/863-3723, www.plowsharing.org
HOURS: Mon.-Thurs. 10am-6pm, Fri. 10am-8pm, Sat. 10am-6pm
Map 6

This volunteer-staffed shop has little in common with the big-box decor stores. Plowsharing doesn't rock the world-music XM station or have storewide sales on throw pillows. Instead, this Loop gem offers unique gifts that enrich lives. Plowsharing partners with Ten Thousand Villages, one of the largest fair-trade organization in the U.S., and money spent here goes right back to artisans in developing nations. In other words, if you spend $30 on a gorgeous hand-carved bracelet from Uganda, your money supports the Ugandan artist who created it. In addition to jewelry, Plowsharing sells home decor, musical instruments, artisanal coffees, and more.

Books and Music

BIG SLEEP BOOKS

239 N. Euclid Ave., 314/361-6100, www.bigsleepbooks.com
HOURS: Mon.-Sat. 11am-6pm, Sun. 11am-5pm
Map 2

Mystery readers are a dedicated and discriminating bunch—and they'll be thrilled by what they find at Big Sleep Books. This cozy Central West End shop specializes in new and used mystery, detective, and espionage tomes (and bibliophiles will love the inventory of rare first editions). Staff members might seem aloof at first, but they're truly happy to direct aimless shelf-wanderers toward personal favorites. Big Sleep also hosts regular book signings with the genre's up-and-comers.

THE BOOK HOUSE

7352 Manchester Rd., Maplewood, 314/968-4491, www.bookhousestl.com
HOURS: Mon. noon-7pm, Tues.-Thurs. 10:30am-7pm, Fri.-Sat. 10:30am-8pm
Map 4

This independent shop, founded in 1986, offers new and used inventory and even rare books. Maybe you'll come across a hard-to-find cookbook, or perhaps you'll rediscover an old favorite among the bargain books. The Book House moved from its old Victorian home in Rock Hill to a new location in Maplewood in 2013. Along with an inventory of more than 200,000 books, the cats who call the shop home made the move, too (and possibly also the ghost who was rumored to watch over the tomes in the old location).

DUNAWAY BOOKS

3111 S. Grand Blvd., 314/771-7150, www.dunawaybooks.com
HOURS: Mon.-Fri. 11am-7pm, Sat. 10am-7pm, Sun. noon-7pm
Map 4

Founded by a professional stamp-and-coin auctioneer who always dreamed of owning a bookstore, Dunaway Books is a true treasure. Walter Morris used his keen collector's eye to fill the cavernous space with books both beloved and unusual, popular and obscure. Browsers will find books from every genre, although the greatest finds are usually in the literary-criticism and nonfiction sections. Be sure to descend to the store's basement level, which boasts hundreds of nifty old textbooks. Morris is always looking to buy, so terrific new books show up daily.

EUCLID RECORDS

19 N. Gore Ave., Webster Groves, 314/961-8978, www.euclidrecords.com
HOURS: Mon.-Thurs. 10am-8pm, Fri.-Sat. 10am-9pm, Sun. 10am-5pm
Map 7

Revered by audiophiles all over the nation, Euclid Records offers a trip through the annals of recorded music. The spacious shop's respectable selection of new and used CDs is eclipsed by its enormous collection of records (there are more than 40,000 titles here). Visitors can also browse shelves of vintage magazines, posters, and other interesting bits of musical ephemera. Jazz is owner Joe Schwab's greatest area of expertise, but shoppers will find a healthy portion of just about everything. Serious collectors may wish to inquire in advance about the un-priced basement stash, which can be browsed by appointment only.

◖ LEFT BANK BOOKS

399 N. Euclid Ave., 314/367-6731, www.left-bank.com
HOURS: Mon.-Sat. 10am-10pm, Sun. 11am-6pm
Map 2

Left Bank Books, the city's oldest independent bookstore, sits at the bustling corner of McPherson and Euclid Avenues. The shop was established in 1969, when its progressive social politics and inventory of gay literature

© KELLY VON PLONSKI

Subterranean Books

were considered risky business. Today, Left Bank serves St. Louis's literati with a thoughtful selection of...pretty much everything. The store carries an estimated 16,000 volumes. New books are upstairs, used books (and a friendly cat) are downstairs, and spirited conversation thrives throughout. Left Bank is a community focal point, thanks to the small but dedicated staff that manages the store's busy calendar of book signings and readings. When well-respected authors come through St. Louis, Left Bank treats them like honored guests and long-lost friends. A second location is downtown (321 N. 10th St., 314/367-6731).

RECORD EXCHANGE

5320 Hampton Ave., 314/832-2249,
www.recordexchangestl.com
HOURS: Mon.-Sat. 10am-9pm, Sun. noon-6pm
Map 4

Devoted, diligent St. Louis music collectors know this shop's cluttered aisles well. On the right day, Record Exchange can be an absolute gold mine, and while the inventory may be less organized and selective than that of local competitor Euclid Records, the great prices reward shoppers who are willing to search. Exploring Record Exchange's room of 45s is a daylong project in itself. Expect to get dusty—but also expect to feel right at home amid the towering stacks of what was once the Southhampton branch of the public library.

SUBTERRANEAN BOOKS

6275 Delmar Blvd., University City, 314/862-6100,
http://store.subbooks.com
HOURS: Mon.-Thurs. 11am-8pm, Fri.-Sat. 11am-10pm,
Sun. noon-6pm
Map 6

Many factors go into making a great bookstore: It has to be inviting without seeming too overbearing, be stimulating enough to rouse both your curiosity and your sense of treasure-hunting, and (most important) be exciting enough to inspire you to want to devour every book in sight. With these criteria in mind, the Delmar Loop's Subterranean Books is a great bookstore. What's more, the staff is knowledgeable, helpful, and happy to let you simply browse the stacks. While the store may not bowl you over with its size, Subterranean takes care to stock both popular favorites and obscure gems. The store's loft space often hosts artwork by local artists, ensuring that both the visual arts and the written word continue to earn their proper respect.

🎵 VINTAGE VINYL
6610 Delmar Blvd., University City, 314/721-4096,
www.vintagevinyl.com
HOURS: Sun.-Thurs. 10am-10pm, Fri.-Sat.
10am-midnight
Map 6

Whether you're seeking a just-released album or something more classic, this Delmar landmark is likely to have it. Want an obscure spoken-word album? A compilation of Swedish pop songs? The newest single from an up-and-coming St. Louis rapper? You're in luck at Vintage Vinyl, where it's easy to spend at least an hour wandering through the meticulously organized inventory. Many of Vintage Vinyl's employees have worked in the shop for years and are tireless boosters of the St. Louis music scene. Don't be afraid to ask questions; the clerks here are incredibly well-informed. Just don't be surprised if they grimace when ringing up your Sting album.

Clothing and Accessories

BEVERLY'S HILL
1309 Washington Ave., 314/621-1633,
www.123underwear.com/beverlys-hill-store.html
HOURS: Mon.-Sat. 11am-6pm
Map 1

If your trip to St. Louis needs a little spicing up, look no further than Beverly's Hill. The super-girly, hot-pink-painted shop serves as the bricks-and-mortar for 123underwear.com, and it has cheekiness in spades. It carries several brands and all manner of underthings for the ladies—from bras and panties to slips and loungewear—so shoppers are certain to find the perfect size, color, style, and coverage for any occasion.

BLUSH BOUTIQUE
110 N. Clay Ave., Kirkwood, 314/965-4411,
www.shopblushboutique.com
HOURS: Mon.-Sat. 10am-6pm, Sun. noon-5pm
Map 7

Sarah King, owner of this inviting Kirkwood boutique, considers herself a disciple of fashion. At Blush, she spreads the good word about affordable, high-quality, leading-edge women's couture. King's preference for up-and-coming designers means you won't be stuck browsing through same-ol'-same-ol' labels, and her

collection of accessories (Virgins Saints and Angels jewelry, Melie Bianco handbags, even Voluspa candles) is one of the best in town. Perhaps best of all, you'll never feel rushed or pressured at Blush. King offers outstanding personalized service in addition to other perks like free gift wrap and after-hours appointments.

IVY HILL
304 N. Euclid Ave., 314/367-7004,
www.ivyhillboutique.com.
Second location: 8835 Ladue Rd., 314/721-7004.
HOURS: Mon.-Wed. 10:30am-6pm, Thurs.-Sat.
10:30am-7pm, Sun. 11am-5pm
Map 2

This pocket-size shop sits smack-dab in the middle of the Central West End shopping district, and though it is not tremendous in size, there's a fair amount of fashion within this boutique's walls. Items from designers including Trina Turk, Lauren Moffatt, and Corey Lynn Calter help fill out Ivy Hill's well-edited racks, providing throngs of neighborhood shoppers plenty of on-trend dresses, tops, and jeans to browse. Elegantly scented candles, one-of-a-kind jewelry, day purses, evening clutches, a rainbow assortment of bandeaus and pashminas, and more round out the shop's offerings.

LAURIE SOLET

18 The Boulevard, Richmond Heights, 314/727-7467, www.lauriesolet.com. Second location: 1176 Town & Country Crossing Dr., Town & Country Crossing, 636/527-4139.

HOURS: Mon.-Sat. 10am-6pm

Map 6

When Laurie Solet returned home to her native St. Louis after living in Los Angeles and London, she wanted to share the zeal she gained for all things fashionable. St. Louisans were grateful. Having opened her first namesake boutique in 2003, Solet now has two shops, and she continues to ensure her stores stay stylish, relevant, and popular among chic St. Louis women by passionately staying attentive to industry news and honing in on customer service. The boutique offers items from designers and brands such as Adrienne Landau, Paige Denim, Vanessa Mooney, and Charlotte Tarantola, and the selection changes frequently.

MISTER GUY CLOTHIERS

9831 Clayton Rd., Ladue, 314/692-2003

HOURS: Mon.-Fri. 10am-6pm, Sat. 10am-5:30pm

Map 7

Mister Guy Clothiers is just the sort of place you can imagine James Bond shopping—the new Daniel Craig-style Bond, that is. Of course, having been in business for more than 30 years, Mister Guy might have clothed Roger Moore, too. Like 007, this Ladue men's shop is not afraid to be both ruggedly manly and perfectly turned out. Case in point: They have cold beer and ESPN in the back, but Vineyard Vines and Robert Talbott in the front (Mister Guy is the exclusive local carrier of the Robert Talbott Estate collection). This high-end shop carries everything from designer jeans to bespoke suits. A full-service boutique, Mister Guy provides free alterations—so while you may not exactly be Bond, you can look like you shop on Bond Street.

MORIS FASHIONS

26 Maryland Plaza, 314/361-6800, www.morisfashions.com

HOURS: Mon.-Sat. 11am-7pm, Sun. noon-5pm

Map 2

St. Louis isn't home to many dedicated men's shops, but what the city lacks in quantity, it makes up for in quality. And Moris Fashions definitely delivers quality goods. The shirts and jackets are fresh takes on the classics, the jeans and hoodies are cool and stylish, and the accessories, including watches and wallets, are perfect for today's modern man. Located in one of the most upscale St. Louis neighborhoods, Moris Fashions can hook you up with something to wear for nearly every occasion. Expect to find items from Modern Amusement, Ted Baker, and more, and note that the owners are the kind of nice guys who often write thank-you notes to their customers.

PAPERDOLLS BOUTIQUE

110 E. Jefferson Ave., Kirkwood, 314/965-3655

HOURS: Mon.-Wed. 10am-6pm, Thurs. 10am-7pm, Fri.-Sat. 10am-6pm, Sun. noon-5pm

Map 7

This mid-priced boutique in Kirkwood carries creative, stylish apparel and great designer jeans. Featured items include the handmade garments of artist Macu and the jeans "Eva Longoria swears by." Sales associates are great at finding your correct inseam amid the heaps of denim, and they are also happy to share stories about Paperdolls' latest featured designers. The philosophy here is that good fashion should be treated as art, and that fashionistas should stay well-informed.

PITAYA

6632 Delmar Blvd., University City, 314/725-2233, www.pitayaonline.com

HOURS: Mon.-Thurs. 11am-9pm, Fri.-Sat. 11am-10pm, Sun. noon-9pm

Map 6

The cool window displays all along the Delmar Loop make this neighborhood prime territory for impulse purchases. You may not *think* you need new clothes, but you're likely to walk away with a bagful. Pitaya is a place full of fun, flirty clothes that look great on many different figures. It's also a place where, when you do find that cute wrap-dress you didn't know you needed, you can afford to buy it anyway.

(Dresses and trousers rarely go above $50, and blouses are even cheaper.) And if you happen to be shopping for, say, a purple top to go with the bracelet you just bought, Pitaya has a clever system made for you: The racks are organized by color. Pitaya makes shopping easy—almost *too* easy.

R·SOLE
6662 Delmar Blvd., University City, 314/721-7653
HOURS: Mon.-Sat. 11am-9pm, Sun. noon-6pm
Map 6

R·Sole has soles—plenty of them: Nike, Vans, Adidas, Artful Dodger, and more. But for a shoe store, the place also has soul. When this retail space debuted in 2006, Delmar Loop shoppers could be forgiven for thinking it was another nightclub, rather than a shoe store. Designed by architects Tobin+Parnes, R·Sole seems to be half-dance club and half-art gallery, displaying high-end, hip-hop-inspired footwear in cut-in niches and on glass ledges lit by color-changing LED. The checkout counter even doubles as a DJ booth, and sometimes music is heard pulsing into the night. These may be sports-styled shoes, but R·Sole's artfully displayed kicks are more for the nightclub than the athletic club.

SKIF
2008 Marconi Ave., 314/773-4401, www.skifo.com
HOURS: Mon.-Sat. 10am-5pm
Map 5

Skif, once famous for outfitting the actors in the second and third *Matrix* movies, now is simply famous for being fabulous. Many of Skif's lovingly knitted, stylish sweaters—which are equal parts funky high school art teacher, cool post-industrial warrior, and comfy, cozy you—are made at this shop/studio on the Hill before they are shipped out to more than 100 boutiques around the country. Visitors are free to browse the casual studio space and pick out a unique piece that perfectly suits them. In addition to knits, Skif also sells a handful of pants, dresses, and shirts.

◖ ZIEZO
6394 Delmar Blvd., University City, 314/752-9602
HOURS: Mon.-Thurs. noon-7pm, Fri.-Sat. 11am-7pm, Sun. noon-5pm
Map 6

On-the-spot decision-making can be difficult when shopping for clothing, particularly when said clothing is of the high-ticket variety (e.g., "Should I buy the $80 T-shirt to complement the $200 jeans?"). But Ziezo demands and rewards quick thinking. The shop's owner, Carol Crudden, buys just four to six pieces of each item on her rack, and the inventory moves quickly. For the fashionista who dreads showing up at a party wearing the same dress as someone else, this definitely has its advantages. This Loop boutique carries such popular lines as Squasht by Les and Miss Sixty, and Ziezo offers more Betsey Johnson designs than any other shop in St. Louis.

Gift and Home

BOTANICALS DESIGN STUDIO

3014 S. Grand Blvd., 314/772-7674, www.botp.com
HOURS: Mon.-Fri. 9:30am-5:30pm, Sat. 10am-4pm
Map 4

This great South City flower and gift shop is a fun place to browse. Visitors can wander amid two floors of beautiful floral and gift displays. Botanical Design Studio's merchandise is as inventive and sophisticated as its plant arrangements, and the staff here is über-friendly. Those looking for the perfect gift will likely find something here, and the awesome gift-wrapping service is always free. In addition, Botanicals' sought-after tropical plant arrangements can be sent anywhere in the country, and their access to a wide variety of suppliers allows them to meet almost any request.

CATHOLIC SUPPLY OF ST. LOUIS

6759 Chippewa St., 314/644-0643,
www.catholicsupply.com
HOURS: Mon.-Sat. 9am-5:30pm
Map 4

You don't have to be Catholic to appreciate the vast inventory of Catholic Supply. Even more important, the employees here make all shoppers feel welcome, and the store's fascinating stash of theology books is downright ecumenical. In St. Louis, Catholic Supply is *the* go-to place for school uniforms, christening gowns, and First Communion gifts. There are also a lot of unexpected delights here, like gorgeous prayer candles, Modernist nativity scenes, and kitschy figurines that put Jesus at the center of basketball games, ski outings, and football matches. A mural on the side of the building commemorates John Paul II's 1999 visit to St. Louis. The city's Catholic heritage is strong, and this southside emporium is a must-see for anyone interested in Catholicism.

CENTRO MODERN FURNISHINGS

4727 McPherson Ave., 314/454-0111,
www.centro-inc.com

HOURS: Mon.-Sat. 10am-6pm
Map 2

Unless you have incredibly deep pockets, you may find yourself doing more browsing than buying at this exclusive modern-furniture gallery. The iconic furnishings on display in CENTRO's bright, 7,500-square-foot gallery space usually don't sport price tags—so bear in mind the old aphorism: If you have to ask, you probably can't afford it. Still, a visit to CENTRO is wonderfully worthwhile. Weekly additions to the museum-quality showroom keep visitors abreast of the latest news in the international design and architecture community. And, despite the super-pricey wares, you won't encounter snobbery here; the very knowledgeable staff is more than happy to answer questions, and the shop's great newsletter is a design resource in itself.

CHEAPTRX

3211 S. Grand Blvd., 314/664-4011, www.cheaptrx.com
HOURS: Mon.-Sat. noon-8pm, Sun. noonam-6pm
Map 4

Those interested in a tattoo or piercing to commemorate their St. Louis trip need go no further than CheapTRX. This friendly Grand South Grand boutique has dedicated its three stories to all those important lifestyle accessories one won't find at Target. In addition to operating the city's oldest and most trusted piercing studio, CheapTRX now runs a clean and professional tattoo shop. The main floor is dedicated to jewelry, alternative clothing, and unique home accessories, while the 18-and-older basement level is a good deal naughtier. Shoppers are invited to use their imaginations, and the store's friendly, open-minded staff is happy to answer any questions about the products on the shelves.

GOOD WORKS

6323 Delmar Blvd., University City, 314/726-2233,
www.goodworksfurniture4u.com

COURTESY OF BOTANICALS DESIGN STUDIO

Botanicals Design Studio

HOURS: Mon.-Thurs. 11am-8pm, Fri. 11am-6pm, Sat. 10am-6pm, Sun. 1pm-5pm

Map 6

Good Works' selection of nicely made, reasonably priced furnishings makes it a popular place for hobbyists and professional designers alike. Every piece—from playfully mod bookshelves to solid-wood coffee tables—reflects topnotch craftsmanship. The majority of pieces on the showroom floor can be custom-ordered in a variety of fabrics and finishes (although visitors should know that delivery is mostly local and can take up to eight weeks). Good Works also sells great gift items, including elegant vases and trendy barware. The staff is exceptionally helpful.

GRINGO JONES IMPORTS
4470 Shaw Blvd., 314/664-1666
HOURS: Daily 10am-6pm
Map 4

Mention Gringo Jones to longtime St. Louisans, and they're likely to break into the store's delightfully cheesy jingle ("Gringo Jooooones

and me," sung to the tune of Counting Crows' "Mr. Jones"). They're also likely to recommend that you head to Gringo Jones ASAP, because just browsing here is highly entertaining. The inventory reflects a guiding aesthetic principal that can best be described as "whatever-chic," as this import store stocks everything from gorgeous teak benches to surreal lawn ornaments. Gringo Jones's proximity to the Missouri Botanical Garden creates some cool synergy—including a variety of Mexican glass bowls inspired by the work of garden mainstay Dale Chihuly.

GROVE FURNISHINGS
3169 Morganford Rd., 314/776-7898, www.grovefurnishings.com
HOURS: Fri. 11am-6pm, Sat.-Sun. 10am-5pm
Map 4

Much of the Grove Furnishings' well-priced collection has been crafted locally, and buyers here have a fondness for the warm, eclectic blend of old and new. Pieces made from salvaged materials are always in rotation, which

JOHN VIVIANO & SONS GROCER

5139 Shaw Ave., 314/771-4645, www.shopviviano.com
HOURS: Mon.-Sat. 8am-5pm
Map 5

Visitors to this historic Italian neighborhood will find a number of old-world Italian grocers, all within a four-block radius of the Hill's nucleus at Shaw and Marconi. If you only have time to visit one, make sure it's J. Viviano & Sons. Established in 1949, this beloved neighborhood shop offers imported cheeses and spices alongside terrific homemade sauces, pastas, and olive salads. Nostalgic locals associate Viviano's with the earthy-sweet smell of bulk spices filling the air. Just look for a green awning and follow your nose.

KITCHEN CONSERVATORY

8021 Clayton Rd., Clayton, 314/862-2665,
www.kitchenconservatory.com
HOURS: Mon.-Sat. 9:30am-5:30pm, Sun. noon-5pm
Map 6

Where can you find a gnocchi board, a spaetzle maker, a tart tamper, a left-handed chef's knife? Where can you find a tagine, a chinois, and the spices to use with them? Where can you find the cookbooks to inspire your gourmet urges? And where, oh where, can you find a "Knork"—that's right, the spork's cousin, the knife-fork hybrid—where, that is, but Kitchen Conservatory? Beloved for its daily cooking classes and culinary expertise, this wonderful shop is the sort of place dreamy gourmands should enter at their own risk (lest they leave a few hundred dollars lighter). From old-school canning supplies to Le Creuset cookware, not only do the folks at Kitchen Conservatory carry it, but they can teach you how to use it.

THE WINE & CHEESE PLACE

7435 Forsyth Blvd., Clayton, 314/727-8788,
www.wineandcheeseplace.com. Other locations:
9755 Manchester Rd., Rock Hill, 314/962-8150; 14748
Clayton Rd., Ballwin, 636/227-9001; 457 N. New Ballas
Rd., Creve Coeur, 314/989-0020.
HOURS: Mon.-Sat. 9am-7pm
Map 6

From a splurge-worthy bottle perfect for

Unleash your inner Food Network star at the Kitchen Conservatory.

© BROOKE S. FOSTER

gracious hosts to an affordable, easy-drinking varietal just right for a picnic, The Wine & Cheese Place has exactly what you seek. Rows and rows of bottles from around the world fill this wine shop, and it all might be too overwhelming to navigate if the staff members weren't so friendly and knowledgeable. And as the store's name indicates, the wine is just the half of it! With cheeses ranging from the familiar to the peculiar, you'll be sure to purchase one that suits your palate and your wine selection—especially since sampling is encouraged here. Plus, the shop offers other snacks and beer as well, making it a most delicious one-stop shop. There are three other locations.

Kids' Stores

THE BUILD-A-BEAR WORKSHOP
Saint Louis Galleria, Brentwood Blvd. and Clayton Rd., 314/725-8282, www.buildabear.com
HOURS: Mon.-Sat. 10am-9pm, Sun. 11am-6pm
`Map 6`

The Build-A-Bear Workshop in the Saint Louis Galleria appears to be just one of many—but it isn't. There are 370 near-identical Build-A-Bear retailers scattered across the country and the world (Japan, Korea, Denmark, Singapore, Germany, Russia, Thailand, Ireland . . .), but this one is the very first. St. Louisan Maxine Clark founded her customizable-teddy-bear company here in 1997, after resigning from her position as president of Payless ShoeSource. Today, Clark is known around the world as one of the retail industry's great innovators—and as a leading female visionary in a sector often dominated by men.

◖ CITY SPROUTS
6303 Delmar Blvd., University City, 314/726-9611, www.citysprouts.com
HOURS: Mon.-Sat. 10am-6pm, Sun. noon-5pm
`Map 6`

Opened by the women who own the Phoenix Rising gift shop, City Sprouts takes that shop's joyful, chic aesthetic and applies it to the toddler set. Find precious clothes with hand-stitched details, or amuse yourself (and your friends) with onesies that say things like "I ate my dreidel" or "Someday, I'll egg a house." City Sprouts also sells beautiful children's books, educational toys, multilingual games, nursery decor, and "survival kits" for new parents. The complimentary gift-wrapping service is chic and efficient.

KANGAROO KIDS
10030 Manchester Rd., 314/835-9200, www.kangarookidsonline.com
HOURS: Mon.-Sat. 10am-6pm, Sun. noon-4pm
`Map 7`

Local parents-on-a-budget absolutely love Kangaroo Kids. The cost of child-rearing adds up quickly, and this Kirkwood shop's selection of gently used, name-brand maternity and children's clothing, toys, books, and equipment is second to none. Parents who bring in items to sell are rewarded either with cash or with store credit. Seasonal items in good condition are purchased at 30-50 percent of their resale value, plus an additional 20 percent if store credit is chosen over cash. Kangaroo Kids also sells some new items, including strollers, breast pumps, and the incredibly popular Slingaroo. These baby slings are handmade locally, and Kangaroo Kids carries them in every color imaginable.

Pet Supplies

GROOMINGDALE'S

3425 Watson Rd., 314/781-6711,
www.groomingdalesstl.com
HOURS: Mon.-Fri. 7:30am-6pm, Sat. 7:30am-4pm
Map 4

Situated behind a massive, neon-pink pawprint marquee, Groomingdale's represents South City's creative streak and proves that St. Louis's pet-care ideals can surpass other places' people-care standards. Offering pet "Playcare" and a full-service pet spa, the folks who invented the now-famous FURminator (a bold tool promising a 90 percent reduction in shedding) will prettify your pooch with special organic treatments for coat, nails, and teeth. And just in case you think little Spot will never be that clean again, Groomingdale's can memorialize that shiny coat in a "Pup-tography" portrait session. They've got plenty of toys and treats to grab on the way home, too.

⬤ LOLA & PENELOPE'S

7742 Forsyth Blvd., Clayton, 314/863-5652,
www.lolaandpenelopes.com
HOURS: Mon.-Fri. 10am-6pm, Sat. 9am-5pm, Sun. noon-4pm
Map 6

Walk down any street in Clayton, and you're pretty much guaranteed to find high-end shopping. Lola & Penelope's puts a fun twist on boutique chic—all of the designer clothes, elegant furniture, and gourmet foods are for four-legged friends. Both levels are filled with items for the discerning dog and cat. Visitors will find Chihuahua-sized cardigans, pink Porsche-shaped cat beds, and organic treats. The shop also offers grooming services, including "paw-dicures," dental cleanings, and heat massages for older pets. Lola & Penelope's frequently hosts events to benefit abandoned pets, and each year the store honors animals that have behaved heroically.

WOLFGANG'S PET STOP

330 N. Euclid Ave., 314/367-8088,
www.wolfgangspetstop.com.
Second location: 1820 Washington Ave., 314/539-9653.
HOURS: Mon. noon-6pm, Tues.-Fri. 10am-6pm, Sat. 9am-5pm, Sun. noon-4pm
Map 2

Wolfgang's is a delightful place for pet-lovers—and for pets themselves. This shop offers everything from designer collars to couture doggie sweaters to customizable birthday parties and "bark-mitzvahs." Purchase one of these canine soirees, and Wolfgang's will provide a homemade party cake, party favors, gift bags, and games. The on-site pet spa offers a number of grooming options, and Wolfgang's also carries gourmet dog food and a line of orthopedic pet beds. Be sure to give a head-scratch to the eponymous Wolfgang, the beautiful rescued dog who often lolls in front of the shop's entrance.

Shopping Centers

THE BOULEVARD

Brentwood Blvd. and Galleria Pkwy.

Map 6

The Saint Louis Galleria is a mall (and a great one at that), but The Boulevard positions itself as a lifestyle center. When you stroll down The Boulevard's brick-paved avenue—the burbling of fountains in the background, the smells from P.F. Chang's and Maggiano's Little Italy beckoning—you can imagine a lifestyle where you (clad in something spiffy from LOFT) can have your hair done at Mitchell James before heading up to your spacious apartment in this mixed commercial-residential development. There are currently 22 shops and restaurants on The Boulevard, but developers plan to expand.

CENTRAL WEST END

Euclid Ave. between Washington Ave. and Forest Park Ave., www.thecwe.com

Map 2

This pedestrian-friendly shopping district is at the heart of one of the city's oldest and most prestigious neighborhoods. The sidewalks along this five-block stretch are canopied by stately trees. Walk down Euclid Avenue (the Central West End's main thoroughfare), and you'll glimpse some of the city's most beautiful homes and gardens.

If you can afford a shopping expedition in the Central West End, by all means go for it. The neighborhood's clothing boutiques are, not surprisingly, upscale—but while some of the prices are astronomical, service is never snobby. Art galleries and high-end furniture showrooms line McPherson Avenue. On Maryland Plaza, you'll find a Design Within Reach flagship store, an exquisite chocolatier, a ritzy nightclub, and several trendy clothing shops. Salons, spas, and specialty gift stores stretch down Euclid Avenue; the street is also home to two great bookstores and many nice restaurants with see-and-be-seen alfresco seating.

Even if you're not looking to drop lots of cash, the Central West End is the perfect place for an afternoon stroll and leisurely browsing. Prime shopping times include Sunday afternoons, when several of the neighborhood's popular eateries open for a late-morning patio brunch.

CHEROKEE STREET

Cherokee St. between Lemp Ave. and DeMenil Pl.

Map 3

Many locals consider Cherokee Street "antiques row." But, in reality, the antiques stores occupy only a portion of this seven-block shopping district. In addition to antique and vintage shops, this thriving stretch plays host to several Central American markets, record sellers, restaurants, and bodega-style convenience stores. Make time to walk Cherokee Street from end to end, and you'll encounter more than 50 businesses. The quiet antiques row is nestled on Cherokee's eastern stretch; the western side is a lively Latino neighborhood, where visitors will find specialty shops and the finest *taquerías* in all of St. Louis.

CLAYTON

Between Maryland Ave., Forsyth Blvd., and Brentwood Blvd.

Map 6

On weekdays, Clayton is a business center, filled with suited-up folks enjoying power lunches. But business isn't being conducted just in the conference rooms of the multistory buildings. Many locally owned galleries and upscale boutiques line the walkable streets of this posh area. Pop into the Duane Reed Gallery to check out the latest art show, and peruse shops like Byrd Style Lounge, a boutique that offers style-consulting services. By night office dwellers emerge for happy-hour drinks at places like The Ritz-Carlton St. Louis's The Lobby Lounge. Join them, or find a quiet table at one of many restaurants for a scrumptious dinner and a relaxing end to a full day of shopping.

DELMAR LOOP
Delmar Blvd. between Trinity Ave. and Des Peres Ave., www.ucityloop.com

Map 6

Arguably the most popular entertainment district in the city, the Loop boasts a variety of restaurants, shops, and live-music venues. It's also home to several indie-rock clubs and the city's alternative newspaper; as such, the area draws a younger, hipper crowd. Vintage Vinyl, one of St. Louis's last remaining record stores, calls the Loop home. The historic Tivoli Theatre is here as well, as are a number of independent bars and coffee shops.

The Loop's fashion boutiques, furniture stores, and gift shops clearly cater to the youthful demographic. The apartments north and south of Delmar are home to hundreds of Washington University students, and Loop businesses lure them in with trendy fashions and abundant drink specials. A number of restaurants are here too, including three Thai spots and the ever-popular Blueberry Hill.

Blueberry Hill has held down the corner of Westgate and Delmar for years. During that time, the restaurant/rock club has grown to encompass an entire block of storefronts. Owner Joe Edwards spearheaded the reimagining of the once-dangerous and rundown Delmar Loop. Today, Blueberry Hill is a tourist flagship, and everything around it hums with life.

GRAND SOUTH GRAND
S. Grand Blvd. between Arsenal St. and Utah St.

Map 4

The Grand South Grand shopping district may appear a little rough around the edges, but it's a vibrant neighborhood that appeals to South City residents and tourists alike. The shops, restaurants, and bars reflect the diversity in this densely populated neighborhood. Visitors could easily spend an entire afternoon perusing the street's many ethnic markets. The most popular and well-stocked market, Jay's International Food Co., sits

at its own pedestrian light in the middle of Grand South Grand's eight-block stretch. Other landmarks include MoKaBe's, a bustling coffee shop across the street from Tower Grove Park; Dunaway Books; and Floored on Grand, where interested parties can receive instruction in everything from tango to pole-dancing.

OLD WEBSTER
Big Bend Blvd. and Lockwood Ave.

Map 7

There are several worthwhile shopping destinations in the idyllic bedroom community of Webster Groves, and they can be found along Big Bend Boulevard and Lockwood Avenue. The two roads meet in a Y. East of here, along Big Bend, visitors will find an upscale fashion boutique as well as longtime resident Music Folk, a folk-instrument shop. West of here, along Lockwood and past a few residential blocks, you'll encounter Old Webster's historic main drag. This stretch is mainly food-oriented, but tucked in amid the casual restaurants are some eclectic gift boutiques, a bookstore, salons and spas, a music store specializing in classical recordings, and a popular high-end grocer.

PLAZA FRONTENAC
1701 S. Lindbergh Blvd., 314/432-0604, www.plazafrontenac.com

HOURS: Mon.-Fri. 10am-8pm, Sat. 10am-7pm, Sun. noon-5pm

Map 7

With Missouri's only Neiman Marcus and Saks Fifth Avenue stores, Plaza Frontenac is where the well-heeled find retail therapy. In addition to these anchor stores, the upscale mall, located in one of the most prosperous parts of the area, also is home to Juicy Couture, Tiffany & Co., lululemon athletica, and St. Louis's own Sam Cavato, as well as Sur la Table and Williams-Sonoma for all manner of quality kitchenware. Local restaurants and chains provide welcome post-shopping sustenance, and a six-screen movie theater shows independent films.

SAINT LOUIS GALLERIA
Brentwood Blvd. and Clayton Rd., 314/863-5500,
www.saintlouisgalleria.com
HOURS: Mon.-Sat. 10am-9pm, Sun. 11am-6pm
`Map 6`

This centrally located shopping mall is one of the most popular in the area, thanks to its variety of shops and its accessibility via MetroBus and MetroLink. The Galleria is anchored by Macy's and Dillard's. On its three levels, the Galleria boasts trendy favorites like Urban Outfitters, the Gap, and Anthropologie, plus a six-theater cinema, a food court, and a few stand-alone restaurants. Visitors tired from a long afternoon of shopping can relax and refuel at outposts of national chains such as California Pizza Kitchen and the Cheesecake Factory. The Galleria recently enacted strict weekend curfew laws—kids age 17 and under must leave the mall before 3pm unless they're accompanied by an adult.

WEST COUNTY CENTER
80 West County Center, Des Peres, 314/288-2020,
www.shopwestcountycenter.com
HOURS: Mon.-Sat. 10am-9pm, Sun. 11am-6pm
`Map 7`

West County Center completed an extensive renovation in 2002. Today, it is one of the area's premier shopping centers. West County Center is anchored by Nordstrom, a flagship Macy's, and Dick's Sporting Goods. Among its 150 other stores are Brooks Brothers, Clarks, The Apple Store, H&M, and Sephora. In addition to having standard food-court fare, the mall caters to hungry shoppers with a California Pizza Kitchen and a see-and-be-seen spot called the Elephant Bar Restaurant.

Spa, Bath, and Beauty

C CASSIE'S
316 N. Euclid Ave., 314/454-1010,
www.cassiescents.com
HOURS: Mon.-Thurs. 10:30am-6pm, Fri.-Sat. 10:30am-8pm, Sun. noon-5pm
`Map 2`

Cassie's is part fragrance shop, part laboratory. Alongside a lovely selection of boutique bath products and handmade soaps, you'll find the scent bar, where you can buy perfume tailored to your exact specifications. The friendly "scent specialists" help patrons mix their own fragrances by combining highly concentrated perfume oils, one drop at a time. The scent can then be purchased as-is or added to lotion or body wash. Locals flock to Cassie's for the inexpensive, spot-on imitations of such designer fragrances as Marc Jacobs and Burberry Touch.

THE FACE & THE BODY
2515 Brentwood Blvd., Brentwood, 314/726-8975,
www.faceandbodyspa.com. Other locations: 1765 Clarkson Rd., Chesterfield, 636/532-2500; 2918 Highway K, O'Fallon, 636/281-2600.

HOURS: Mon.-Fri. 8am-9pm, Sat. 8am-6pm, Sun. 10am-5pm
`Map 7`

Loyal spa-goers don't just *like* The Face & The Body's house-brand cosmetics and skin products. They love them, adore them, evangelize about them. Founder Peggy Mitchusson developed the line to complement her services at St. Louis's first full-service day spa. The Face & The Body has grown since its doors opened in 1979, with one location expanding into three and luxurious products selling like hotcakes. Travel-weary tourists looking for true indulgence will find it here. Stop in for a mud wrap, manicure, facial, or massage—or spring for a medical spa treatment, such as laser hair removal or a microdermabrasion session that will leave your skin baby-smooth.

K. HALL DESIGNS
8416 Manchester Rd., Brentwood, 314/961-1990,
www.khalldesigns.com
HOURS: Mon.-Sat. 10am-6pm
`Map 7`

The handmade olive oil and shea-butter soaps

St. Louis spa-goers swear by The Face & The Body's luxurious treatments.

© BROOKE S. FOSTER

at K. Hall Designs in Brentwood are worth the trip alone. The shop's divinely scented, all-natural home and bath products are made at a small-scale manufacturer less than five miles away, but fans of K. Hall's merchandise hail from all over the globe. This operation distributes its products to more than 1,200 stores—from New York to Hong Kong—and has been featured in nearly every garden- and food-related publication on the newsstand. Inspired by her own garden, the tranquil, breezy little apothecary on Manchester is owner Kelley Hall-Barr's home showcase.

NATURALLY PURE

8195 Big Bend Blvd., Webster Groves, 314/963-7101, www.naturallypuresalon.com

HOURS: Tues.-Thurs. 9am-9pm, Fri.-Sat. 9am-5pm
Map 7

This cozy converted house, located near Webster Groves' main drag of shops and restaurants, is a favorite getaway for frazzled locals. A full-service Aveda salon, Naturally Pure offers everything from super-soothing scalp massages to eyebrow shaping to exceptionally good haircuts. Stylists here take the time to make you look perfect, so be sure to set aside three hours if you want, say, highlights and a blowout. Naturally Pure sells the complete line of Aveda cosmetics, plus tons of hair products, facial masques, and body lotions.

Vintage and Antiques

AVALON EXCHANGE
6388 Delmar Blvd., University City, 314/725-2760, www.avalonexchange.com
HOURS: Mon.-Thurs. 11am-8pm, Fri.-Sat. 11am-9pm, Sun. noon-7pm
Map 6

This good-size thrift store offers funky, eclectic dresses and skirts; jeans and tops for everyday wear; fun costumes; shoes and bags; and tons of jewelry. The racks are always packed with recently recycled wardrobe items and beloved retro-wear for both men and women, and sorting through everything has the feel of a treasure hunt. You might even spot some tags—on items that have never been worn! Prices here aren't as bargain-basement as your average charity-run thrift shop, but the pieces are still easily affordable and worth the hunt.

RETRO 101/CHERRY BOMB VINTAGE
2303 Cherokee St., 314/762-9722
HOURS: Daily noon-5pm
Map 3

Cherry Bomb Vintage is St. Louis's largest mid-century antique shop. The city's alternative weekly has voted Cherry Bomb "Best Vintage Store" five years running, and it's quite easy

to see why. Not only is the selection great, but the location (the heart of the Cherokee Street antiques district) is wonderful, and the service is charming and gracious. A visitor could spend hours browsing Cherry Bomb's three jam-packed floors of vintage clothing, accessories, housewares, furniture, jewelry, and books. The market for great vintage in St. Louis hasn't yet been sapped, and out-of-towners are likely to appreciate the veritable gold mine of Mod and kitsch found on every lovingly arranged display.

T.F.A. THE FUTURE ANTIQUES
6514 Chippewa St., 314/865-1552, www.tfa50s.com
HOURS: Mon., Wed.-Thurs. 11am-6pm, Fri.-Sat. 10am-7pm, Sun. noon-5pm
Map 4

The Future Antiques, or T.F.A., specializes in midcentury home furnishings: Think Danish Modern, astro-blue vinyl, and the blond-wood decor of 1950s California ranch homes. Fashionable folks looking to re-create life in the Atomic Age will be impressed by the great selection here. Thanks to its ever-increasing inventory, T.F.A. was recently forced to move to its new, much larger space on Chippewa Street.

HOTELS

Because of the sheer number of universities, medical complexes, and conference centers in St. Louis, there are plenty of hotel rooms. Most of the hotels are located in downtown and in the city's central corridor, although there are also delightful bed-and-breakfasts nestled in St. Louis's residential areas. As can be expected in a city of St. Louis's size, the majority of downtown hotels are outposts of pricey chains, but even these have plenty of local touches (not to mention a great location). Travelers looking to indulge themselves will find a healthy number of options, from the astonishing minimalist beauty of the Four Seasons to the old-world elegance of the Chase Park Plaza. Visitors should know that, because much of the downtown hotel business comes from large, well-funded conventions, there are very few budget options in this area. Tourists looking to spend the night for less than $100 are very unlikely to find such a deal downtown (except in the rare instance of an off-season discount).

The more budget-friendly hotel options are a bit farther from the city center, although there are plenty of affordably priced bed-and-breakfasts. In fact, a stay in a St. Louis B&B promises both a restful night and a glimpse into local history and architecture, as most bed-and-breakfasts in town are tucked inside lovely old homes. The budget-conscious traveler who wants to stay close to tourist attractions, restaurants, and entertainment venues will definitely want to look into one of St. Louis's many B&Bs. Those looking for a boutique hotel won't find an abundance of options, but the boutique hotels St. Louis *does*

HIGHLIGHTS

LOOK FOR (TO FIND
RECOMMENDED HOTELS.

(**Best Place to Pamper Yourself:** The **Four Seasons Hotel St. Louis** is undoubtedly the most luxurious hotel in the city. Soak in the marble bathtub, stretch out on the chaise longue (while taking in a stellar view of the Arch and the Mississippi River), or head to the seventh floor for a spa treatment (page 128).

(**Best Room with a View:** The **Hilton St. Louis at the Ballpark** brings new meaning to "field of dreams." Spacious, pretty rooms overlook the city—or, if you're lucky, provide the perfect view of Busch Stadium's infield (page 128).

(**Most Historic Hotel:** Built in 1922, **The Chase Park Plaza** is a true St. Louis landmark. But this hotel doesn't rest on its laurels: Rooms are large and luxuriously appointed, on-site dining is first-rate, and visitors will find plenty of entertainment options, including live music and a five-screen movie theater (page 131).

(**Most Chic Bed-and-Breakfast:** Forget frilly bedspreads and outdated plumbing fixtures: **Dwell 912** is a bed-and-breakfast for the 21st century. The furniture is sleek and chic, and amenities like wireless Internet and flat-screen televisions will delight the modern traveler (page 132).

(**Most Romantic Accommodations:** The stunning **Fleur-de-Lys Mansion** is an object lesson in opulence and romance. Ask for a room with a Jacuzzi—and consider springing for the Ultimate Romantic Getaway Package, which includes a four-course dinner, a carriage ride, and in-room massages (page 133).

(**Best Getaway in the Middle of It All:** For years, the bustling Loop district went without a hotel—which was quite the bummer, considering this area's designation as one of "America's Great Streets." Activist, entrepreneur, and tireless Loop-booster Joe Edwards changed that when he built the **Moonrise Hotel,** a chic hotel that puts you at the center of all that the Loop offers (page 135).

(**Best Boutique Hotel:** Life is sweet at the Tudor-style **Seven Gables Inn.** Rooms are meticulously decorated, with an eye toward beauty and comfort, and gourmet candies from local chocolatier Bissinger's await each night (page 136).

HOTELS

have are great—particularly the Seven Gables Inn in Clayton and the Moonrise Hotel in the Delmar Loop. Hotels in these areas rarely fall in the "budget" category, but their chic ambiance and in-the-middle-of-it-all location make them worth the price.

PRICE KEY

$ Less than $150 per night
$$ $150-250 per night
$$$ More than $250 per night

Downtown   Map 1

DRURY PLAZA HOTEL $$
2 S. 4th St., 314/231-3003, www.druryhotels.com
The 10-story Drury Plaza Hotel ($119-180) offers one of the best values downtown. It

occupies three beautifully restored 1919 buildings at the corner of 4th and Market, offers great views of the Arch, doesn't charge for its WiFi, and serves a free hot breakfast every morning. Other amenities include a 24-hour business center, exercise room, and indoor pool. Although rooms are run-of-the-mill, they are squeaky clean, and the staff is always friendly. The Drury is only a few blocks from a MetroLink stop, a mile from the Amtrak station, and within walking distance of several important visitor sites, including the Gateway Arch, Busch Stadium, the Old Courthouse, and Union Station.

FOUR SEASONS HOTEL ST. LOUIS ⑤⑤⑤
999 N. 2nd St., 314/881-5800, www.fourseasons.com/stlouis

Simply one of the most exquisite hotels in the city, the Four Seasons Hotel St. Louis ($305-1,310) brings a much-needed update to downtown lodging. The hotel, which adjoins Lumière Place Casino & Hotels, is a work of art. Enter the first-floor foyer, with its stunning minimalist design, and take the elevator to the eighth-floor lobby. There, floor-to-ceiling windows provide one of the best views in the city. Guest rooms offer equally excellent vistas, in addition to plush accommodations and abundant amenities. The marble bathrooms (with glass-enclosed rain showers and LCD televisions) are particularly impressive. Ask about the "hotel credit" when you reserve your room; when the Four Seasons isn't booked to capacity, you can usually get a $50 credit to the spa or to Cielo, the upscale on-site restaurant.

HILTON ST. LOUIS AT THE BALLPARK ⑤⑤
1 S. Broadway, 314/421-1776, www.hiltonstlouis.com
Find baseball heaven at Hilton St. Louis at the Ballpark ($169-309), which is right next to Busch Stadium. The hotel's proximity to David Freese and the gang makes it a popular "staycation" spot for St. Louis residents, although the halls also hum with convention business. Rooms are large and nicely appointed, with luxe bedding, MP3 player docks, and wireless Internet access. Choose between a city-view or a stadium-view room, but do know the latter can be hard to come by when the Cards are

on a winning streak. This Hilton boasts both universally known amenities (a gigantic lobby Starbucks) and local favorites (an outpost of Imo's Pizza).

HOTELUMIÈRE ⑤⑤
999 N. 2nd St., 314/881-7777, www.lumiereplace.com
A stone's throw from the Four Seasons, HoteLumière ($109-399) is the more budget-friendly option in the Lumière Place complex. HoteLumière's accommodations aren't nearly as plush as those at the Four Seasons, but the location is good. This is a former Embassy Suites (frequent travelers will recognize that chain's open floorplan in a heartbeat) with a few fun updates, like mod furniture, flat-screen televisions, and a chic bar. Plus, you're just a few steps away from the casino floor and its cadre of restaurants, including the Stadium Sports Bar and Grill. Service at HoteLumière is not as polished as that at the Four Seasons—but at around 100 bucks less per night, that's more of an observation than a complaint.

HYATT REGENCY ⑤⑤
1 St. Louis Union Station, 314/655-1234, www.stlouis.hyatt.com
The Hyatt Regency ($119-219), inside historic Union Station, gives guests the opportunity to spend a night in a national landmark. The old-world beauty of this turn-of-the-20th-century train station remains intact, and its Grand Hall serves as the hotel's lobby. Outstanding features include the hall's stately marble arches, its towering barrel-vaulted ceiling, and period furnishings, although the visual impact here is mostly reserved for common spaces. Rooms offer a few deluxe accoutrements (comfy pillowtop mattresses, Egyptian cotton sheets, super-fast in-room Internet connections), and some have nice garden views, but are nothing to write home about. Hotel amenities include a 24-hour business center, fitness center, and outdoor pool. Guests can have a drink or casual meal at the adjoining shopping center (waaay touristy) or go upscale at the Station Grille, the Hyatt's on-site steakhouse.

COURTESY OF FOUR SEASONS HOTEL ST. LOUIS

Four Seasons Hotel St. Louis

THE MAYFAIR HOTEL $$

806 St. Charles St., 314/421-2500,
www.robertsmayfairhotel.com

Situated at the corner of 8th Street and St. Charles Street, just one block south of bustling Washington Avenue, the elegant Mayfair Hotel ($89-285) brings a bit of old-world charm to St. Louis's burgeoning downtown. Stained-glass windows, marble floors, and wooden handrails give this historic hotel a romantic ambiance and make it a truly charming place to stay. The Mayfair's state-of-the-art amenities are impressive as well, and include premium 42-inch plasma flat-screen TVs, Aeron chairs, down pillows, thick terry towels, and spacious spa-like bathrooms stocked with Bath & Body Works products. Guests will love the fresh, bright, modern feel of these rooms (and the comfort of the crisp luxury linens). The hotel also boasts free WiFi in every room, a fully equipped workout facility, and sparkling rooftop swimming pool. The Roberts Brothers, who own the gorgeous Roberts Orpheum Theater and a large amount of real estate on the city's north side, bring elegance to all of their projects—and the Mayfair is no exception.

OMNI MAJESTIC $$

1019 Pine St., 314/436-2355, www.omnihotels.com

Omni hotels are almost always a great bet, and the Omni Majestic ($135-239) is a particularly bright feather in that chain's cap. This boutique hotel, constructed in 1913, is full of old-world beauty. Mahogany furnishings lend an air of drawing-room elegance, and the service—from the front-desk staff to the caterers to the porters—is outstanding. A perennial favorite with St. Louis couples seeking nice accommodations for their wedding guests, the Omni offers large rooms and suites at reasonable prices. The charming hotel bar is several steps up from most others in the area, and the grand piano in the lobby is a lovely touch.

RENAISSANCE ST. LOUIS GRAND HOTEL $$

800 Washington Ave., 314/418-5600,
www.marriott.com

Because of its proximity to the city's convention center and downtown commerce district, the Renaissance St. Louis Grand Hotel ($149-250) is a very popular choice with business travelers.

© TOM PAULE/ HILTON ST. LOUIS AT THE BALLPARK

Hilton St. Louis at the Ballpark

The service is pleasant and efficient, and the rooms—while nothing extraordinary—are comfortable. Bathrooms are lavish and spa-like. While common spaces are sometimes an afterthought in midrange hotels, the sitting areas and lobby at the Renaissance are beautifully appointed. Request a top-floor room, and you'll be rewarded with panoramic city views and easy access to the rooftop pool. This hotel is also home to a Starbucks outpost and two restaurants. Before you book a reservation, be sure to visit the Renaissance Grand's website for great "weekend getaway" packages.

SHERATON ST. LOUIS CITY CENTER $$
400 S. 14th St., 314/231-5007,
www.sheratonstlouiscitycenter.com
Breathe easy at the Sheraton St. Louis City Center ($109-199), a completely smoke-free hotel. This quiet property is a good bet for business travelers, although its proximity to the Edward Jones Dome and Scottrade Center also make it popular with football and hockey fans. The digs aren't particularly fancy, but service is

friendly, amenities are thoughtful, and rates are reasonable. Swim laps in the huge heated pool, or stretch out with a book on the sundeck. The Sheraton St. Louis isn't known for its restaurants (a recently shuttered hockey-themed restaurant was particularly ill-conceived), so avoid the dark hotel dining room and head instead to a downtown eatery.

WESTIN ST. LOUIS $$
811 Spruce St., 314/621-2000,
www.starwoodhotels.com
The Westin ($169-322) is one of the city's newest luxury hotels, enjoying a premier location in the center of downtown. It is directly across the street from Busch Stadium and within walking distance of several important St. Louis sights, including the Gateway Arch, the Old Courthouse, and Washington Avenue. The plush, spa-inspired rooms have a clean, Modernist design and pamper guests with fluffy towels and super-high-thread-count bedding. The marble bathrooms, with glass-enclosed showers and separate soaking tubs, are

particularly nice. Enormous arched windows in many rooms offer outstanding views of the city skyline. The hotel's many amenities include a full-service spa, health center, and late-night lounge and grill. Potential guests should make particular note of the Westin's proximity to the baseball stadium: On game nights, this place can be a zoo.

Midtown and Central West End   Map 2

■ THE CHASE PARK PLAZA $$$
212-232 N. Kingshighway Blvd., 314/633-3000, www.chaseparkplaza.com
This stately four-star hotel is both a civic treasure and a historic landmark. When the Chase Park Plaza ($149-389) opened its doors in the 1920s, it welcomed the crème de la crème of celebrity society. For years, the Chase was *the* destination for upscale business and leisure travelers. The hotel hosted the Rat Pack, Bob Hope, and every visiting United States president from the 1920s to the 1980s. The Chase fell into disrepair toward the end of the 20th century, but a $100 million renovation restored the legendary hotel to its former glory, and there are enough luxurious amenities to make this hotel a destination in itself. Popular with wealthy socialites and brides on an unlimited budget, the StarlightBallroom and Khorassan Ballroom are state-of-the-art event facilities. The hotel is also home to a quaint five-screen cinema, a bistro and lounge, a beautiful pool and patio, and a full-service salon and spa.

MARRIOTT RESIDENCE INN $$
525 S. Jefferson Ave., 314/289-7500, www.marriott.com
The Residence Inn ($126-259) near downtown St. Louis is conveniently located off US-40/64, at the Jefferson exit, and is a five-minute drive from several important tourist sites, including Forest Park, the Missouri Botanical Garden, the Arch, and Busch Stadium. The beautiful

and historic Lafayette Square neighborhood is just around the corner, as are the neighborhoods of South City and Soulard. The Residence Inn is in a centrally located (though particularly unattractive) corridor of the city and is a good choice for travelers who place a premium on convenience. Amenities include a fitness center, a lounge, an indoor pool, free continental breakfast, and private galley kitchens with a coffeemaker, toaster, microwave, refrigerator, and utensils. The Residence Inn offers guests a complimentary cocktail hour on weekdays.

THE PARKWAY HOTEL $
4550 Forest Park Ave., 314/256-7777, www.theparkwayhotel.com
The Parkway Hotel ($139-151) is, to quote Ernest Hemingway, "a clean, well-lighted place." You won't find mod chaise longues or commissioned art here, but you *will* find comfortable rooms and a helpful staff. The hotel's proximity to the Barnes-Jewish Hospital and St. Louis Children's Hospital complex makes it a logical choice for visiting surgeons and for families with loved ones undergoing medical procedures. The Parkway is also quite close to a MetroLink station, making it a good choice for visitors traveling without a car. Avoid the adjacent Applebee's and walk a few blocks into the Central West End, where the options are far more interesting. Special rates for AAA members, AARP members, and government employees are available.

HOTELS

Soulard and Lafayette Square   Map 3

◖ DWELL 912 ❸❸

912 Hickory St., 314/599-3100, www.dwell912.com

Stay at Dwell 912 ($150-175), and you can almost pretend that it's your own fabulous apartment in the heart of the city. This private two-story guesthouse, nestled in historic LaSalle Park, is just a half mile from the must-visit neighborhoods of Soulard and Lafayette Square. Dwell 912 sleeps up to four people on its second floor and is ideal for extended stays. This urban oasis is styled like a five-star boutique hotel—but without the boutique-hotel price. Amenities include 600-thread-count linens, an oversized Egyptian bath, a wood-burning fireplace, and such aesthetic delights as 13-foot ceilings and original modern art. On the first floor, you'll find an art library, a gorgeous lounge-style sitting area (with HDTV and free WiFi), and a kitchen stocked with gourmet treats and breakfast items.

THE LEMP MANSION RESTAURANT & INN ❸❸

3322 DeMenil Pl., 314/664-8024, www.lempmansion.com

Travelers looking for a night's stay unlike any other will certainly find it at The Lemp Mansion Restaurant & Inn ($125-295). This historic home once belonged to the powerful and suicide-prone Lemp family, a clan of beer barons whose trajectory went from incredible success to heartbreaking tragedy. The Lemp Mansion is a beautiful example of historical preservation, and guests who like a few ghost stories with their stay will certainly be delighted. Each of the inn's suites is decorated with period furnishings, fixtures, and artwork—much of it original to the house—and is named after a departed member of the Lemp family. Three of the suites have private baths, and two connected suites on the third floor boast Jacuzzi tubs. The amenities

are thoughtful, but it's the fascinating history of the place that draws visitors here year after year.

NAPOLEON'S RETREAT ❸❸

1815 Lafayette Ave., 314/772-6979, www.napoleonsretreat.com

Located just outside of downtown in the historic Lafayette Square neighborhood, Napoleon's Retreat ($149-229) entices visitors with its charm and history. Built in 1880, this French Second Empire Victorian home was highlighted in *Better Homes and Gardens*. Jeff Archulata is the B&B's amicable innkeeper, and his thoughtful hospitality draws guests back again and again. After a restful night's sleep, indulge in a breakfast of fresh fruit, juice, and gourmet teas. Savor the quiche, Napoleon French toast, and Belgian waffles, then head for Lafayette Park. Weekend reservations at Napoleon's Retreat require a two-night minimum stay.

PARK AVENUE MANSION BED AND BREAKFAST ❸❸

2007 Park Ave., 314/588-9004, www.parkavenuemansion.com

Picture-perfect suites make the Park Avenue Mansion Bed and Breakfast ($135-289) a favorite with locals celebrating special occasions. Gracious hosts Kathy and Mike Petetit prepare a gourmet breakfast every morning, and guests dine in the tranquil English garden whenever weather permits. Every room here is unique and has its own bathroom, complete with whirlpool bath. A gourmet coffee, tea, and snack bar is open in the kitchen around the clock, and a candle-lit dinner in Park Avenue's elegant dining room is available upon request. Front rooms offer a view of Lafayette Park, and downtown is only a mile and a half away. A two-night minimum stay is usually required.

COURTESY OF NAPOLEON'S RETREAT

Napoleon's Retreat

South City   Map 4

CASA MAGNOLIA BED AND BREAKFAST ⑤

4171 Magnolia Ave., 314/664-8702,
www.casamagnoliabandb.com

Travelers looking for a home away from home will truly appreciate Casa Magnolia ($125). This carefully restored 1906 Shaw Park home enjoys an outstanding view of Tower Grove Park and is around the corner from the Missouri Botanical Garden. Every beautifully appointed room is unique. The house showcases warm wooden furnishings and the owners' impressive antique collection. Each of the three guest rooms has its own bathroom, and guests share a second-floor study with a library and fireplace. Breakfast is prepared every morning by Casa Magnolia's gracious hosts, Lillabet and Jordi. The hot meal is served every morning at 8am and can be enjoyed poolside during summer months.

◖ THE FLEUR-DE-LYS MANSION ⑤⑤

3500 Russell Blvd., 314/773-3500,
www.thefleurdelys.com

The beautiful accommodations within this historic South City mansion are as gracious as its hosts. Jan and Dave Seifert welcome every guest personally, and their much-loved Fleur-de-Lys Mansion ($160-305) at Russell and Grand has been voted one of the city's top bed-and-breakfasts by countless local and national polls. Each of this home's four spacious, carefully appointed suites is unique and offers views of the gardens below or Reservoir Park across the street. A gourmet breakfast is available to guests every morning, and a four-course dinner can be served in the elegant dining room on any night, upon special request. The Fleur-de-Lys also offers a handful of special weekend packages that change regularly. Carriage rides and in-room massages are often available, too.

Dogtown and the Hill Map 5

DRURY INN & SUITES $$

2111 Sulphur Ave., 314/646-0070,
wwwc.druryhotels.com

The convenient central location of the Drury Inn & Suites near Forest Park ($109-129) makes this brand-new economy lodge one of the best bargains in the area. Located just off the Hampton Avenue ramp at I-44, Drury is a five-minute drive from Forest Park, the Missouri Botanical Garden, and the city's historic South City and Southampton neighborhoods. Downtown is a mere 10-minute drive from here, as are the suburban enclaves of Maplewood and Webster Groves. Though this standard chain hotel is anything but fancy, rooms here are quiet and kept immaculately clean, and the hotel's menu of amenities covers all the basics, from a lounge and restaurant (the locally owned Italian restaurant Bartolino's Osteria) to a workout room and free daily breakfast. (And there's a certain local pride surrounding the Drury chain, since it started in southeast Missouri.) Ask about the Drury's St. Louis Weekend Fun packages. Special discounts are available to those in town for sightseeing and sports events.

HAMPTON INN & SUITES $$

5650 Oakland Ave., 314/655-3993,
www.hamptoninn.hilton.com

Travelers looking for a hotel conveniently located amid the city's many sightseeing destinations will appreciate the clean, comfortable, and affordable accommodations of the Hilton-owned Hampton Inn ($129-189). Though the property itself is not much to write home about, the Hampton Inn's location is great. This mid-priced hotel is right near Forest Park and all of its attractions, including the Saint Louis Zoo, the Saint Louis Art Museum, and the Missouri History Museum. Hotel amenities include a complimentary breakfast, indoor pool, and 24-hour business and fitness centers. The suites afford more room to spread out than a typical Hampton Inn.

RED ROOF INN ST. LOUIS-HAMPTON $

5823 Wilson St., 314/645-0101, www.redroof.com

What the Hampton Red Roof Inn lacks in panache, it makes up for in cost and convenience. The clean, simply furnished rooms here rent for around $74 a night, and access to the motel's WiFi network is available for only $5 extra a night. Most of the rooms also have a small walk-out patio, a great little attribute not often found on the St. Louis hospitality scene. In addition to great rates and the outdoor space, the motel's location couldn't be any better. The Red Roof Inn is just off I-44, at the Hampton Avenue exit, and is less than a 10-minute drive from downtown.

Delmar Loop and University City Map 6

CROWNE PLAZA ST. LOUIS-CLAYTON $

7750 Carondelet Ave., Clayton, 314/726-5400,
www.cpclayton.com

The St. Louis Crowne Plaza ($115-183) offers great rates, plus the centralized convenience of a downtown Clayton location. This executive-class hotel resides in the heart of the Clayton business district and is just three blocks from a MetroLink stop. The Crowne Plaza caters to the corporate set with abundant conference rooms, a business center, a 24-hour fitness room, a restaurant, and same-day dry-cleaning service, but it's kid-friendly, too. Spacious adjoined suites, an indoor/outdoor swimming pool, a free arcade, and dog-friendly rooms are among Crowne Plaza's family-oriented offerings. Luxury features in each room, from the two-bedroom executive suite to the single-room double, include Italian marble showers, Simmons pillow-top mattresses, and plush bathrobes. Hungry guests should bypass the just-okay on-site grill and head instead for one of Clayton's great restaurants.

MARRIOTT RESIDENCE INN ST. LOUIS GALLERIA $$

8011 Galleria Pkwy., 314/862-1900, www.marriott.com

Sure, it's part of a big chain, but the Marriott Residence Inn ($169-189) does offer home-like accommodations. This is a good option for businesspeople or for families who want to save a bit of money by preparing a few meals in their hotel room. Every suite at this Brentwood hotel comes equipped with a full kitchen, comfortable work and seating areas, satellite TV, free WiFi, a daily newspaper, and complimentary parking arrangements. This Residence Inn boasts close proximity to some of the city's finest shopping destinations, including downtown Clayton and the Saint Louis Galleria

Moonrise Hotel

Mall. Guest amenities available upon request include on-site laundry, an inexpensive grocery-shopping service, and dinner delivery from a handful of area restaurants. A complimentary hot breakfast is served every day off the lobby.

MOONRISE HOTEL $$$

6177 Delmar Blvd., 314/721-1111, www.moonrisehotel.com

A standout among St. Louis's crop of high-concept boutique hotels, the Moonrise Hotel ($209-309) fills a too-long-vacant niche in one of the city's most popular entertainment districts. This plush, sophisticated hotel is located on the Delmar Loop, just steps from The Pageant. Opened in 2009, the Moonrise was the first hotel in this area in years. Envisioned and bankrolled by Loop entrepreneur Joe Edwards, this boutique hotel puts visitors within shouting distance of a MetroLink stop, not to mention the neighborhood's myriad restaurants and shops. LCD flat-screen televisions, luxury bedding, and Aveda bath products are standard in every one of the hotel's unique moon-themed suites (and the all-important WiFi is free). Nice in-room St. Louis touches include locally roasted Kaldi's premium coffee and Bissinger's chocolates. Guests are also welcome to take advantage of Moonrise's bike-rental service and a complimentary shuttle to Clayton, the Central West End, and Midtown.

THE RITZ-CARLTON ST. LOUIS $$$

100 Carondelet Plaza, Clayton, 314/863-6300, www.ritzcarlton.com

The Ritz-Carlton St. Louis ($299-429) lives up to the implicit promises made by its brand name. This downtown Clayton hotel represents the height of luxury and elegance—and, if you can pull yourself away from your beautiful room and the snazzy piano lounge, you'll find you're within walking distance of dozens of restaurants and shops. Every room includes a broad private balcony, offering lovely views of the city below. The hotel houses three restaurants, one of which serves the most sumptuous Sunday brunch in the area. The Ritz-Carlton is

HOTELS

a good option for guests traveling sans car; it is directly across from a MetroLink stop.

SEVEN GABLES INN $$$

26 N. Meramec Ave., Clayton, 314/863-8400, www.sevengablesinn.com

Seven Gables Inn ($148-199) is a 32-room boutique hotel in the middle of downtown Clayton. Guests spending the night here will revel in the attention to detail. There are always freshly baked cookies in the lobby, Bissinger's chocolates accompany the turn-down service, and a copy of Nathaniel Hawthorne's *The House of Seven Gables* comes standard with every room. Staying here is a little like visiting your hip grandmother, and you can't beat the Seven Gables' location and extras. This cozy Tudor-style chalet is only two blocks from the Clayton MetroLink stop, has its own restaurant (American eclectic), provides free WiFi, offers a complimentary continental breakfast, and serves free wine and cheese on the weekends.

SHERATON CLAYTON PLAZA HOTEL $$

7730 Bonhomme Ave., Clayton, 314/863-0400, www.sheratonclaytonhotel.com

The suburban location of the Sheraton Plaza Hotel in Clayton ($139-189) puts guests within blocks of this ritzy borough's busy downtown—and shopaholics should note that it's just a mile away from the Saint Louis Galleria and only five miles northeast of the super-spendy Plaza

Frontenac. Every room here features updated yet classic decor. There aren't many surprising twists here (with few exceptions, a Sheraton is a Sheraton is a Sheraton), but service is great and rooms are comfy. Among the Sheraton Plaza Hotel's many convenient amenities are a full-service salon, a car-rental service, a business center, a lounge, and a heated pool and sundeck. Those who travel with their pets should know that furry critters are welcome here for just a small deposit.

SPRINGHILL SUITES ST. LOUIS BRENTWOOD $

1231 Strassner Dr., Brentwood, 314/647-8400, www.marriott.com

The spacious, South Beach-style rooms of the Marriott-owned SpringHill Suites ($129) boast a clean, modern decor and abundant amenities at some of the area's most reasonable rates. Visitors will love this stylish hotel's close proximity to Lambert-St. Louis International Airport, the Saint Louis Galleria, and downtown Clayton. Springhill is off of Brentwood Boulevard, one block west of I-170, and three minutes from the Clayton business district. In addition to the hotel's great location and friendly, eager-to-please staff, complimentary services include a daily continental breakfast, in-room coffee, a coin-operated laundry center, and valet dry-cleaning. The views aren't much, but you just can't beat the price or the location.

EXCURSIONS FROM ST. LOUIS

St. Louis is great in a lot of ways: low cost of living, strong diversity, world-class universities and health care, ample cultural experiences, wonderful restaurants. Still, sometimes even the most proud St. Louisans just want to see their city in the rear-view mirror. Fortunately, there are several great day- and weekend-trip options that are as convenient as they are affordable. Three of the most popular options—the collegiate streets of Columbia, the rolling hills of Missouri wine country, and the family-friendly shores of Lake of the Ozarks—are also three of the closest.

Columbia is the quintessential college town. About two hours from downtown St. Louis, this collegiate burg offers many cultural events, great dining, fun boutique shopping, and—of course—the chance to see the Mizzou Tigers on the hardwood and the gridiron. Hotel options are limited in downtown Columbia, but there are affordable lodging places just off the main drag. Proximity to downtown Columbia is key, as the town's many restaurants and shops are concentrated in these 43 square blocks.

Many St. Louisans own timeshares at Lake of the Ozarks, as this in-state vacation destination offers plenty of recreational options (including boating, golfing, hiking, and waterskiing). Visitors looking for a quiet weekend at the lake are wise not to go at the peak of summer, when many of the boats turn into floating keg parties. Most of the time, though, the Lake of the Ozarks is a pleasant getaway.

In the wonderfully temperate fall and spring months, many St. Louisans head to Missouri wine country for a mini-retreat. This area is

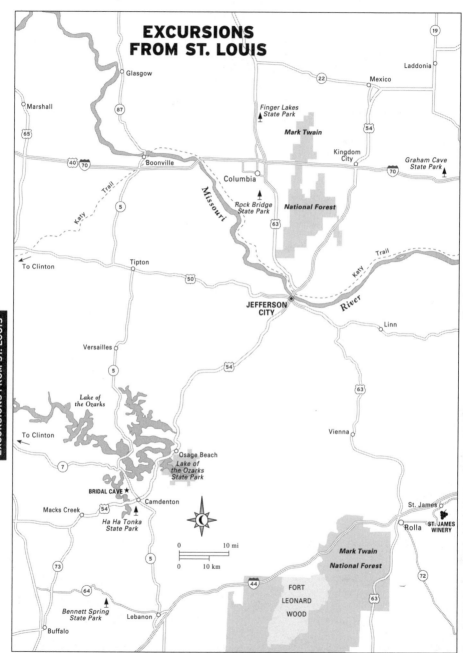

EXCURSIONS FROM ST. LOUIS

Laddonia

Glasgow

Mexico

Marshall

Finger Lakes
State Park

Mark Twain

Boonville

Kingdom
City

Graham Cave
State Park

Columbia

National Forest

Rock Bridge
State Park

To Clinton

Tipton

Katy Trail

Missouri River

JEFFERSON
CITY

Linn

Versailles

Lake of
the Ozarks

To Clinton

Vienna

Osage Beach
Lake of
the Ozarks
State Park

BRIDAL CAVE ★

Macks Creek

Camdenton

St. James

Rolla

ST. JAMES
WINERY

Ha Ha Tonka
State Park

Mark Twain

National Forest

0   10 mi

0   10 km

FORT

LEONARD

WOOD

Bennett Spring
State Park

Lebanon

Buffalo

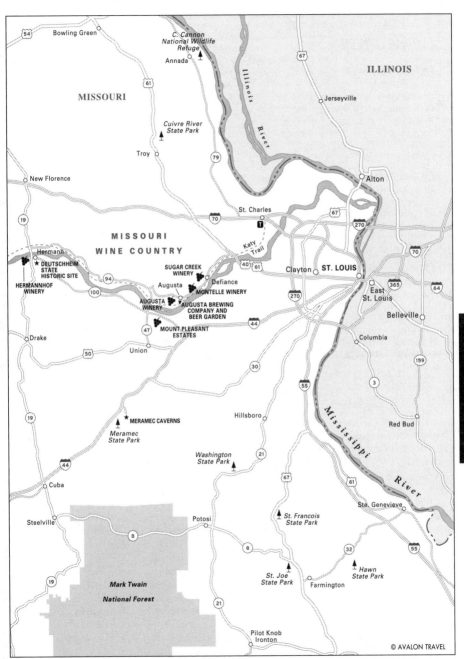

© AVALON TRAVEL

HIGHLIGHTS

LOOK FOR ◖ TO FIND RECOMMENDED SIGHTS, ACTIVITIES, DINING, AND LODGING.

◖ **Best Folk-Art Collection:** Lauded by arts-and-crafts publications nationwide, **Bluestem Missouri Crafts** in downtown Columbia is a can't-miss stop. The gallery-caliber work and artful displays make Bluestem a great place to browse, and the prices are so reasonable that visitors can afford to take something home (page 141).

◖ **Best Place to Feel Like a Student Again:** The **University of Missouri** campus is pretty much the Platonic ideal of a university. Stroll along the broad lawns, taking in the lovely Peace Park and the affecting Memorial Union. Wear a Mizzou sweatshirt and you'll fit right in (page 141).

◖ **Best Underground Attraction:** While some caverns are little more than cheesy tourist traps, **Bridal Cave** near Lake of the Ozarks is a truly stunning sight. This series of subterranean rooms got its name from the delicate "veils" of stalactites–and from the Osage Indian marriage ceremonies that were once performed here (page 144).

◖ **Best Golf Excursion:** There are plenty of nice golf courses in the St. Louis area, but

Osage National Golf Resort is a true golf getaway. The course, which was designed by no less a golfer than Arnold Palmer, is both challenging and gorgeous. Thirsty players can repair to the bar inside the 20,000-square-foot clubhouse (page 145).

◖ **Most Picturesque Winery:** When St. Louisans think about Missouri wine country, they usually conjure up images of **Hermannhof Winery.** This idyllic German-style vineyard is the perfect place to relax, picnic, and (of course!) drink wine (page 148).

◖ **Best Wine Innovators:** The winemakers at **Sugar Creek Winery** do things a bit differently. Rather than bottling the same varietals that are available at other wineries, they take those varietals and create bold and bright blends. The results are nothing short of delicious (page 149).

◖ **Best Place to Commune with Nature:** The **Katy Trail** just might be Missouri's most beautiful hike-and-bike path, with a perfect view of the Missouri River below. Lush greenery and the occasional darting eagle complete the tableau (page 149).

also well worth the trip for out-of-towners; the vistas are gorgeous, and the wines are affordable and often quite good. Antiques buffs will find browsing bliss in the antiques shops of Hermann and Augusta.

PLANNING YOUR TIME

Although Columbia, Missouri wine country, and Lake of the Ozarks are all just a pleasant drive or train ride away, visitors should take caution while planning their time. If you have just three or four days to explore St. Louis, you'll find plenty to do in the city itself and may want to save day trips and weekend excursions for a later visit. Missouri wine country's bed-and-breakfasts are lovely, but the area can also be enjoyed in an afternoon.

Consider arriving in Hermann or Augusta around lunchtime, savoring a light meal at one of the area restaurants, and then heading to a winery for a tour and tasting. You can be back in St. Louis by supper. Columbia is about two hours away and, as such, could feasibly be explored in a day. The only downside to that strategy is that—as is true of most college towns—the main thoroughfare really comes alive at night. Lake of the Ozarks is a little over three hours away, so making the round-trip in a single day would be rather exhausting and impractical. Plan on staying at least one night at the lake, to give yourself time to enjoy the steak-and-seafood restaurants, the fun bars, the great golf, *and* the lovely hiking and biking trails.

Columbia

Spend even a few days in St. Louis, and you will see a great many "Mizzou" bumper stickers, T-shirts, and ball caps. As home to the University of Missouri's flagship campus, Columbia holds a special place in the hearts of countless St. Louisans and offers visitors the vitality of any great college town: buzzing coffeehouses, funky boutiques, dusty used bookstores, and live music almost every night. The annual True/False Film Fest draws filmmakers and movie buffs from around the world. And, of course, sports are a huge draw, with the university's football team having recently emerged from years of futility to become a national-title contender.

As hard as it might be to imagine when you see the throngs of students walking through downtown and packing the (smoke-free) bars, Columbia is more than just a college town. Its best restaurants match up course-for-course with St. Louis's standouts, and the nearby parks and trails offer a sense of escape from the urban bustle. Families will want to plan trips around outdoor recreation because there are very few kid-specific attractions.

SIGHTS

◖ Bluestem Missouri Crafts

The downtown location of **Bluestem Missouri Crafts** (13 S. 9th St., 573/442-0211, www. bluestemmissouricrafts.com, Mon.-Thurs. and Sat. 10am-6pm, Fri. 10am-8pm, Sun. noon-5pm), named "Top Retailer of American Crafts" by *Niche* magazine, features the work of more than 300 artists and craftspeople from Missouri and neighboring states. Here you can browse jewelry, ceramics, quilts, paper vases, and glass art; the selection is limited only by the artists' imaginations. The staff is handy with information about the artists, and custom gift-wrapping is offered. You can preview and order much of Bluestem's inventory on its website, but work this unique really should be seen in person.

Columbia Art League

The **Columbia Art League** (CAL, 207 S. 9th St., 573/443-8838, www.columbiaartleague. org, Tues.-Fri. 11:30am-5:30pm, Sat. 11am-5pm) is both an exhibition space and an ambassador of the arts. Exhibitions run for six weeks on average. Shows have featured "The Horse in Fine Art" and the work of art professors from Missouri colleges and universities, and each year CAL hosts several juried competitions. CAL also offers classes for kids and adults, including weekend workshops that visitors could include on a trip. Each June CAL hosts the Art in the Park Festival at Stephens Lake Park, with more than 100 artists, live music, and interactive activities.

Columbia Cosmopolitan Recreation Area

Covering 533 acres, the **Columbia Cosmopolitan Recreation Area** (1615 Business Loop 70 West, 573/874-7460)—more commonly known as Cosmo Park—is the largest park in Columbia. There are fields for football, soccer, and softball as well as a golf course, tennis courts, and a roller-hockey rink. Kids might enjoy the skate park and the track for remote-control cars. The 1.75-mile Cosmo Nature Trail winds through wetlands and, if you're lucky, might include the sight of dam-building beavers. Each summer Cosmo Park hosts the Show-Me State Games. This Olympics-inspired competition gathers amateur athletes in nearly three dozen events, from the triathlon to paintball, over three consecutive weekends in July and August.

◖ University of Missouri

The University of Missouri—the first public university west of the Mississippi—sprawls over 1,358 acres in the heart of Columbia. No visit to the campus is complete without a stop in front of the Columns, the only part of Academic Hall to survive an 1892 fire. Other

EXPERIENCE THE DISTRICT

Every college town worth its salt needs a bustling arts-and-culture hub, and The District gives Columbia plenty of cool cachet. Shops, clubs, coffeehouses, galleries, cafés, and bars are packed into a wonderfully walkable 43 square blocks. (The District's website claims the area has 5,900 parking spaces, and while that's probably technically true, parking in Columbia is rarely convenient or free.)

Feel like a college kid again when you get your caffeine fix at **Lakota Coffee Company** (24 S. 9th St., 573/874-2852, www.lakotacoffee.com), a lodge-inspired coffeehouse with abundant laptop space and the best espresso in town. Grab a groovy, earth-friendly bite at **Main Squeeze Natural Foods Café and Juice Bar** (28 S. 9th St., 573/817-5616, www.main-squeeze.com); the vegetarian fare here is so good that even carnivores are won over (seriously).

Shops in The District range from wink-wink incense-and-lava-lamp stores to high-end boutiques—there are hours' worth of browsing here. **Britches** (130 S. 9th St., 573/499-1401) carries au courant clothes that don't tip into super-trendy territory (think good denim and lines by stalwarts like Kenneth Cole). The clothes at **Elly's Couture** (914 E. Broadway, 573/499-4401, www.ellyscouture.com) are a bit more trend-hugging, but the cruise-cute pieces from Lacoste are hard to resist. Feel the collegiate love by stopping in **Tiger Spirit** (111 S. 9th St., 573/449-0608, www.tigerspirit.

com), where Mizzou memorabilia fills every bit of the shop's 2,400-square-foot space. Other great specialty shops in The District include the yummy parfumerie **Makes Scents** (19 S. 9th St., 573/445-1611, www.makesscentsonline.com); the superbly stocked **Top Ten Wines** (111 S. 9th St., 573/442-2207, www.toptenwines.net), which is worth a visit just to chat with the incredibly knowledgeable staff; and **A la Campagne** (918 E. Broadway, 573/815-9464), an antiques shop that is always chic and never fussy.

Of course, a college's cultural district must also be graded by its nightlife, and The District passes (with honors). At Columbia's cultural core is **The Blue Note** (17 N. 9th St., 573/874-1944, www.thebluenote.com), a live-music venue that books the best of the best. Performances here tend toward indie-rock (TV on the Radio, Ani DiFranco, Sonic Youth) and alt-country (Wilco, Avett Brothers, Old 97s), but the Note also lets folks in for live broadcasts of political speeches and Mizzou sporting events. Great nightlife continues at college-student faves like **Harpo's** (29 S. 10th St., 573/443-5418, www.harposcomo.com) and **Quinton's & Tonic** (124 S. 9th St., 573/815-1047, www.quintonsandtonic.com). Looking for something a little less Animal House? Consider a nightcap at **Sycamore** (800 E. Broadway, 573/874-8090, www.sycamorerestaurant.com), where the bar stays open till midnight on Fridays and Saturdays.

notable spots include the Memorial Tower, a Gothic structure intended as a memorial to alumni killed in World War I, and the lovely Peace Park (once the locus of student protests against the Vietnam War and now a popular gathering spot). The university's athletic facilities are south of the main academic campus. The Missouri Tigers play on Faurot Field at Memorial Stadium, while the men's and women's basketball teams call the 15,061-seat Mizzou arena home. The campus is an easy walk from downtown Columbia. With many of

Mizzou's 27,000 undergraduate students living on campus or nearby, the entire city can often seem like university property.

RESTAURANTS
Booches Billiard Hall (110 S. 9th St., 573/874-9519, entrées less than $10) is a 125-year-old treasure: a bar and pool hall that happens to serve some of the best burgers not just in Columbia, but in the whole country. The burgers are rather small—most diners order more than one—and each is served without fanfare

on a sheet of wax paper. Not in the mood for a burger? Come back to Booches another time. The kitchen (a grill behind the bar) doesn't turn out much else, not even French fries. Booches is cash-only, and you can buy a T-shirt proclaiming its famous policy: "Closed on Sundays. See you in church."

Stories abound of University of Missouri alumni having frozen pizza from ◖ **Shakespeare's Pizza** (225 S. 9th St., 573/449-2454, www.shakespeares.com, Sun.-Thurs. 11am-10pm, Fri.-Sat. 11am-11pm, bar opens daily at 4pm, entrées $15) shipped halfway around the globe. It's *that* good. The dough is made from scratch each day, the cheese is aged provolone, and the pepperoni is hand-sliced nice and thick. The restaurant itself is the Platonic ideal of the college hangout: dim, loud, and drowning in pitchers of beer. Drinks are served in plastic souvenir cups—most St. Louisans own at least one. Shakespeare's is open "past your bedtime," making it a perfect end to a night on the town.

Step inside ◖ **Sycamore** (800 E. Broadway, 573/874-8090, www.sycamorerestaurant.com, Mon.-Fri. 11am-2pm and Mon.-Sat. 5pm-10pm, bar Mon.-Thurs. 5pm-11pm and Fri.-Sat. 5pm-midnight, entrées $22), and you could suddenly be in a city two or three times Columbia's size. This large, high-ceilinged restaurant has a cosmopolitan feel, from the beautiful bar to the open kitchen situated on a mezzanine above the dining room. The menu features contemporary American bistro fare, with a focus on local produce and meat. Pork dishes are a sure bet. Or you can build a meal out of several of the fantastic appetizers, like the thick-cut fries dusted with Parmigiano-Reggiano cheese or the homemade gnocchi. The lunch menu offers salads, soups, and sandwiches at very reasonable prices.

The name is literal: You enter **The Wine Cellar & Bistro** (505 Cherry St., 573/442-7281, www.winecellarbistro.com, Mon.-Fri. 11am-2pm and Mon.-Sat. 5pm-10pm, Sun. 5pm-9pm, entrées $27) at ground level and then descend into the casually elegant dining room.

The atmosphere is perfect for either a romantic dinner or a relaxed get-together with friends. Owner and executive chef Craig Cyr's menu reflects his traditional technique and his interest in exotic ingredients and unexpected flavor combinations: lamb, duck, wild-boar, and seafood dishes as satisfying as they are dazzling. Cyr's wife, Sarah, is in charge of the wine list, which *Wine Spectator* magazine has honored with its Award of Excellence. Beer connoisseurs will want to check out the restrooms, which are decorated with old beer cans.

HOTELS

When it comes to Columbia hotels, the main three selling points are: location, location, location. Visitors to this college town won't find much in the way of historic B&Bs or chic boutique hotels, but most lodging options are clean, well priced, and very close to downtown.

The **Hampton Inn & Suites** (1225 Fellows Pl., 573/214-2222, hamptoninn3.hilton.com, rooms start at $129) is within walking distance of the University of Missouri campus, as well as downtown shops and restaurants. Free parking, fast WiFi, and a complimentary breakfast make for a comfy and hassle-free stay. Other hotel options include the **Hilton Garden Inn** (3300 Vandiver Dr., 573/814-5464, hiltongardeninn3.hilton.com, rooms start at $119), just a five-minute drive from downtown, and a **La Quinta Inn & Suites** (2500 I-70 Dr. SW, 573/445-1899, www.lq.com, rooms start at $75), which is the most affordable of the bunch.

PRACTICALITIES
Tourist Office
The **Columbia Convention and Visitors Bureau** is located at 300 South Providence Road (573/875-1231, www.visitcolumbiamo.com).

Media
The *Columbia Missourian* (www.columbiamissourian.com) and the *Columbia Daily Tribune* (www.columbiatribune.com) are the area's two daily newspapers.

EXCURSIONS FROM ST. LOUIS

Getting There

The drive from downtown St. Louis to downtown Columbia is straightforward. From St. Louis, take I-70 west for approximately two hours to Exit 128. Turn left at North College Avenue and then right onto East Broadway, and you'll be on downtown Columbia's major thoroughfare. You can ride **Greyhound** (www.greyhound.com) from St. Louis to Columbia; buses depart in the early morning and early evening from the Downtown station. An even cheaper option is the **MegaBus** (www.megabus.com/us). The Chicago-Kansas City line makes a daily stop in Columbia. Round-trip tickets are around $30 per person.

Getting Around

Downtown Columbia and the University of Missouri campus are wonderfully walkable. Parking is another matter, especially when the university is in session. Make sure to have change and cash on hand to feed meters and pay for garage spots. The Columbia Transit provides bus service throughout the area, but outside of downtown a car is useful.

Lake of the Ozarks

A weekend at the Lake of the Ozarks means different things to different people. Some St. Louisans have many fond memories of childhood summers spent on the lake's sandy shores. Others think of it as a business conference destination, thanks to plentiful golf courses and convention-center-huge hotel ballrooms. Still others will wink knowingly at a mention of Lake of the Ozarks—they're undoubtedly thinking of the secluded area called Party Cove, which *The New York Times* dubbed a "floating bacchanal."

The reasons for going to Lake of the Ozarks are varied, but the fact is that people flock there in droves. The body of water itself—one of the largest man-made lakes in the nation—is great for boaters and water-skiers. (Swimmers, on the other hand, should be advised that this isn't exactly the cleanest place around.) The glittering lake and hilly topography make the region a truly lovely place, particularly once you get off the main tourist drag and away from the bars and tchotchke shops. The higher-end restaurants serve good steaks and seafood in heaping portions, and the resorts offer a variety of spa treatments. Lake of the Ozarks prides itself on being a family-friendly destination, and with the exception of Party Cove and a few other boozy hangouts, it truly is. Water parks, swimming pools, and miniature golf courses abound.

SIGHTS

◖ Bridal Cave

More than 2,000 couples have wed in **Bridal Cave** (526 Bridal Cave Rd., Camdenton, 573/346-2676, www.bridalcave.com), which is full of veil-like stalactites and was once the site of Osage Indian marriage ceremonies. Even if you're not interested in a subterranean wedding, the Bridal Cave is worth seeing. The cool temperatures make it a nice escape from southwestern Missouri summers, and the rock formations are truly lovely. The Bridal Cave contains more onyx formations than any other cavern. "Soda-straw" formations and enormous columns fill each room of the Bridal Cave. Guided tours, which leave every few minutes and last about an hour, are the best way to see and learn about the cave. Admission is $16 for visitors age 13 and up, and $8 for ages 5-12.

Lake of the Ozarks State Park

At 17,626 acres, the beautiful **Lake of the Ozarks State Park** (304 Hwy. 134, Kaiser, 573/348-2694, www.mostateparks.com/park/lake-ozarks-state-park) is the largest park in Missouri. This is a great place to escape the touristy noise of the lake's bars and resorts, as the emphasis here is truly on nature. Hikers and bicyclists can take advantage of the park's 12 trails, which wind along 85 miles of shoreline

© 123RF.COM

rushing natural spring flowing into the Lake of the Ozarks

and through old-growth hickory forests. Many families opt to camp here rather than stay at a resort, and there are nearly 250 campsites (some are super-primitive, while others offer electricity hookups). The park's two public beaches are prime spots for fishing, swimming, and boating. Boaters should pick up an informational booklet about the Lake of the Ozarks Aquatic Trail, a buoy-marked boat trail that highlights significant spots.

GOLF
Old Kinderhook

The stunning **Old Kinderhook golf course** (20 Eagle Ridge Rd., Camdenton, 573/317-3500, www.oldkinderhook.com), designed by Tom Weiskopf, offers a golfing experience that capitalizes on the natural land features of southwest Missouri. The course welcomes players of all skill levels, and you don't have to be a birdie-shooting superstar to appreciate the waterfalls and flowering trees that dot Old Kinderhook's landscape. Amenities here include a clubhouse and pro shop, a health and

fitness area, and meeting rooms. Both fine and casual dining are offered. Play 18 holes for $55 to $69 Monday through Thursday; on Friday, Saturday, and Sunday, the fee is $55 to $95.

◖ Osage National Golf Resort

Golfers from throughout the Midwest make it a point to play at **Osage National Golf Resort** (400 Osage Hills Rd., Lake Ozark, 866/365-1950, www.osagenational.com). Living legend Arnold Palmer designed the course in 1992, and the bentgrass greens and zoysia fairways provide an experience as lovely as it is challenging. Because of the popularity of this course, it's recommended that prospective golfers reserve a tee time no less than 48 hours in advance. Eighteen holes will cost you $45 to $65 Monday through Thursday, and $45 to $80 Friday through Sunday. The 20,000-foot clubhouse houses the Eagle View Sports Bar & Grille, a restaurant that offers everything from onion rings to blue-point mussels.

RESTAURANTS

Dinner at the 🏰 **Blue Heron** (Business Hwy. 54 and Horseshoe Bend Pkwy., Lake Ozark, 573/365-4646, http://theblueheronrestaurant.net, Tues.-Fri. 5:30pm-10pm, Sat. 5pm-10pm, closed in winter, entrées $40) is a treat. Everything about the place is oversized and opulent, from the gilded dining room to the house specialty—a huge deep-fried lobster tail served atop shoestring potatoes. If you're looking to indulge while at Lake of the Ozarks, this is the place to do it. Other restaurants tout their own deep-fried lobster, but the Blue Heron did it first and does it best. The lengthy menu is meat-centric, with generous cuts served in classical preparations. There are also quite a few European options (schnitzel, Dover sole meunière), no doubt thanks to owner Joseph Boer's Dutch heritage. A first-generation American, the delightful, avuncular Boer circulates through the dining room every night, offering after-dinner cordials to everyone (although pretty women seem to get first dibs).

At **J. Bruner's** (5166 Hwy. 54, Osage Beach, 573/348-2966, www.jbruners.com, daily 5pm-9pm, cocktail lounge opens daily at 4:30pm, entrées $25), the recipe for success is a straightforward one: Serve luxurious food in an unpretentious setting. Cultivate a strong wine list, offer weekend specials, and throw in a few unexpected twists—like a selection of adults-only ice-cream drinks. J. Bruner's hasn't changed much in its several decades of operation, and for its many faithful patrons that's a *good* thing. It's worth making sure your trip to the lake falls on a Friday or Saturday, as those are the nights that J. Bruner's offers its outstanding prime rib.

Whether you've built up an appetite waterskiing or just need a big meal to soak up last night's margaritas, **J.J. Twig's Pizza & Pub** (1815 Bagnell Dam Blvd., Lake Ozark, 573/365-9911, www.jjtwigs.com, Mon.-Fri. 11am-midnight, Sat. 11am-1am, Sun. 10am-4pm, entrées $10) has you covered. This family-run pizza place serves up the best pies in town and specializes in "double-deckers": hubcap-sized pizzas stacked with two layers of crust, cheese, and toppings. Other options, such as

lasagna and chicken parmesan, are serviceable but not nearly as good as the pizza.

Some area restaurants deserve the following backhanded compliment: "Pretty good—for Lake of the Ozarks." Not so with 🏰 **On the Rise Bakery** (5439 Osage Beach Pkwy., Osage Beach, 573/348-4224, www.ontherisebakery.com, Wed.-Mon. 7am-3pm, entrées $10), which could be plunked down in the middle of St. Louis or Chicago and still be one of the best spots in town. Helmed by Culinary Institute of America graduate Michael Castle and his wife, Cheryl, On the Rise represents a welcome departure from typical lake fare. You won't find deep-fried seafood or neon-hued shooters here. Instead, you'll be served delicious freshly baked breads and pastries in addition to Kobe burgers, wood-fired pizza, and lobster pot pie. Wine is available; wet T-shirt contests are not.

HOTELS

The 🏰 **Lodge of Four Seasons** (315 Four Seasons Dr., Lake Ozark, 573/365-3000 or 888/265-5500, www.4seasonsresort.com, rooms start at $109, condos at $349) is one of the Lake's spiffiest overnight options. There are 350 guest rooms at the Lodge of Four Seasons, and furnished condominiums are also available. Many rooms feature lake views, natural-rock walls and gas fireplaces. Nightly turndown service is available. The Lodge of Four Seasons caters more to the adult set than to kiddos, so don't expect lots of kid-friendly options. That's a plus for people who just want to relax, and the on-site Spa Shiki offers a full menu of luxurious treatments. There are several restaurants on the property, and—as is true at most Lake of the Ozarks eateries—the fare is almost hilariously over-the-top. Think batter-fried turkey, chicken Oscar, and a massive lamb porterhouse. Healthier options are available, of course, but for most folks the lake is all about indulgence.

The sprawling **Tan-Tar-A Resort** (494 Tan Tar A Dr., Osage Beach, 573/348-3131, www.tan-tar-a.com, $110-173; call for special packages and conference rates) is a favorite destination for family reunions and business conferences. The rolling golf course is perfect for on-the-green client meetings, and Tan-Tar-A offers plenty of kid-friendly options (including multiple swimming pools and a water park). Choose a standard hotel room in the main complex, or reserve a small house in the "Estates" section of the resort. The main hotel complex is within walking distance of Tan-Tar-A's shops and restaurants; guests staying in the Estates must drive a few miles. The rooms themselves are nothing special (think early-'90s decor and spartan bathrooms), but they're clean and, for the most part, quiet. The on-site Black Bear Lodge offers a great full breakfast, and there's also a food court (with a Burger King and Sbarro) for late-night snacking. Avoid Wind Rose, Tan-Tar-A's "fine dining" option, and head to Blue Heron or J. Bruner's instead.

PRACTICALITIES
Tourist Office
The **Lake of the Ozarks Convention and Visitor Bureau** is at 5816 Osage Beach Parkway in Osage Beach (573/348-1599, www.funlake.com).

Media
The **Lake News Online** (www.lakenewsonline.com) is the area's news website.

Getting There and Around
The drive from St. Louis to Lake of the Ozarks is a very pretty one. From the city, take I-44 west to Exit 195 toward St. James. Make a right at MO-68, and then make another right at US-63. Then, take a left at MO-42. This route, also known as West 5th Street, is beautifully bucolic. The gentle hills of MO-42 lead up to US-54. Take a left at US-54, drive for about 10 minutes, and you'll be in the heart of Lake of the Ozarks. Do know that neither trains nor buses make the St. Louis-to-Lake of the Ozarks trip, so you will need to rent a car if you would like to visit the lake.

The best way to get around Lake of the Ozarks is by car. There's very little in the way of public transportation.

Missouri Wine Country

Missouri's wine country is a cherished getaway for St. Louisans looking to escape the noise and stress of city life. The rolling hills and bluffs of this picturesque region are less than an hour from the city, making a wine-country jaunt the ideal day trip. Visitors wishing to spend a weekend in this pastoral paradise certainly can, as there are many quaint and affordable bed-and-breakfasts. Augusta and Hermann, the small towns nestled among the wineries, boast a handful of lovely inns. There are also plenty of restaurants and antiques shops.

Visitors to Augusta and Hermann will find old-world charm in spades. Hermann centers around a Main Street that's straight out of a Norman Rockefeller print, but be advised that there's little in the way of grocery-shopping or entertainment (outside of drinking wine, of course). But it's precisely this lack of hubbub that makes Hermann so appealing; pack a picnic and capitalize on the opportunity to enjoy true serenity. The views here are outstanding, and sweeping vistas can be enjoyed from many vantage points throughout the region.

The wine-making operations here are still young (which explains why some people do a double-take at the mention of "Missouri wine"). The area was established as a wine region in the 1850s, but progress was halted by Prohibition and then stymied by economic depression for a full 40 years after that. Despite this late start, Missouri winemakers have made some notable achievements. The zinfandel-style reds made from the region's own Norton grapes have earned acclaim in international competitions. The Missouri Vignole, a lovely dry white with notes of gardenias and peach pits, has been garnering praise as well. Winemakers throughout the region are friendly, knowledgeable, and unfailingly generous—tastings are free at all wineries.

WINERIES
Augusta Winery

Augusta Winery (5601 High St., Augusta, 888/667-9463, www.augustawinery.com, Mon.-Fri. 10am-5:30pm, Sat. 10am-6pm, Sun. noon-6pm) may not have the old-world elegance of other area wineries, but it offers some fantastic wines at the lowest per-bottle price in the region. There's not much more to the place than a small tasting room, bottling facilities, and a narrow patio, but the tasting counter is always packed. The award-winning wines start at $7 per bottle and peak around $20 (Augusta's luscious pinot noir-style Chambourcin is a real bargain at just $12 a bottle). Visitors may notice some similarities between the wines sold here and those sold at the Montelle Winery, and with good reason: Augusta's owner purchased Montelle in 1998 and oversees both operations.

ⓒ Hermannhof Winery

As its name suggests, the **Hermannhof Winery** (330 E. 1st. St., Hermann, 800/393-0100, www.hermannhof.com, Mon.-Sat. 10am-5pm, Sun. 11am-5pm) is in the historic small town of Hermann and has a German lineage. The winery's cozy red-brick manor, Bavarian-style guest houses, and stone cellars were built in the 1850s and are a testament to the craftsmanship of Hermannhof's founders. Picnickers can sit beneath the grape arbor near the main house or snag a shady spot on the winery's rolling lawn. Beneath this lawn are 10 stone cellars, which produce 15,000 cases of wine each year. Hermannhof's casks are made from white oak harvested in France and Missouri, and the winery is a two-time winner of the Brown-Forman trophy for "Best New World White," but buyers should always taste first. Vintages vary greatly in quality, and at upwards of $25 a bottle, you don't want to get a bum year. In addition to a host of reds, whites, and sparkling wines, Hermannhof

sells a selection of cheeses and locally made German-style sausages.

Montelle Winery

Montelle Winery (201 Montelle Dr., Augusta, 636/228-4464, www.montelle.com, Mon.-Thurs. 10am-5:30pm, Sat. 10am-10pm, Sun. 11am-6pm), off of Highway 94, offers some of the area's absolute best views. Visitors can see all the way to the Missouri River from the winery's expansive, multi-level deck. Coolers and picnic baskets are prohibited beyond the parking lot, but the gift shop sells a nice selection of domestic cheeses, sausages, sandwiches, and pizzas. Fruit and sandwich trays can be ordered in advance, and a three-course dinner is offered on weekend evenings (just be sure to reserve a spot at least 48 hours prior to arrival). Montelle was opened in 1970 by Clayton Byers, one of the pioneers responsible for revitalizing the entire Missouri wine region. In addition to making some great Vignoles and a number of fruit wines, Montelle distills grappa and a brandy made from Golden Delicious apples. These, too, are available for tasting—although at a small additional charge.

Mount Pleasant Estates

Mount Pleasant Estates (5634 High St., Augusta, 636/482-9463, www.mountpleasant.com, Mon.-Fri. 11am-5pm, Sat.-Sun. 11am-5:30pm) is the oldest operating winery in Augusta and the most popular winery in the region. Manicured grounds and stone paths weave their way through an assemblage of quaint cottages, which house a tasting room, banquet facilities, a market, and a grill. Drinking at Mount Pleasant is no bargain, as visitors must pay restaurant-markup prices to enjoy a bottle of house wine on the grotto-like patio. Don't even try to buy a bottle at the retail counter and drink it on the patio, as that is strictly prohibited. The rule seems a bit unfair, but the view from the bluffs is worth the extra bucks. Grapes grown at Mount Pleasant include cabernet, merlot, and chardonnay, and the winery's ports have won several awards in recent years. Tours of the winery's cellar and bottling facility are offered at noon and 1pm on Saturdays and Sundays (April-October).

St. James Winery

St. James Winery (540 State Route B, St. James, 800/280-9463, www.stjameswinery.com, Mon.-Sat. 8am-7pm, Sun. 9am-7pm) is in the Ozark Highlands, which makes it a little out of the way for visitors doing a tour of Missouri's wine country. It's off of Highway 44, between the towns of Cuba and Rolla, and is about an hour's drive from Hermann. An early Italian settlement left behind a strong Italian heritage and an equally strong winemaking tradition. St. James Winery's "School House"-label wines are named for the one-room schoolhouse built by the town's original settlers. Complimentary wine tastings and tours are offered daily, and the expansive gift shop boasts an array of gourmet gift items, baskets, and juices. Most of the wines produced here are on the light-bodied side, and the catawba-grape dessert wine is one of St. James's best sellers.

🍷 Sugar Creek Winery

The tasting room at **Sugar Creek Winery** (125 Boone Country Ln., Defiance, 636/987-2400, www.sugarcreekwines.com, Mon.-Sat. 10am-5:30pm, Sun. noon-5:30pm) is nestled inside a charming turn-of-the-20th-century Victorian home. On cold days, visitors are invited to enjoy the hospitality of the home's cozy parlor. When the weather turns warm, wine-drinkers head to the terrace patio, which overlooks the vineyards and the Katy Trail below. Sugar Creek produces a handful of estate wines but is most well-known for its unique blends of the four popular Missouri varietals grown on the premises: Chambourcin, Chardonel, Cynthiana, and Vidal. French and American hybrid grapes are grown here and blended to coax out each varietal's best qualities and brightest notes. The results have been praised by some of the industry's toughest critics. On weekends between April and October, the winery hosts live music, and picnic baskets are welcome.

SIGHTS
Deutschheim State Historic Site

The **Deutschheim State Historic Site** (109 W. 2nd St., Hermann, 573/486-2200, www.mostateparks.com/park/deutschheim-state-historic-site, April-Oct. daily 10am-4pm, Nov.-March Thurs.-Sun. 10am-4pm, free) is dedicated to the preservation of Missouri's rich German heritage. An on-site gallery explores the lives of early German immigrants, who came to Missouri by the thousands between 1820 and 1850. Visitors can also check out a half-timbered barn, a print shop, a faithful re-creation of an 1830s kitchen garden, and two typical 19th-century German-style homes. The park is open during all seasons and hosts some great festivals throughout the year. Among these is Hermann's popular Weihnachtfest, an outdoor winter festival and market that celebrates the Christmas season. Guided tours of the Deutschheim State Historic Site are available daily and depart from the park's main office at 10am, 12:30pm, and 2:30pm.

🍷 Katy Trail

This 225-mile recreational trail, encompassed by Katy Trail State Park and built on the bed of a former railroad track, is one of the longest of its kind in the nation. The **Katy Trail** (www.bikekatytrail.com) hugs the Missouri River and leads hikers and cyclists through some of the state's most beautiful rural corners. Trailheads are located in St. Charles and in the tiny town of Clinton. The trail is made of crushed limestone, and bike-friendly bridges allow one to cross the Missouri River into Hermann, Washington, or Jefferson City for lunch or a night's respite. The trail's outstanding website offers downloadable maps, trail FAQs, up-to-date information on trail conditions, and links to several Katy Trail trip-planning services. To get to St. Charles from St. Louis, take I-70 west to the 5th Street exit. Make a slight right on Boone's Lick Road. Follow Boone's Lick until it turns into Riverside Road. Trailhead parking lots are on the right.

EXCURSIONS FROM ST. LOUIS

RESTAURANTS

A welcoming Augusta restaurant, **Ashley's Rose Restaurant & Lone Eagle Pub** (5567 Walnut St., Augusta, 636/482-4108, Tues.-Thurs. and Sun. 11am-7pm, Fri.-Sat. 11am-9pm, entrées $18) resides in an early-20th-century frame building known as "the white house" and sports a quirky aviation theme. It is cozy (seats about 60 people) and has a fully stocked bar. The menu features about 20 entrées and is fairly straightforward in its aims. Ashley's grills a great steak and offers a popular weekly wiener schnitzel special with homemade sweet-and-sour red cabbage and potato pancakes. The restaurant also offers a handful of nice regional wines and runs some additional specials that change with the season. Come early on the weekend—this tiny place fills up fast.

Augusta Brewing Company (5521 Water St., Augusta, 636/482-2337, www.augusta-brewing.com, Sun.-Mon. and Wed.-Thurs. 11am-6pm, Fri.-Sat. 11am-9pm, entrées $12) is a popular stop for cyclists on the Katy Trail; the restaurant's shady beer garden is just 30 steps from it. Fare here is American pub food with a few traditional German beer haus items thrown in, like the freshly baked Bavarian pretzel served with Tannhauser mustard and a beer brat smothered in house-made sauerkraut. Several locally produced wines are offered in addition to the microbrewery's own handcrafted ales, wheats, and lagers, and the menu recommends several great pairings. In addition to a friendly atmosphere and beautiful surroundings, the restaurant also has a great summer schedule of country and bluegrass music.

A cozy little family restaurant in historic Hermann, **The Cottage Restaurant & Studio** (1185 Hwy. H, Hermann, 573/486-4300, http://cottagerestauranthermann.com, Mon. and Thurs.-Sat. 11am-2pm and 5pm-8pm, Sun. 10am-2pm and 3pm-6:30pm, closed in winter, entrées $15) is a perennial favorite. The food here isn't fancy, but it's very well-prepared—don't miss the golden-brown fried chicken, served with a heaping mound of home-style mashed potatoes. (Also on the Do Not Miss list: homemade pie.) Outdoor seating is available on The Cottage's lovely patio, which overlooks 22 acres of forest. Want to take a painting home with your leftovers? All of the art decorating the walls is for sale, and some of it's great. Besides, the restaurant's motto is "Fried Chicken, Fine Art"—and there's just something undeniably appealing about that.

HOTELS

The hosts of the **◐ H.S. Clay House and Guest Cottage** (219 Public St., Augusta, 314/504-4203, www.hsclayhouse.com, $150-235) bring 50-plus years of hotel-hospitality experience to this B&B. Each spacious suite here offers luxurious amenities on par with a four-star hotel. Covered porches, private balconies, whirlpool tubs, fireplaces, and flat-screen TVs with surround sound are only a few of the inn's great features. Outdoor amenities include an 18,000-square-foot double-tiered deck, swimming pool, and hot tub. The careful clutter and lush landscaped grounds of this whimsical place draw guests back again and again. Hosts Leigh and Alan Buerhe are happy to arrange a romantic gourmet dinner for two in the home's elegant dining room or to recommend a local restaurant. And guests are sent off every morning on the right foot: A gourmet breakfast served in the first-floor common space features handmade specialties like shirred eggs, sage sausage, and custard French toast.

The inviting suites of **The Iron Horse Inn** (207 E. 4th St., Hermann, 573/486-9152, www.theironhorseinn.net, $125-165) exude warmth and comfort—all within walking distance of Hermann's historic Main Street. Each suite in this beautifully restored 1898 Victorian Queen Anne home is completely self-contained (a plus for those not keen on sharing the bathroom with strangers). Visitors here will love the combination of old-fashioned elegance with modern amenities. Some of the suites offer whirlpool baths big enough for two, while others have lovely claw-foot tubs—and every suite is furnished with heirloom antiques. Rhiannon, the Iron Horse's innkeeper, is perhaps the most gracious host in the area. She is happy to give shop and restaurant recommendations to newcomers, and will also make dinner reservations for guests upon their request. In addition to its proximity to Main Street, the Iron Horse is near the riverfront and the Amtrak station.

The School House Bed and Breakfast in Rocheport (504 3rd St., 573/698-2022, www.schoolhousebb.com, $149-279) is a little off the beaten path—about an hour's drive west of Hermann—but well worth a side trip. This unique inn is an expertly converted, turn-of-the-20th-century schoolhouse, and it offers some great modern amenities. The school's original oak floors and 13-foot ceilings accentuate every addition, including private luxury baths complete with whirlpool tubs, fireplaces, antique furnishings, and luxury down bedding. Abundant windows flood every room with great morning light, and during the warm-weather months guests usually begin their day with gourmet coffee in the School House's serene garden. This bed-and-breakfast has been featured in numerous national publications, including *Midwest Living* and *Southern Living*. It is two blocks from the Katy Trail and a mile from Les Bourgeois Vineyards and Winery. Travelers should check the website for last-minute deals, particularly in the off-season.

PRACTICALITIES
Tourist Office
Information about Missouri wine country can be found in the Central region of the **Missouri Division of Tourism** website (www.visitmo.

com). The **Hermann Chamber of Commerce** (312 Market St., 573/486-2744) maintains a tourism web presence at www.visithermann.com. You'll find the **Augusta Chamber of Commerce** (636/228-4005) on the web at www.augusta-missouri.com.

Media
Keep up-to-date on Hermann happenings with the town's weekly newspaper, the *Hermann Advertiser-Courier* (www.hermannadvertisercourier.com). Augusta distributes a bimonthly community newspaper, the *Augusta Neighborhood News* (636/228-4821).

Getting There and Around
Highway 94 is the route to take. This scenic two-lane stretch south of US-40/64 is nicknamed the Weinstrasse, or "Wine Street." There are four family wineries along this road and eight more within a 10-mile radius. Simply take US-40/64 to I-94 and travel south. Numerous signs are posted to point visitors in the right direction.

It is recommended that travelers rent a car and drive, but train service is available as well. **Amtrak** provides train service to Hermann from the historic Kirkwood station and back again, via the *Kansas City Mule* and *Ann Rutledge*. The fare is approximately $20 each way. Visit www.amtrak.com for a complete timetable.

Cyclists should check out the **Katy Trail** (www.bikekatytrail.com), as a 30-mile stretch of this bike route runs directly alongside the Weinstrasse.

EXCURSIONS FROM ST. LOUIS

BACKGROUND

The Setting

GEOGRAPHY AND CLIMATE

St. Louis is located near the geographical center of the United States and stands at the confluence of the Missouri and Mississippi Rivers. Together with the Meramec River, these major waterways constitute the city's most outstanding geographical (and ecological) feature and border the city on nearly every side. The Mississippi River forms much of St. Louis's eastern border, the Missouri forms its northern boundary, and the Meramec River runs along its southern edge. Together, these rivers' broad floodplains have shaped St. Louis's gently rolling topography—and, despite plenty of human intervention, they continue to affect it today. In 1993, a "500-year" flood devastated the area, and in 2008 the waters rose once again, swelling the Meramec River to three times its normal size.

Not surprisingly, St. Louis is built upon the material of riverbeds. Beneath the city's surface is a thick crust of limestone and dolomite, corkscrewed with sinkholes and caves. St. Louis's 62 square miles of zoysia lawn, pavement, and parkscapes hide a vast network of naturally occurring limestone caverns, as well as the seam of two major tectonic plates. The New Madrid Fault Line is a hair's breadth

from the city proper and has been threatening St. Louis with a devastating, non-elective remodeling for the past century. In 1811, one of the largest earthquakes in recorded history toppled chimneys and reversed the flow of the Mississippi River. Residents have felt occasional rumblings ever since—including a spring 2008 quake that measured 5.2 on the Richter scale—and experts predict that an earthquake of even greater magnitude will occur before the year 2040.

The climate of this otherwise landlocked region is characterized by four full seasons and lengthy periods of high heat and humidity. Spring weather arrives as early as March, and July typically brings the year's highest temperatures. On average, St. Louisans suffer temperatures of 100-plus degrees five days out of every year (and temperatures hit record highs during the devastating, statewide drought of summer 2012)—but, on the plus side, growing seasons are long and winters are relatively mild. Winter temperatures hover around 30 degrees Fahrenheit, while summer temps average 80 degrees. St. Louis receives an average of 23 inches of snow per year and more than 46 inches of rain.

The collision of the humid Gulf Stream and cool Canadian air masses helps keep St. Louis's median temperature at approximately 55 degrees—and also causes frequent shifts in weather conditions. Throughout the spring and summer months, severe thunderstorms strafe the city with damaging straight-line winds and (sometimes) golf ball-sized hail. They also whip up an occasional tornado, such as the one that destroyed significant parts of Lambert-St. Louis International Airport in spring 2011. Thunderstorms can cause travel delays, as can the fairly frequent ice storms that occur throughout the winter months. No matter the

season, visitors to St. Louis should check the forecast and come prepared.

ENVIRONMENTAL ISSUES

While St. Louisans often joke about the area's unpredictable weather, the air quality here is no laughing matter. During the summer months, the region is blanketed by warm, heavy air that creates a less-than-ideal environment for allergy sufferers. People who believe themselves to be allergy-free are sometimes proven wrong when they move to St. Louis—thanks to abundant allergens like the yellow-green pollen that dusts windshields beginning in May.

In terms of air pollution, the region's record is fairly clean. St. Louis was the first major city in the nation to enforce a set of laws meant to reduce air pollution. During the 1940s, in an effort to reduce the smog created by coal-burning, St. Louis launched one of the most effective clean-air campaigns to date. Today, the St. Louis Regional Clean Air Partnership continues this breathe-easy mission by monitoring the city's air quality and enforcing measures to reduce harmful vehicle emissions. The organization posts its findings daily via special billboards throughout the area, as well as on its website at www.cleanair-stlouis.com.

The city is also adopting LEED (Leadership in Energy & Environmental Design) standards for much of its new construction. The membership of the Missouri LEED chapter is growing quickly, and the United States Green Building Council has certified a dozen projects throughout the area. Of particular note is the Alberici headquarters, a beautiful wind-powered, sunlit office building not far from Lambert-St. Louis International Airport. For more information on the Missouri Gateway Chapter of the U.S. Green Building Council, visit http://chapters.usgbc.org/stlouis.

History

THE FOUNDING OF ST. LOUIS

St. Louis has acquired quite a few nicknames over the years. "Mound City" is a nod to the area's first inhabitants, ancient tribes who shaped the river valley's topography with elaborate patterns of mounded earth. "Gateway City," St. Louis's more common nickname, refers both to its middle-of-the-country location and to its history; St. Louis was a trailhead during the great western migration. The city's full name is Saint Louis, a moniker bestowed by French settlers in honor of their king, Louis IX.

The French heritage here is strong, and it's particularly evident in the architecture of the city's oldest neighborhoods. In 1673, French explorers Louis Joliet and Jacques Marquette surveyed the Mississippi River Valley, the geographical feature from which St. Louis would rise. Five years later, Robert La Salle claimed the entirety of the river's banks for France and named the territory Louisiana (in honor of King Louis XIV). In the years that followed, the French government established settlements throughout this territory, but it wasn't until 1763 that France decided to make St. Louis the first stop on a north-south trade route.

The following February, French settler Auguste Chouteau laid out the city's New Orleans-inspired grid pattern. St. Louis's life as a successful river city had begun. Trade along this important river route flourished over the next 150 years, thanks in no small part to the introduction of the steamboat. Great infusions of wealth pushed the city's boundaries west (the Paris Treaty of 1763 had granted the territory east of the Mississippi to Britain). In 1780, as the American Revolution ground on, the British attacked St. Louis and were soundly defeated by combined French and Spanish forces. In 1804, the United States obtained the area as part of the Louisiana Purchase, and St. Louis was incorporated as an American city soon after.

By the middle of the 19th century, St. Louis's thriving economy had transitioned from trade to manufacturing. The city's burgeoning industry was driven largely by incoming German and Irish immigrants, who took full advantage of St. Louis's proximity to the Mississippi River. This proximity, in conjunction with the ever-expanding railroads, gave manufacturers easy access to raw materials and affordable means for shipping. By the time the Civil War began, northern St. Louis had emerged as a major provider of furniture, machinery, lumber, coal, and livestock. The flourishing garment district along historic Washington Avenue supplied the nation with much of its first ready-to-wear apparel. In Midtown, manufacturers began producing some of the country's first Brass Era automobiles.

COURTESY OF THE MISSOURI HISTORY MUSEUM

The past comes alive at the Missouri History Museum.

POPULATION DECLINE

It was at the height of this manufacturing era that St. Louis would see its largest population spike. By 1956, the city's population had reached nearly 900,000—but it began to decline soon after. By the mid-1980s, the city proper had lost 50 percent of its population. In fact, between 1957 and 2006, St. Louis experienced the sharpest population decline of any American city. There are many theories about this rapid loss, but the easiest theory to defend is also the most general: St. Louis simply could not adapt quickly enough to compete in a changing market. As more efficient means of transportation turned steamboats into antiquities, businesses began to leave the area in pursuit of better opportunities.

ST. LOUIS TODAY: BACK IN BUSINESS

Today, St. Louis is experiencing a re-emergence—thanks to another industry altogether. Leading biotech firms and world-class medical facilities are filling in the once-abandoned warehouse district between Forest Park Southeast and the Central West End. Bioengineering giant Monsanto continues to prosper in suburban St. Louis. Pfizer, the world's largest pharmaceutical company, operates one of its major U.S. research complexes in West St. Louis County. In conjunction with the Washington University School of Medicine, the Saint Louis University School of Medicine, and the St. Louis College of Pharmacy, Pfizer has helped establish St. Louis as a respected center of medical technology. Optimists project that a "Silicon Valley of biotechnology" will someday stand in the place of departed stalwarts like TWA, McDonnell Douglas, and Chrysler.

In the meantime, local government and the St. Louis Regional Chamber and Growth Association (RCGA) are developing incentive programs meant to encourage business development and preservation—particularly in the city proper, where population loss has taken its greatest toll. In 1998, Missouri adopted a tax credit for the redevelopment of historic buildings, which made large-scale development more financially feasible. The incentive attracted dozens of developers from all over the nation; as a result, areas such as Midtown Alley and downtown's Washington Avenue have been redeveloped into mixed-use residential and retail districts. The city's redevelopment strategy received international recognition in 2007, when it was given the World Leadership Award for Urban Renewal by the World Leadership Forum. St. Louis also receives frequent accolades for its implementation of LEED's strict, eco-friendly development standards.

Government and Economy

Despite the common (mis)perception that the Midwest is politically conservative and primarily Republican, St. Louis is dominated by the Democratic Party—and has been for years. The city has not had a Republican mayor since 1949, nor have St. Louisans elected a Republican to a major city office since the 1970s. All of the city's twenty-eight aldermen are Democrats. St. Louis's mayoral office has set some important precedents, including an exceptionally even distribution of executive powers among nine elected city officials. The often-overlooked offices of comptroller, treasurer, and collector of revenue have significant influence here, as do the city's aldermen.

EDUCATION

St. Louis is home to several dozen colleges and universities, both public and private. Washington University and Saint Louis University enjoy the greatest renown on both local and national levels. Other major area institutions include Fontbonne University, Webster University (home to a terrific fine arts program), the University of Missouri-St. Louis, and Southern Illinois University-Edwardsville.

The University of Missouri's flagship campus is located two hours west in Columbia, while the University of Illinois at Urbana-Champaign is three hours northeast.

Washington University is a significant economic force. The university reported $2.2 billion in expenditures in 2012, including approximately $1 billion in payroll. A study commissioned in 2002 found that the university's overall economic impact on the region is $2.2 billion. In 2010 Saint Louis University, a Jesuit institution located in Midtown, boasted an operating revenue of $356 million and an endowment of $708 million. The university's Chaifetz Arena is home to the school's popular Division I men's basketball team and also hosts national touring acts.

HEALTH CARE

St. Louis benefits from some of the nation's best and most affordable health care. Its impact on the local economy is substantial. The 13 hospitals of the BJC HealthCare network boast more than 27,000 employees and an annual net revenue of $4 billion, and BJC estimates that its contribution to the region's economy is $1.8 billion per year. BJC's flagship facility, Barnes-Jewish Hospital, is consistently ranked among the nation's top hospitals by *U.S. News & World Report* and is also home to Washington University's renowned medical school. *U.S. News & World Report* has also named BJC's St. Louis Children's Hospital one of the country's top pediatric facilities.

SSM Health Care employs more than 11,000 at seven hospitals in the St. Louis area, including SSM St. Mary's Health Center and SSM Cardinal Glennon Children's Medical Center. Several SSM facilities are teaching hospitals affiliated with Saint Louis University School of Medicine, as is Saint Louis University Hospital.

People and Culture

At the beginning of the 20th century, the population of St. Louis City was well over half a million and climbing. One-fifth of this population was foreign-born, and nearly half of it was German, but the demographics and population of the area have changed drastically in the past 100 years.

When considering St. Louis's census statistics, it's important to note that the populations of the city and the county are surveyed separately—and have been since St. Louis City separated from the larger St. Louis County in 1880. Today, a majority of St. Louisans live in the suburbs rather than in the city proper. Although the 2012 population of St. Louis City was just 318,172, the population of St. Louis County was 1,000,438. The massive migration to the suburbs began shortly after World War II, when the population boom created an outsized demand for housing. By 1950 there were 856,796 people living in St. Louis proper. By 2000, the number had dwindled dramatically, to 348,189. It was during those five decades that St. Louis experienced the largest population decrease of any American city. Today, the numbers aren't exactly up, but the population decline has slowed down significantly.

St. Louisans are keenly aware of their city's history. They take pride in its rapid ascension as one of America's great early cities, and they smart at its mid-20th-century decline. As is true in most "second cities"—large metropolitan areas that aren't as wealthy or as culturally diverse as places like New York or San Francisco—St. Louisans subject their city to some good-natured teasing. For the most part, though, civic pride is strong. That pride can morph into occasional snobbery, as evidenced by native St. Louisans' favorite breaking-the-ice question: "So, where did you go to high school?" (St. Louis high schools vary widely in quality, reputation, and cost, so sometimes the inquisitor is actually asking a loaded question about socioeconomic standing.) The high-school question is only asked by one St. Louisan of another, though, so out-of-towners need not worry. St. Louisans are gracious and friendly and almost always eager to share advice with visitors.

IMMIGRANT GROUPS

Many residents and urban planners are optimistic about St. Louis City's future, and a thriving immigrant culture plays a big part in that revival. Planners predict that the city will soon see a population surge, thanks to residential development downtown and to the unexpected revival in South City's once-beleaguered Bevo Mill neighborhood. In the 1990s, Bevo Mill's surplus of inexpensive housing (coupled with St. Louis's overall low cost of living) attracted more than 15,000 Bosnian refugees. The Bosnian community here is one of the largest in the United States; only Chicago has a bigger Bosnian population.

According to 2010 statistics gathered by the United States Census Bureau, St. Louis City is home to more than 11,000 Latinos and more than 9,000 people of Asian descent. There is also a strong Ethiopian and Eritrean community, and many Indian and Pakistani families live in both the city and in West St. Louis County.

AFRICAN AMERICAN CULTURE

In the city, African American and Caucasian populations are about equal. In the county, however, African Americans compose just a fifth of the population—which is disheartening evidence of the "white flight" that took

place in St. Louis City in the mid-20th century. St. Louis owes much of its success and its cultural strength to the African American community. Scott Joplin, Maya Angelou, and Chuck Berry are just a few of the internationally known luminaries who hail from St. Louis, and St. Louis's historical role in the Dred Scott case makes it a crucial birthplace of the civil-rights struggle.

Although some areas of the city are well-integrated—particularly the neighborhoods surrounding Tower Grove Park and South Grand—St. Louis is plagued by de facto segregation. The city's north side is almost entirely African American, and while some neighborhoods are thriving, others suffer. Many in the community—both African American and Caucasian—feel that the mayor's office does little to support and strengthen north-side neighborhoods, and many of the once-beautiful buildings have fallen prey to speculators who blight entire areas with no real intention to develop.

Despite the aforementioned obstacles, St. Louis's African American community is a significant force in the city's cultural development and business growth. Groups like the St. Louis Black Leadership Roundtable—a nonprofit composed of African American politicians, attorneys, journalists, law-enforcement officers, and educators—work to build voter awareness, to support the growth of black-owned businesses, and to "advocate for an improved climate of justice and fairness." Another force for change is the *St. Louis American,* the city's outstanding African American newspaper.

The Arts

ARTS, CRAFTS, AND FOLK TRADITIONS

Any city with a history as rich as St. Louis's is bound to have a strong folk-art tradition. Whether they're preserving centuries-old practices or putting new twists on the form, St. Louis's folk artists are a talented and dedicated bunch. Visitors to the city have many opportunities to see the tradition for themselves.

Many of St. Louis's most talented artisans create, display, and sell their work at the **Craft Alliance** (www.craftalliance.org). Since its establishment in 1964, this cooperative has helped artists make a living—and has educated a whole city in the process. The bright, funky Craft Alliance building in the Delmar Loop hosts classes for all ages and skill levels, and the retail shop features beautiful wares made by local hands. Unlike studios that only feature work in a specific medium, the alliance is broad in its definition of the word "craft." Glass, metal, fiber, clay, and wood crafts are all created and sold here. Craft Alliance funds itself through tuition, sales, and membership fees, and local groups such as the St. Louis Regional Arts Commission often give grants to help the Alliance continue its excellent educational mission.

Despite its rather catch-all name, the **St. Louis Artists' Guild** (www.stlouisartistsguild.org) focuses primarily on classic and modern folk art—and does an outstanding job of it. Exhibits here vary from found-object collections to stunning metal sculptures to fascinating displays of "tattoo paintings." Particularly excellent are the frequent book-arts shows, which gather talent from all around the nation. The guild also houses the only non-university printmaking studio in the area, and visitors are welcome to rent space in the studio for $15 for the day. Local artists frequently teach classes at the artists' guild, and children's work is displayed in the Monsanto Children's Gallery.

The **Portfolio Gallery & Education Center** (http://portfoliogallerystl.org), on the northern edge of Midtown, features work in both the fine- and folk-art tradition. The gallery's mission is to preserve and foster the work of local African American artists, and talents on display here include watercolor painter Henry Dixon and the great portrait artist Cbabi Bayoc. Founded by sculptor Robert A. Powell, the Portfolio Gallery has been a vibrant part of the St. Louis art scene for more than 20 years.

On the south side of town, **Skif International** (www.skifo.com) is creating some of the most exciting, earth-friendly textiles around. While most of Skif's artwork is of the wearable variety, its beauty is just as impressive as its functionality. The owners of this folk-arty collaborative are part of a growing movement in St. Louis, one that takes the DIY ethos seriously and creates amazing art as a result. Dozens of like-minded artisans get together at the annual **Rock N Roll Craft Show** (www.rocknrollcraftshow.com), a roving bazaar stocked with every cool handmade item imaginable. Many, many St. Louis shops carry items made by local craftspeople—and it's that kind of community support that makes the city's folk-art scene so continually viable.

LITERATURE

Although St. Louis's literary importance sometimes flies under the radar—even in the consciousness of the city's own residents—the literary history here is rich. Many of America's most important authors, poets, and playwrights have called the Gateway City home, and St. Louis is the subject of and setting for dozens of works.

Much of St. Louis's literary history survives in its very buildings. The childhood home of T. S. Eliot (*The Wasteland, The Love Song of J. Alfred Prufrock*) is at the corner of Westminster Place and Euclid Avenue in the Central West End. Eliot claimed that the Missouri and Mississippi Rivers made a deeper impression

ST. LOUIS'S FAMOUS FACES

On the whole, St. Louisans are welcoming and down to earth–but don't let that humble facade fool you. This river city has produced dozens of famous people, from major-league sluggers to matinee idols. If the St. Louis Walk of Fame included all of the area's celebs, it would likely stretch for a few more miles. Following are people who were born in St. Louis or lived here for a significant part of their lives.

Actors and other Hollywood types: Kate Capshaw, Phyllis Diller, Jenna Fischer (of *The Office* fame), Redd Foxx, Bob Gale (co-writer of *Back to the Future*), John Goodman, Betty Grable, Robert Guillaume, Jon Hamm (*Mad Men*'s Don Draper), Ellie Kemper (also of *The Office*), Kevin Kline, supermodel Karlie Kloss, Vincent Price

Artists and writers: Maya Angelou, William S. Burroughs, Kate Chopin, Charles Eames, Stanley Elkin, Jonathan Franzen, William H. Gass, Al Hirschfeld, A. E. Hotchner, Marianne Moore, Gyo Obata, Irma Rombauer, Ernest Trova, Mona Van Duyn, Tennessee Williams

Athletes and broadcasters: Cool Papa Bell, Yogi Berra, Jack Buck, Joe Buck, Harry Caray, Jimmy Connors, Bob Costas, Dwight F. Davis, Joe Garagiola, Jackie Joyner-Kersee, Sonny Liston, Stan Musial, "Cowboy" Bob Orton, Ozzie Smith, Rusty Wallace, Dick Weber

Singers and musicians: Josephine Baker, Fontella Bass, Chuck Berry, Grace Bumbry, T-Bone Burnett, Miles Davis, Grant Green, Julius Hemphill, Johnnie Johnson, Scott Joplin, Albert King, Oliver Lake, Nelly, David Sanborn, Clark Terry, Ike and Tina Turner

upon him than any other part of the world. Another award-winning poet, Sara Teasdale, fondly referred to the city throughout her body of work and even named a poem in its honor: *Sunset: St. Louis.*

Novelists and playwrights also found inspiration in St. Louis. Kate Chopin (*The Awakening*) spent her young married life here before moving to New Orleans. Chopin is buried at Cavalry Cemetery in North St. Louis, as is Tennessee Williams (*The Glass Menagerie, A Streetcar Named Desire*). Maya Angelou, American poet and best-selling author of *I Know Why the Caged Bird Sings,* spent many childhood summers visiting her mother in St. Louis; several of her stories are based on time spent in the city.

Young literary lights also focus on St. Louis. Gifted postmodern novelist Jonathan Franzen, who grew up in Webster Groves, set his ambitious political thriller *The Twenty-Seventh City* in St. Louis and lived in the Central West End while composing the novel. Mystery writer Ridley Pearson (*The Body of David Hayes, No Witnesses*) divides his time between St. Louis and Sun Valley, Idaho. Talented young author (and *New York Times* bestseller) Curtis Sittenfeld (*Prep, American Wife*) also called St. Louis home upon graduating from the Iowa Writers' Workshop.

Thanks to its rich history and still-thriving community of up-and-coming authors, the city's literary tradition continues to this day. Also key to St. Louis's literary success are its great universities and network of notable literary publications. The imitable William Gass (*Omensetter's Luck, The Tunnel*) resides here and for years was a professor of humanities at Washington University. Wash. U.'s program for English graduate studies is one of the top in the country. The faculty has included novelist Stanley Elkin, 1988 U.S. Poet Laureate Howard Nemerov, and the remarkable husband-and-wife poets Donald Finkel and Constance Urdang. Today, the faculty roster boasts some of the academic scene's most promising newcomers.

The English department at Webster University, in the suburban enclave of Webster Groves, is a hidden gem. Although MFAs in writing are not yet offered here, the undergraduate department has snapped up a sharp staff of Ivy League-educated instructors from all over the country, and the program's reputation in the community is growing. Excellent literary publications dedicated to preserving the area's written heritage include the University of Missouri's *Missouri Review* (www.missourireview.org) and the local quarterly *River Styx* (www.riverstyx.org).

MUSIC

Despite its struggles with population decline and limited visibility in the professional music world, St. Louis's contribution to American music has been immense. There is simply no way to overstate music's impact on St. Louis—and St. Louis's music's impact on the nation. The Gateway City has served as a musical incubator, fostering both young artists and young movements. Many St. Louis musicians have been very successful, even revolutionary.

St. Louisan Scott Joplin chartered a movement. He is widely considered the father of ragtime, and he composed the most famous example of that genre: "Maple Leaf Rag." Visitors can tour the modest 19th-century walkup where Joplin wrote many of his legendary songs. The visionary Miles Davis—who was born across the river in Alton, Illinois, and spent much of his life in East St. Louis—changed the face of jazz. Josephine Baker, the extraordinary chanteuse and civil-rights proponent, was born here and got her start with the St. Louis cabaret scene.

As the city approached its population peak in the mid-20th century, it was contributing more than its fair share to the emerging rock and soul genres. Recording studios popped up all over the city. Chuck Berry, one of rock's most influential forefathers, grew up in north St. Louis. In the 1950s, he recorded the now-legendary songs "Johnny B. Goode" and "Maybelline." After decades of history-making collaboration, Berry returned to his hometown, and to this day he plays monthly shows at Blueberry Hill in the Delmar Loop.

Many blues giants have also called the St. Louis area home. The St. Louis blues—a unique, piano-driven sound with roots in

ragtime and Delta blues—can be heard almost any night of the week at beloved joints like B.B.'s Jazz, Blues, and Soups and Beale on Broadway. Sadly, many of the genre's most talented musicians have passed on in recent years, owing to advanced age and limited health care. Their torch is carried, though, by incredible blues prodigies like Marquise Knox.

Funk and soul were also nurtured in St. Louis. In 1959, Ike Turner met Anna Mae Bullock (known to millions by her adopted stage name, Tina Turner) in a St. Louis nightclub. The pair became the Ike & Tina Turner Revue and turned out hit after hit, including the barn-burning "Proud Mary." While Ike's poor treatment of Tina often overshadowed the music itself, the Turners' impact upon soul and R&B music cannot be underestimated.

In recent years, St. Louis and its surrounding suburbs have produced many successful musicians. After studying at the University of Columbia, Grammy-winning musician Sheryl Crow taught elementary-school music classes in the St. Louis exurb of Fenton. Story of the Year, a post-grunge outfit currently signed to the major label Epitaph Records, formed in St. Louis. Musicians from the local twang scene are responsible for some of alt-country's most respected bands, including Wilco, Son Volt, and the Bottle Rockets. Members of the successful glam rock-psychobilly band 7 Shot Screamers grew up in Fenton (and tour with the legendary Exene Cervenka under the *nom du stage* The Original Sinners). Members of the funk-reggae-rock hybrid The Urge attended high school together nearby, as did the Grammy-winning hip-hop artists Nelly, Chingy, and Murphy Lee.

FILM

The most iconic St. Louis film is, of course, *Meet Me in St. Louis*—the classic 1944 Judy Garland film that added ditties like "The Trolley Song" and "Have Yourself a Merry Little Christmas" to the American show-tune canon. With the 1904 World's Fair as its backdrop, *Meet Me in St. Louis* made its title city look at once progressive, romantic, and whimsical (never mind the fact that most of it was shot on a Culver City back lot).

Films released after St. Louis's early-20th-century heyday provide a more realistic, if not always Chamber of Commerce-approved, glimpse into the city. *The Great St. Louis Bank Robbery,* a Steve McQueen vehicle released in 1959, capitalized on St. Louis's late-'50s noir appeal (the bank in question is Southwest Bank, a gorgeous building that's still in business, now as BMO Harris Bank, at the corner of Kingshighway Boulevard and Southwest Avenue).

In 1981, action-adventure director John Carpenter filmed much of *Escape from New York* in St. Louis. This decision was the ultimate in backhanded compliments: Carpenter chose St. Louis because much of its downtown looked like a bombed-out, apocalyptic New York. (Fortunately for downtown boosters, Carpenter would be out of luck today.) Crucial scenes were filmed at the old Chain of Rocks Bridge, the Civil Courts Building, and Union Station. *National Lampoon's Vacation* (1983) took another swipe at St. Louis: The Griswolds' car breaks down in St. Louis and, in a scene that now seems cringe-inducingly racist, a cadre of young African American kids strip the vehicle.

One of the more interesting St. Louis film stories revolves around *White Palace,* the steamy Susan Sarandon-James Spader movie

that came out in 1990. The original name was *White Castle,* a real Midwest burger chain mentioned in the novel upon which the movie is based. The folks at White Castle corporate refused to lend their name to the racy flick, so Universal Pictures shot the film at a downtown St. Louis diner. The diner was renamed "White Palace" for the duration of filming—but when the owners asked to keep the name, Universal Pictures said no. The restaurant changed its name to "White Knight" and slings steak-and-egg platters to this day.

A few recent movies have been better for civic pride. *The Game of Their Lives,* released in 2005, is based on the true story of the 1950 United States soccer team that unexpectedly beat England in a World Cup match. Because many of the team members grew up on the Hill, St. Louis's predominantly Italian neighborhood, much of the film was shot here. Merchants and restaurant owners willingly altered their facades to lend a true 1950s feel to the film, turning one of St. Louis's most charming neighborhoods into a picture-perfect backdrop. That same year, St. Louis had another (brief) star turn in *Fever Pitch,* the Jimmy Fallon-Drew Barrymore romantic comedy about an over-the-top Boston Red Sox fan. In 2010, George Clooney took up residence in St. Louis while filming *Up in the Air,* and the sport of Clooney-sighting became nearly as popular as Cardinals baseball.

ESSENTIALS

Getting There

Coast-dwellers may consider St. Louis "flyover country," but it's precisely that on-the-way-to-everywhere status that makes the city so accessible. Lambert-St. Louis International Airport is short on creature comforts but quite navigable. Visitors can also arrive in and depart from St. Louis via train, bus, or automobile; several major highways (including I-70, I-55, I-64, and I-44) run right through the city.

BY AIR

Located 15 miles from downtown, **Lambert-St. Louis International Airport** (314/890-1333, www.flystl.com) was once one of the busiest hubs in the nation. Before it stopped offering direct international flights, this airport welcomed more than 20 million passengers and 460,000 flights each year. These numbers have dwindled significantly in the past decade, but Lambert still hosts a few major air carriers, including **American Airlines** (www.americanairlines.com), **Continental** (www.continental.com), and **Delta** (www.delta.com) in the Main Terminal (Terminal 1) and **Southwest** (www.southwest.com) in Terminal 2. In 2008, the airport inked a $16 million expansion contract with its concessions provider, and many new eateries have

been added, including an outpost of the wildly popular Schlafly Tap Room and an upscale tapas restaurant. Otherwise, Lambert's conveniences (basic magazine stands, pay-as-you-go Internet access) are sufficient if not impressive. One particularly welcome amenity is the business center (with computer docking stations, printers, copiers, and fax machines) on the lower level of the Main Terminal. An interfaith chapel is next to the Main Terminal's baggage claim. This chapel, which is staffed by a chaplain seven days a week, offers a Catholic mass on weekends.

Lambert-St. Louis International opened in the 1930s. The Main Terminal's striking domed structure, considered a forerunner in modern airport design, was built in the mid-'50s to the specifications of architect Minoru Yamasaki. While passing through the airport, you may want to visit the reproduction of the legendary *Spirit of St. Louis*—the single-engine monoplane that Charles Lindbergh piloted across the Atlantic Ocean. *Spirit* is suspended above Lambert's central security checkpoint. Also of note is the beautifully vibrant mural near the baggage-claim area.

To and From the Airport

Visitors looking for cheap transportation to and from the airport will likely be most pleased with **MetroLink,** the city's efficient light-rail system. The station is a five-minute walk from the Arrivals gate, and trains depart every 25 minutes. You can catch a ride on MetroLink between 4:30am and 11:10pm Monday through Friday, and between 5am and 11pm Saturday and Sunday. One-ride tickets are $2.25, and all-day passes (which include bus rides as well) are $7.50. Alternatively, a two-hour pass from the airport is available for $4 (inclusive of bus rides as well) and comes with a free transfer at the Central West End/DeBaliviere station. From this point, you can transfer to trains headed to multiple destinations, including downtown and Grand Boulevard.

Cabs queue up right outside the Main and East Terminals' baggage claims, but be aware

that the ride is a rather expensive one. The fare from Lambert-St. Louis to downtown is rarely less than $40, and the cab companies tack on an additional $3 "airport use fee." The popular SuperShuttle service does not operate at Lambert, but many area hotels offer a similar service for a nominal charge (or for free). Limousines and private cars are also available.

Long- and short-term parking options are abundant at Lambert, and prices vary fairly widely. One of the cheapest options—just $7 a day for remote parking in an uncovered lot—is available through **SuperPark** (314/890-2800, www.superparkinglot.com). For $15 per day, SuperPark offers parking in a lot that is much closer to the Main Terminal. SuperPark's garage-parking option gets you the closest and costs $23 per day. **The Parking Spot** (314/426-4510 or 314/428-5146, www.theparkingspot.com) offers remote covered and uncovered parking (valet service is also available) and a free, nonstop shuttle to the airport. Daily rates range $11.95-18.95, and the website always features a coupon.

Car Rental

Travelers arriving at Lambert-St. Louis International Airport have their pick of rental-car agencies. Outside the baggage claim, you'll find representatives from eight of the major companies, including **Hertz** (800/654-3131, www.hertz.com), **Budget** (800/527-0700, www.budget.com), and St. Louis-based **Enterprise** (800/261-7331, www.enterprise.com).

BY CAR

Many major highways run right through St. Louis, making the city very accessible to road warriors. Those traveling on **I-44** will want to take Exit 208 (Park Avenue), which will deposit them in downtown St. Louis. Travelers on **I-55** can reach downtown by connecting with **I-64/U.S. 40** (watch for signs for St. Louis/U.S. 40 W/I-64 W) and then exiting at 40A (9th Street). From I-70, take Exit 250B to merge onto North Memorial Drive.

BY TRAIN

At the turn of the 20th century, visitors to St. Louis arrived in style, as locomotives chugged into elegant Union Station. Today, the structurally stunning Union Station houses chain restaurants and a lackluster mall, and those who choose to travel by train will arrive in and depart from St. Louis's newly built **Amtrak station** (430 S. 15th St., 314/331-3309, www.amtrak.com). The fares are reasonable, and the trains are pleasant. Popular destinations include Kansas City ($29, 5.5 hours) and Chicago ($26-48, 5.5 hours), for which there are several departures daily. The ride to Chicago is particularly lovely, as it wends through tiny Illinois towns and verdant countryside. The volunteer-run, historic train station in Kirkwood is far more charming than the downtown depot, but daily train service is limited to day-trip jaunts to places like Alton, Illinois, and Washington, Missouri.

BY BUS

You won't find an operational train service at Union Station (1820 Market St.), but you *will* find the pickup point for **Megabus** (877/462-6342, http://us.megabus.com). A Scottish concept that came to the U.S. fairly recently, Megabus offers nonstop service to and from Chicago, twice a day, for fares as low as *one dollar*. Other destinations in its affordable intercity network include Kansas City, Columbia, and Bloomington-Normal. (Do note that tickets must be purchased online in advance.)

Located downtown in the same building as the new Amtrak station, **Greyhound** (450 S. 15th St., 314/231-4485, www.greyhound.com) offers a much more complete, though less expedient, service. Here, visitors will find buses headed for most major cities, as well as popular Midwestern destinations such as Columbia and Kansas City. Route and ticket information are available at Greyhound's website.

Getting Around

PUBLIC TRANSPORTATION

Getting around St. Louis is inexpensive and fairly convenient thanks to **Metro,** the area's transit authority. Metro operates both the bus and the MetroLink (the region's light-rail system), and together these can take you practically anywhere—for cheap. Metro passes allow travelers to transfer from bus to light rail as needed, and every light-rail station is conveniently near a bus stop. A one-ride ticket aboard MetroLink is $2.25 (bus fare is $2), while a two-hour, multi-use pass (useful for short return trips and transfers and inclusive of both MetroLink and bus) is $3. For visitors planning to do most of their sight-seeing via public transportation, a one-day pass is probably the best deal: For just $7.50, the pass allows unlimited, all-day use of both the bus and the light-rail system. If you are staying in St. Louis for more than a couple of days, consider a weekly (seven-day) pass, which is available for $25. The majority of MetroLink stations (with the exception of the downtown stops) offer free or inexpensive public parking, making light rail a great alternative for drivers looking to save money and fuel.

At www.metrostlouis.org, travelers can view route maps, plan their trips, check bus and MetroLink time tables, and purchase passes in advance with a credit card.

The MetroLink has two lines that meet in the West End, at the Forest Park/DeBaliviere station. From this point, one can travel as far east as Fairview Heights, Illinois, and as far west as Shrewsbury. MetroLink trains also run to such inner suburbs as Maplewood. Points of interest made easily accessible by the MetroLink include tourist favorites such as the Gateway Arch and Busch Stadium, shopping destinations like the Galleria and the Promenade at Brentwood, and the Delmar Loop and Washington Avenue entertainment districts.

© BROOKE S. FOSTER

Bike St. Louis's clearly marked routes are a dream come true for two-wheeled tourists.

DRIVING

Unfortunately—in light of current fuel prices—a car is the most convenient way to get around St. Louis. There are some perks to assuage your driving headache, though. In all but Clayton and the downtown area, parking is readily available and frequently free. Traffic congestion is minimal outside of peak drive times, and a car offers the convenience of not having to abide by the Metro timetable (buses often run in excess of 30 minutes apart). Be forewarned, though, that newcomers often find St. Louis's long, name-shifting streets confusing. A good street guide is highly recommended; the *Rand McNally St. Louis Street Guide* is particularly useful.

TAXIS

St. Louis is not a cab-hailing sort of town. Visitors seeking a taxi will have to call for one; restaurants and bars always keep a few companies' numbers on hand. Locals don't frequently use taxis, so the only place cabs converge en masse is at the airport. Popular taxi companies servicing the area include **Laclede Cab** (314/652-3456) and **Metropolitan Cab** (314/773-1000). For journeys outside of St. Louis proper, a traveler's best bet is **St. Louis County Cab** (314/991-5300).

BICYCLING

Less than five years ago, St. Louis was declared one of the nation's most dangerous cities for cyclists, but nonprofit groups such as **Bike St. Louis** and **Trailnet** have worked to turn the tide. Visit their useful websites (www.bikestlouis.org and www.trailnet.org) for guides to the city's existing bike lanes, tips for mapping out trips, and downloadable maps. Bike St. Louis, one of the city's largest public-interest groups, has established more than 77 miles of dedicated bike and shared-traffic lanes. On a regional level, the **Great Rivers Greenway District** has established a wonderful, Missouri-wide system of interconnected parks and trails. Information can be found at www.greatriversgreenway.org.

ACCESS FOR TRAVELERS WITH DISABILITIES

All Metro buses are equipped with wheelchair lifts and universal wheelchair tie-down systems. Metro also offers small, similarly outfitted vans for door-to-door service, but interested parties must prove they meet eligibility requirements by applying for a Metro Call-A-Ride ADA Eligibility ID card. The process usually takes a week, and reservations for rides need to be made at least 24 hours in advance. For more information, call 314/652-3617 or visit www.metrostlouis.org.

Tips for Travelers

WEATHER

The weather in St. Louis can be very unpredictable, particularly as the seasons shift from winter to spring. Those planning a March or April visit are advised (only half-jokingly) to bring shorts, tank tops, long underwear, and galoshes. If locals overhear visitors complaining about the weather, they'll likely advise the out-of-towners to "just wait a few hours." Often, this advice is spot on.

The growing season here is long, which explains the many farms and orchards that dot the landscape just outside St. Louis. Still, the area fully experiences all meteorological extremes. St. Louis receives an average of 43 inches of rain per year and has an average of 164 cloudy days. Visitors with a strong distaste for heat and humidity will likely be uncomfortable in July and August, when temperatures can break 100 degrees. Winters aren't quite as harsh here as in other Midwestern burgs, although the mercury can dip into the single digits. Spring brings a lot of rain (often accompanied by a lot of thunder), but it also ushers in the city's most beautiful days, along with temperatures around 70 degrees. Autumn in eastern Missouri is absolutely dazzling, as golden light falls across the numerous bright-red trees. Check out weather updates and related travel tips at www.weather.com, or read the local forecast at www.stltoday.com.

HOURS

True to its Midwestern roots, St. Louis is a city that goes to bed rather early. Only a handful of bars—mostly concentrated downtown and in South City—stay open until 3am, with the majority closing at 1am (or even earlier, if business is slow). South Grand Boulevard can become particularly chaotic on weekend nights, as revelers migrate en masse from the 1am bars to the 3am bars. Cops patrol the area on foot and in squad cars, but visitors who dislike drunken shouting (and the occasional fight) may want to call it a night after 1am.

Most St. Louis restaurants also close up shop fairly early. Some places do offer limited late-night menus, but be advised that dinner service typically ends by 10pm on weeknights and 11pm on weekends. In St. Louis, it's usually best to eat dinner before any other evening activities—by midnight, your choices narrow to fast food joints and 24-hour diners.

The financial and business center of downtown St. Louis shuts its doors around 6pm, but visitors will find plenty of dining and entertainment options on Washington Avenue, downtown's vibrant main drag. Drinking and dancing last till 3am at most Wash. Ave. hotspots, and even many of the boutiques stay open till 9pm or 10pm on weekend nights.

TIPPING

The tipping standard for full-service dining in St. Louis is 15-20 percent of the total bill, including alcohol. Today, many in the service industry consider 15 percent to be insulting, but rude or inattentive servers shouldn't expect much more. Good servers average about 18 percent over the course of an evening by being knowledgeable and courteous. (Remember, too, that tips make up the bulk of a waitperson's income; servers in Missouri currently earn $3.68 per hour.) Bartenders are tipped between $1 and $2 per drink, or 20 percent of the tab. At many St. Louis bars, particularly the popular ones, your generous tips will be rewarded with faster service. Sommeliers are generally tipped 15 percent of wine sales. Standard gratuity for takeout and delivery is 10 percent. At nicer restaurants, where preparing a takeout order is an exception to the usual routine, you may want to tip closer to 15 percent.

Practically every popular restaurant downtown and in Clayton offers valet service. Because this service is often complimentary, it's nice to be a bit generous with the tip (between $3 and $4 is standard). Coat-check attendants typically receive $1 per checked item. If you travel by taxi, tip your driver 10-15 percent of the total fare. (Note: Cab drivers are legally obligated to accept credit cards, although some may argue vehemently about it.)

Hair stylists and salon technicians (such as manicurists) are usually tipped 15 percent, as are masseurs. Feel free to tip above that, though, for particularly good service—or if the salon or spa is high-end. In hotels, tipping expectations vary significantly. Consider leaving between $2 and $10 per day for the housekeeping staff, depending on the quality of the hotel and the work required to put your room back in order. Room-service attendants typically receive 10-15 percent of the total bill, and bell-desk employees are often given $2-3 per bag. It's perfectly fine

to ask a hotel's concierge about tipping procedures—and, in all tipping situations, it's nice to err on the side of generosity.

SMOKING

Thanks to its lax smoking laws (and abundance of fried foods and beer), St. Louis long held a reputation for being one of America's most unhealthy cities. However, a 2011 ban means that smoking is prohibited in most bars, restaurants, and hotels in the city. Be aware (or beware): The ban does not apply to establishments where food counts for less than 25 percent of total sales (or to casino floors and some bowling alleys), meaning that most corner taverns are viewed through a smoky haze.

Health and Safety

CRIME

When Morgan Quitno Press announced that St. Louis was one of the most dangerous cities in the nation, St. Louisans responded with a mixture of anger and disbelief. From South City to Webster Groves, from Richmond Heights to Dogtown, the St. Louis area is imbued with strong civic pride. Many residents have spent their entire lives here. They went to school here, raised families here—and they can't imagine living anywhere else. On many of St. Louis's tree-lined avenues, nothing bad *ever* seems to happen. Still, the statistics (particularly in relation to property crimes and nuisance crimes) tell a slightly different story. As would be true in any large city, visitors are advised to exercise caution, particularly when exploring unfamiliar places on foot.

The revitalization of St. Louis's urban core is an ongoing success story, and most neighborhoods are perfectly safe by day. Still, there are areas that should be avoided altogether. The once-thriving outdoor mall across from Crown Candy Kitchen in North City fell victim to neglect and abandonment and now exists in a seemingly permanent state of deterioration. Entire neighborhoods of condemned and

dilapidated homes in this area (just north of downtown's Washington Avenue) have met the same fate, and the result is both eerie and sad. Areas that are reasonably safe during the day but require extra vigilance at night include the northernmost edge of the Central West End, the quiet fringes of Soulard and downtown, the area surrounding South Broadway, and the neighborhoods due east of Grand Boulevard.

The best rule to apply is that of common sense: If an area appears dangerous or abandoned, tourists should avoid it. As in any large city, visitors should be equal parts adventurous and vigilant. At night, stick to well-lit, pedestrian-friendly areas. Explore less-familiar areas during the day and with a friend or two, and don't be shy about asking the locals for advice. Most St. Louisans love to talk about their city and are more than happy to help tourists.

HOSPITALS AND PHARMACIES

BJC HealthCare (www.bjc.org) operates several major hospitals in the area, including **Barnes-Jewish Hospital** and **St. Louis Children's Hospital** in the Central West End. BJC also operates health-care centers in the suburbs, including **Missouri Baptist Medical Center** in West County, the **Christian Hospital** in St. Charles County, and **Progress West HealthCare Center** in O'Fallon.

St. Louis is fortunate to have world-class health care, particularly in the area of pediatrics. Both St. Louis Children's Hospital and **SSM Cardinal Glennon Children's Medical Center** (on Grand Boulevard) continually rank among the best children's hospitals in the country. Cardinal Glennon is operated by SSM Health Care (www.ssmhc.com), which also runs **SSM St. Joseph Health Center** in Kirkwood, **SSM DePaul Health Center** in Bridgeton, and **St. Mary's Health Center** in Richmond Heights. Hospitals outside of the huge BJC and SSM systems include **St. Luke's Hospital** in Chesterfield (www.stlukes-stl.com), **St. John's Mercy Medical Center** on New Ballas Road (www.mercy.net), and **St. Anthony's Medical Center** (www.stanthonys-medcenter.com), which maintains urgent-care facilities in the suburbs of Arnold, Fenton, and Lemay. The Saint Louis University School of Medicine operates the **Saint Louis University Hospital** (www.sluhospital.com) and its neighboring state-of-the-art cancer center.

Popular insurance providers in St. Louis include **Aetna, Aflac, Blue Cross Blue Shield,** and **UnitedHealthcare.** The national drugstore chain **Walgreens** operates locations all over the area, and several locations offer a 24-hour pharmacy. **Rite Aid** and **CVS** also operate pharmacies in the area. For a complete listing of Walgreens, Rite Aid, and CVS pharmacies, as well as the many independently owned pharmacies in the area, visit www.yellowpages.com.

EMERGENCY SERVICES

To call the police, or in the case of a fire or a medical emergency, dial 911. (Call 314/231-1212 for nonemergency police services.) If you experience a power outage or other electrical emergency in St. Louis, dial 314/342-1000. Direct any calls about gas emergencies to 314/342-0800 (if this number is busy, dial 314/621-6960). The Missouri Poison Center can be reached at 314/772-5200. To report a water or sewer emergency in St. Louis, dial 314/768-6260. The toll-free number for the St. Louis Regional Crimestoppers is 866/371-8477.

Information and Services

MEDIA AND COMMUNICATION
Phones and Area Codes

The area code for the city of St. Louis and its innermost suburbs is 314. In May 1999, many towns in West St. Louis County transitioned from 314 to 636. The 636 area code serves eastern-central Missouri, including the West County suburbs of Chesterfield, Ballwin, and Wildwood; the cities of Union and Troy; and all of St. Charles County and Jefferson County. The 618 area code serves the Metro East, a swath of Illinois considered part of the Greater St. Louis region. Towns using the 618 area code include Belleville, Alton, and Granite City. It is not necessary to dial an area code when calling from within that code's region.

Internet Services

Visitors can go online at all branches of the **St. Louis Public Library** (314/241-2288, www.slpl.org). Internet access is free at each branch, although a temporary library card is required and can be obtained by showing a state-issued driver's license or valid passport. Wireless access is available at numerous cafés, bars, and restaurants around town. Some of the most popular places—think strong signals, lots of electrical outlets, and staff who won't rush you away from your table—include all **Saint Louis Bread Co.** locations (www.panerabread.com), the two cafés of **Companion** bakery (www.companionstl.com), and all **Kaldi's Coffee House** locations. Most major hotels also offer free high-speed wireless, and the entire city center of Clayton is a wireless hot spot.

Mail and Messenger Services

Visitors will have little trouble finding a convenient post office, as the **United States Postal Service** operates branches in nearly every St. Louis neighborhood. To find a specific location, visit www.usps.com or call 800/275-8777. For international shipping or overnight delivery, consider using **UPS** (800/742-5877, www.ups.com), **FedEx** (800/463-3339, www.fedex.com), or **DHL** (800/225-5345, www.dhl—usa.com). All three of these companies have St. Louis stores and drop boxes; visit the websites to find the nearest location. Post office boxes may be rented at **The UPS Store** (4579 Laclede Ave., 314/361-5505, www.theupsstorelocal.com/0532) or **Pak Mail** (12545 Olive Blvd., 314/469-6116, www.pakmail.com). The majority of Pak Mail locations are in St. Louis County and the Metro East, while The UPS Store has locations all throughout the city and county. Copying, faxing, packing, and shipping services are available at The UPS Store as well as at **FedEx Office** (800/463-3339, www.fedex.com/us/office).

Bike messengers are fairly uncommon in St. Louis, but there are several courier companies that deliver by car. Your choices include **Access Courier** (314/962-8000, www.accesscourier.com), **Ontime Express** (314/729-7878, www.ontimeexpress.net), and **JS Logistics** (800/814-2634, www.jslogistics.com).

Magazines and Newspapers

The **St. Louis Post-Dispatch** is the city's only major daily, although the area once boasted several. A good source for local news and weather, the *Post-Dispatch* is hanging in there—and adapting to 21st-century journalism at its website, www.stltoday.com.

Despite the *Post-Dispatch*'s tenacity, however, there is some discontent in the newsroom. Once celebrated for its liberal, humanist leanings and top-notch editorial staff, the daily lost some of its cachet after a hotly contested 2005 buyout. The *Post-Dispatch* was founded by Joseph Pulitzer in 1878 and, for more than a century, enjoyed the auspicious reputation associated with the good Pulitzer name. Today, the paper is owned by the publicly traded media company Lee Enterprises, one of the largest newspaper conglomerates in the nation. Many old-guard staff members were laid off or accepted buyouts, and the *Post-Dispatch* is frequently criticized for its heavy reliance on wire-service stories and guest editorials. Additional massive layoffs in 2007, 2008, and 2012 did little to quell people's fears about this rapidly declining dynasty.

The *Globe-Democrat,* St. Louis's last competing daily, was shuttered in 1986 after more than 130 years in operation. It enjoyed a brief resurrection as an Internet-only publication, but folded (again) not long after. **The St. Louis Beacon** (www.stlbeacon.org), an online publication founded by veterans of the *Post-Dispatch,* proved to be formidable competition and is a far better publication, with some of the most thorough and original reporting in town.

St. Louis also has a number of weeklies. The **Suburban Journals of Greater St. Louis** (http://suburbanjournals.stltoday.com) is the umbrella company for dozens of community publications in the region (such as the **St. Charles County Suburban Journal,** the **Collinsville Herald,** and the magazine-style **Ladue News**). The **St. Louis Business Journal,** published each Friday, offers comprehensive coverage of the region's business news. On Thursdays, St. Louis's alternative weekly, the **Riverfront Times** (www.riverfronttimes.com), hits the streets. The *Riverfront Times* features in-depth reporting and the most exhaustive arts and entertainment coverage in the area. Owned by national conglomerate Village Voice Media, the *Riverfront Times* has social commentary and extensive music listings that make it particularly popular with twenty- and thirtysomethings. The paper is free and can be found at bars, restaurants, shops, and clubs all over the city.

Strong reporting and excellent opinion columns are par for the course in the **St. Louis American** (www.stlamerican.com), the city's

African American weekly. Established in 1928, the *American* covers news, politics, entertainment, and more. Other African American weeklies include the **St. Louis Argus** (www.stlouisargus.com) and the **St. Louis Sentinel** (www.stlouissentinel.com). **Limelight,** the region's African American monthly, addresses current issues with insight and historical perspective.

Visitors to St. Louis should seek out a copy of the **Evening Whirl** (www.thewhirlonline.com). The 70-year-old *Whirl,* which reports on local crime using delightfully over-the-top purple prose, has earned an enormous cult following. At the hands of *Whirl* scribes, local politicians earn 1930s-gangster-style nicknames, and crimes are recounted in cartoonishly lurid detail.

Red Latina (www.redlatinastl.com) serves the city's Hispanic community, and the **St. Louis Jewish Light** (www.stljewishlight.com) focuses on issues of importance to Jewish St. Louisans. **The Vital Voice** (www.thevitalvoice.com) is a biweekly paper serving the lesbian, gay, bisexual, and transgendered communities throughout the city and the state.

Over the past two decades, regionally focused magazines have flourished in St. Louis. **Sauce,** a tabloid-sized monthly, covers the city's dynamic restaurant scene and includes the sort of food and travel writing made popular by *Saveur* and *Bon Appétit.* You can pick up *Sauce* (it's free) at most restaurants and specialty food shops in the region. And be sure to peruse the excellent website, www.saucemagazine.com; it's an invaluable tool when making St. Louis dining plans. Its competitor, **Feast** (www.feaststl.com), is an equally nice publication with wonderful, award-winning food photography. **Alive Magazine** (www.alivemag.com) is a luxury lifestyle publication. Available for free at many area locations, *Alive* focuses on the trends and desires of St. Louis's young and upwardly mobile. **St. Louis Magazine** (www.stlmag.com) is a subscription-based monthly with plenty of great information and increasingly substantive reporting. Beautiful photography and

an exhaustive events calendar make *St. Louis Magazine* perfect for visitors.

St. Louis has a strong cultural history, and several small-scale art and literary magazines operate here. The poetry quarterly **River Styx,** published since the early 1970s, was one of the first journals to print such poets as Czeslaw Milosz, Yusef Komunyakaa, Howard Nemerov, and Derek Walcott. In nearby Columbia, **The Missouri Review** (www.missourireview.com) continues to enjoy its stellar national reputation; the *Review* publishes fiction, poetry, plays, essays, and author interviews. The award-winning **Boulevard** (www.boulevardmagazine.org) is based at Saint Louis University and has printed works by such luminaries as Joyce Carol Oates, John Updike, Charles Simic, and Philip Levine. **MESH** covers the latest happenings at the Contemporary Art Museum St. Louis and is available with a one-year museum membership.

Radio and TV

St. Louis carries affiliates of every major television network. **Nine Network of Public Media** (http://ninenet.org), the city's PBS station, has been providing educational and community-focused programming to residents since 1954. **STL TV** (http://stltv.net) is the city's oldest community television station; it often broadcasts programs about cultural and entertainment options in St. Louis.

KDHX, the not-for-profit media organization that provides St. Louis's excellent community radio, also operates public-access stations on channels 21 and 22.

St. Louis has many radio stations; a complete listing and links to each station's site can be found at www.ontheradio.net/metro/Saint_Louis_MO.aspx. A combined listing of television and radio stations is available at www.macrosign.com/stlouis/tv.htm. Some of the more popular area stations include **KDHX 88.1 FM** (noncommercial community radio, with both talk and music programming), **KMOX 1120 AM** (news and talk), **KFNS 590 AM** (sports news), **WSIE 88.7 FM** (jazz), **KTRS 550 AM** (sports—all Cardinals games are broadcast here), **KWMU 90.7 FM** (St. Louis's NPR affiliate), **KSHE 94.7 FM** (classic rock), **WHHL 104.1 FM** (hip-hop), **KPNT The Point 105.7 FM** (alternative rock), **KWUR 90.3 FM** (college eclectic), and **KFTK 97.1 FM** (news and talk).

PUBLIC LIBRARIES

The St. Louis Public Library (SLPL) is a full-service public library that, with the help of 15 satellite branches throughout the city, provides invaluable information to a diverse array of residents and visitors. The SLPL educates its community not just through an enormous catalog of books, music, videos, and databases, but also through free events, exhibits, and programs. Educational offerings are abundant and eclectic; the SLPL hosts seminars on such topics as traditional Japanese flower arranging, classic motorcycle design, and local bass fishing.

Central Library (1301 Olive St., 314/241-2288, http://central.slpl.org), SLPL's main branch, is one of the city's great architectural treasures. Designed by renowned architect Cass Gilbert, dedicated in 1912, and grandly restored and reopened in 2012, the Italian Renaissance-inspired building features beautiful stained-glass windows, Tennessee marble, elaborate hand-carved moldings, painted ceilings, and glass floors. Today, this busy hub houses several special research divisions within its walls, including a fine-arts library, pop library, rare-books library, and books-on-tape library. The genealogy department here is one of the best in the country; this library-within-a-library is staffed with specialists working to trace and preserve the history of St. Louis through the lineages of its families.

Many of the genealogy department's resources are now available online at library's main website (www.slpl.org), alongside its extensive catalog and an "electronic city hall" that provides access to local government information. Those interested in doing business in St. Louis will find this meticulously organized history of current and past legislation particularly useful. Also of great use is the St. Louis Area Studies Center, which brings together pamphlets, periodicals, and other clippings on the history of the city.

All of the SLPL's satellite locations offer an up-to-date selection of books, CDs, and films. Nearly every neighborhood boasts a library branch. The **Schlafly** location in the heart of the Central West End (225 N. Euclid Ave., 314/367-4120) and the **Buder** location in South City (4401 Hampton Ave., 314/352-2900) offer beautiful, brand-new facilities and convenient parking. The **Carpenter** (3309 S. Grand Blvd., 314/772-6586) branch is just a five-minute walk from South Grand's busy main drag, and the elegant old-world building underwent a complete renovation in 2007. Most excitingly, the Central Library just underwent a renovation that wrapped up in 2012; it is now more beautiful and visit-worthy than ever. Visit www.slpl.org for a complete list of library locations and events.

MAJOR BANKS

St. Louis is home to several locally owned banks, and many St. Louisans choose to keep their accounts and investments at these institutions. One of the best-known was Southwest Bank (visitors might recognize the branch at Kingshighway and Southwest from the Steve McQueen vehicle *The Great St. Louis Bank Robbery*), which unfortunately fell victim to two mergers in recent years and lost its local cachet. Travelers need not worry about finding a branch of their home institution; US Bank, Regions Bank, Bank of America, Commerce Bank, and other financial institutions maintain offices and ATMs here. If you use an ATM that belongs to a bank other than your own, be prepared to pay $2-5 in fees. (Fees are particularly steep at the airport and in entertainment districts.)

PLACES OF WORSHIP

Today, St. Louis is home to more than 300,000 people from diverse religious and ethnic backgrounds. Nearly all of the world's religions are represented here, but from the time of its founding in the 1700s, the city has been predominantly Christian. Many consider St. Louis a "Catholic town," thanks to its deep French roots, its strong communities of Irish-Catholic and Italian-Catholic immigrants, and its excellent Jesuit schools.

In 1829, the widely read German travel writer Gottfried Duden published an account in which he compared the Mississippi and Missouri River Valleys to Germany's famous Rhine Valley. Inspired by what he saw, Duden urged his countrymen to settle where the two great rivers met, and many German Catholics did. As America received its first large wave of immigrants in the 1840s, hundreds of thousands came to St. Louis. Cities such as Boston, New York, and Philadelphia were considered "tolerant" of Catholics, whereas St. Louis truly welcomed them. Within a few decades— thanks to the large number of Catholic immigrants—St. Louis's population had doubled.

Today, there are more than 339 parishes in the St. Louis Archdiocese, including the **Cathedral Basilica** (4431 Lindell Blvd., 314/373-8200, www.cathedralstl.org), **Saint Pius V** in South City (3310 Grand Blvd., 314/772-1525, www.stpiusv.org), and **Little Flower Catholic Church** in Richmond Heights (1264 Arch Terrace, 314/645-1445, www.little-flower-parish.org). For a complete directory, visit the archdiocese's website at www.archstl.org.

Gottfried Duden's exhortation evidently made an impact on Germany's Lutherans, as well. The Missouri Synod Lutheran Church—a denomination that split off from the Catholic church during Martin Luther's reformation—thrives here. The Synod's headquarters, Concordia Seminary, and Concordia Publishing House are all located in St. Louis, as are dozens of Lutheran congregations. To view the complete list of these churches, including the city's oldest (**Historic Trinity Lutheran Church St. Louis** in Soulard, 812 Soulard St., 314/231-4092, www.trinitystlouis.com) and largest (**Concordia Lutheran Church** in Kirkwood, 505 S. Kirkwood Rd., 314/822-7772), visit www.lcms.org.

The St. Louis area is also home to a large Jewish population. At the turn of the 20th century, the Jewish Federation of St. Louis formed to help meet the needs of new immigrants. Now, more than 100 years later, the Jewish community continues to expand in both size and influence. One of the city's largest and most culturally active temples is the progressive **Central Reform Congregation** (5020 Waterman Blvd., 314/361-3919, www.centralreform.org). Information about other congregations (as well as an events calendar and a wealth of community news) can be found at the Jewish Federation's website, http://jewishinstlouis.org. The **Jewish Community Center** in Creve Coeur (2 Millstone Campus Dr., 314/432-5700, www.jccstl.com) provides educational, recreational, and cultural programming—including consistently excellent theatrical productions—to people of all faiths.

The African Methodist Episcopal (A.M.E.) Church is a vital spiritual and cultural wellspring for many of St. Louis's African American residents. The A.M.E. church is the nation's oldest historically black denomination, and congregants are known for their faith-based altruism within the community. St. Louis congregations include **Ward Chapel** (2840 Locust St., 314/652-1990) and the **St. James African Methodist Episcopal Church** (4301 St. Ferdinand Ave., 314/371-0687, www.stjamesstl.org).

St. Louis has a relatively small but active Muslim population; the heart of St. Louis's Islamic community is the **Daar-ul-Islam Masjid** in Manchester (517 Weidman Rd., 636/394-7878, www.islamicfoundationstl.org). This important and architecturally stunning complex is home to the large **Daar-ul-Islam mosque** and the **Al-Salam Day School.** Other Muslim congregations include the **Masjid Al-Mu Minun** (1434 N. Grand Blvd., 314/531-5414) and the **Masjid Qooba** (1925 Allen Ave., 314/771-3548), a South City mosque that provides assistance to Muslim refugees.

Those interested in an ecumenical, humanist service should visit the **Ethical Society of St. Louis** (9001 Clayton Rd., 314/991-0955, www.ethicalstl.org). This outstanding community resource offers lectures and seminars by noted educators, scientists, and social reformers. The society's motto, "Deed Before Creed," emphasizes its desire to put good works before doctrine.

Hindus in St. Louis are well served by the **Hindu Temple of St. Louis** in Ballwin (725 Weidman Rd., 636/230-3300, www.hindutemplestlouis.org), which offers a full complement of services and activities. Many Buddhists congregate at the **Wat Thai Buddhist Temple** in Florissant (890 Lindsay Ln., 314/839-3115, www.stlthaitemple.org), and a **Baha'i Faith Information Center** has been established in the heart of Webster Groves (30 W. Lockwood Ave., 314/963-1415).

RELOCATION

Thinking about making the Gateway City your permanent home? You can begin your research before you even arrive in St. Louis. You'll find a compendium of relocation resources via the **St. Louis Regional Chamber** (www.stlrcga.org/x3981.xml). The St. Louis page at About.com (http://stlouis.about.com) offers moving-service advice, cost-of-living statistics, and a list of real-estate and employment agencies. While the About.com page can be useful, do know that, unlike the two aforementioned sites, it is supported by advertisers and may present biased information.

To learn more about the city's real estate and neighborhoods, visit **STL Agent** (www.stlagent.com), a great home-buyer's resource that offers guided tours designed to introduce new residents to St. Louis's diverse properties. STL Agent even sends out free "relocation kits" by mail—just be prepared for a sales pitch or two.

Finding a Job

The *St. Louis Post-Dispatch,* like any other large daily paper, offers job listings. The paper keeps its print classified section fairly small, so job seekers will fare better by visiting www.stltoday.com, where the *Post-Dispatch* lists hundreds of jobs.

Those seeking service-industry jobs would do well to peruse the *Riverfront Times* (www.riverfronttimes.com), St. Louis's alternative weekly paper. Like the *Post-Dispatch,* the *Riverfront Times* lists the bulk of its positions online. Many St. Louis employers use Craigslist—particularly when seeking applicants for creative jobs such as marketing, writing, or graphic design. Local government positions are posted at http://stlouis-mo.gov/government/departments/personnel/city-jobs.cfm.

In addition to conducting research, job-seekers should consider joining professional organizations with ties to their field. The Internet-based Ad Club STL (www.adclubstlouis.org), for example, is a great resource for researching and networking in the city's advertising industry. The St. Louis Metropolitan Medical Society (www.slmms.org) is a well-regarded Web community for those in the medical field—the city's largest, fastest-growing employment sector. Find other useful networking groups (as well as labor organizations) by performing a search at stlouis.citysearch.com.

Some favorite employers in the St. Louis area include Ameren, AG Edwards, BJC HealthCare, Brown Shoe, Monsanto, and Washington University.

Housing

Roommate matching services (such as www.roommates.com and www.roomiematch.com) offer thousands of listings, but the hits for St. Louis are relatively few. Newcomers seeking a roommate are likely to have better luck on Craigslist—or by checking out the bulletin boards at colleges and coffee shops.

If the national roommate-search sites don't really provide an accurate picture of St. Louis, then the same must be said for the advertiser-run apartment sites. Visits to sites such as www.apartments.com and www.apartmentfinder.com/Missouri/St-Louis will yield many listings for complexes—but, in reality, the nicest and most affordable apartments in St. Louis are often in two- and four-family flats. You'll find these spacious abodes throughout the city, and many are privately owned and leased for less than their market value. Do a search on Craigslist (most apartment listings are accompanied by pictures), and then set up appointments. You may also want to take a walking tour of areas that appeal to you. Landlords with property in some of the more desirable city neighborhoods, such as Shaw and Tower Grove, simply advertise with a sign.

Apartment-seekers who know little about St. Louis or just want some extra advice will appreciate the one-on-one attention provided by Stl-Apartments.com (www.stl-apartments. com). This locally run service matches renters with apartments and makes every effort to find housing that suits a person's needs and preferences. Best of all, the service is free. **Red Brick Management** (314/361-7067, www. redbrickmanagement.com) and **FrontDoor LLC** (314/446-4501, www.frontdoorstl.com) are St. Louis's largest property-management companies, and both broker nice, updated apartments in the city's most desirable areas. Comprehensive apartment listings can be found in the *Apartment Guide,* which is published quarterly and distributed at local retailers.

Those interested in exploring the St. Louis real-estate market certainly should. The city is known for its abundant, affordable housing stock and beautifully distinct neighborhoods. Newcomers who want to work with a real-estate agency should begin at the St. Louis Association of Realtors' website (www.stlrealtors.com). Here, you'll find a complete listing of local agents and agencies, as well as an abundance of useful sales statistics. Favorite agencies include locally owned **Coldwell Banker Gundaker** (314/298-5000www.cbgundaker. com) and **Janet McAfee Inc.** (314/997-4800, www.janetmcafee.com). Both are popular agencies with strong reputations, sound financial relationships, and numerous properties throughout the region.

Information about grants, housing tax credits, and assistance programs meant for home buyers can be found at the state's **U.S. Department of Housing and Urban Development** site (www.hud.gov). The **St. Louis Rehabbers Club** (www.rehabbersclub. org) is also an outstanding resource for potential home buyers—this nonprofit offers the perspective of some of the city's most preservation-minded homeowners and developers.

RESOURCES

Suggested Reading

HISTORY AND GENERAL INFORMATION

Gordon, Colin. *Mapping Decline: St. Louis and the Fate of the American City.* Philadelphia: University of Pennsylvania Press, 2009. Gordon's book is both a thorough explanation of St. Louis's modern history and a harsh indictment of its politics. This story of urban decline isn't exactly fodder for the Convention & Visitors Commission, but it is a brilliant and vital work nonetheless. Gordon's use of maps is quite effective.

Hernon, Peter and Terry Ganey. *Under the Influence: The Unauthorized Story of the Anheuser-Busch Dynasty.* New York: Avon Books, 1992. This is a wonderfully compelling (if at times breathless) history of the Busch family. *Under the Influence* has something for history buffs, true-crime junkies, and mystery lovers alike. A great read that serves as a nice companion piece to broader histories of St. Louis.

McNulty, Elizabeth. *St. Louis Then and Now.* San Diego: Thunder Bay Press, 2000. This beautiful coffee-table book reveals St. Louis's history through its iconic structures. *St. Louis Then and Now* might be of particular interest to visitors who take a downtown architecture tour; the photos reveal the former lives of downtown's many rehabbed lofts and condos.

Primm, James Neal. *Lion of the Valley: St. Louis, Missouri, 1764-1980.* Columbia, MO: University of Missouri Press, 1998. Primm's exhaustive history of St. Louis is one of the best resources available. Visitors seeking to truly understand the city's complicated past are wise to pick up *Lion of the Valley.* The clear writing and abundant photos make this a must-have book for urban historians and tourists alike. If you only read one book about St. Louis's rich history, make it this one.

LITERATURE AND FICTION

Angelou, Maya. *I Know Why the Caged Bird Sings.* New York: Random House, 1969. St. Louis native Maya Angelou is the author of some of the most beautiful, lyrical prose in the American canon. Maya's autobiographical *I Know Why the Caged Bird Sings* tells the story of her difficult upbringing in Arkansas and St. Louis.

Elkin, Stanley. *George Mills.* New York: E. P. Dutton, 1982. For years, Elkin taught at Washington University in St. Louis. Elkin's poignant, acerbic, and downright funny observations are on display in *George Mills,* which traces the lives of people named George Mills throughout human history—including a furniture mover from St. Louis.

Franzen, Jonathan. *The Twenty-Seventh City.* New York: Farrar, Straus & Giroux, 1988. While not as critically acclaimed as his National Book Award-winning *The Corrections,* Jonathan Franzen's *The Twenty-Seventh City* is a fun, fascinating look at the seedy side of St. Louis politics. Webster Groves native Franzen writes about the Midwest with a mixture of affection and derision, and *Twenty-Seventh City* shows the stark contrast between abandoned city neighborhoods and the affluent enclaves of St. Louis County.

Hamilton, Laurell K. The *Anita Blake: Vampire Hunter* series. New York: Jove Books. Hamilton's long-running *Anita Blake* series (she's currently on the 22nd installment) is a hit with supernatural-thriller fans. Each of the books is set in a parallel St. Louis, where the streets are besieged by vampires and werewolves.

Pearson, Ridley. *Cut and Run.* New York: Hyperion, 2006. Affable St. Louis author Ridley Pearson has found incredible success with his crime novels—but not many take place in the River City. Enter *Cut and Run,* which focuses on a U.S. marshal from St. Louis. The storyline is standard crime thriller, but Pearson's smart literary style elevates the writing. A quick airplane read for visitors making the journey to St. Louis.

Williams, Tennessee. *The Glass Menagerie.* Premiered in 1944. Available in paperback (New York: New Directions, 1999). Williams's legendary autobiographical play is the perfect companion piece for a trip to St. Louis's Central West End and old Gaslight Square areas.

Index

Restaurants Index

Nightlife Index

Shops Index

Hotels Index

www.moon.com

DESTINATIONS | ACTIVITIES | BLOGS | MAPS | BOOKS

MOON.COM is ready to help plan your next trip! Filled with fresh trip ideas and strategies, author interviews, informative travel blogs, a detailed map library, and descriptions of all the Moon guidebooks, Moon.com is all you need to get out and explore the world—or even places in your own backyard. While at Moon.com, sign up for our monthly e-newsletter for updates on new releases, travel tips, and expert advice from our on-the-go Moon authors. As always, when you travel with Moon, expect an experience that is uncommon and truly unique.

KEEP UP WITH MOON ON FACEBOOK AND TWITTER
JOIN THE MOON PHOTO GROUP ON FLICKR